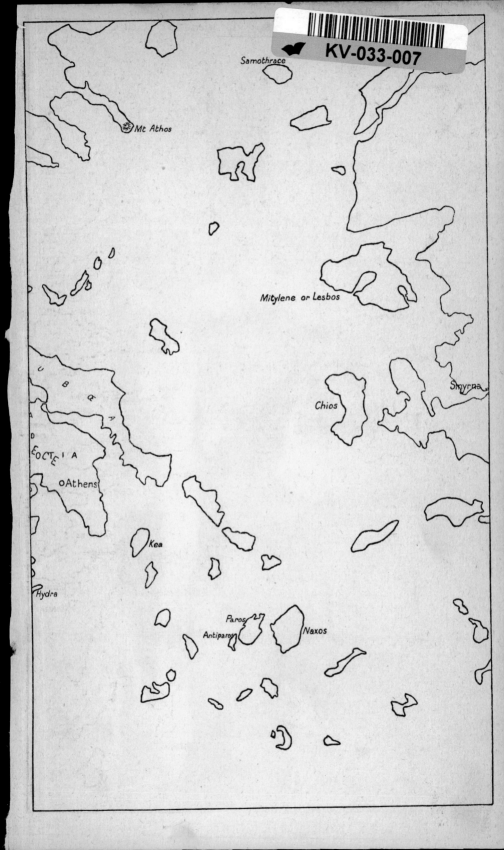

BYRON

BYRON

THE LAST JOURNEY
APRIL 1823—APRIL 1824

BY

HAROLD NICOLSON

CONSTABLE & CO. LTD.
LONDON

First Published 1924
Second Impression, 1924

PRINTED IN GREAT BRITAIN BY RICHARD CLAY & SONS, LIMITED,
BUNGAY, SUFFOLK.

EPIGRAPHS

"With false ambition what had I to do?
Little with love, and least of all with fame ;
And yet they came unsought, and with me grew,
And made me all which they can make,—a Name.
Yet this was not the end I did pursue ;
Surely I once beheld a nobler aim.
But all is over :—I am one the more
To baffled millions which have gone before."
                                        Epistle to Augusta, xiii.

                          " ' We might be all
We dream of ; happy, high, majestical.
Where is the love, beauty, and truth we seek
But in our mind? And if we were not weak
Should we be less in deed than in desire?'
'Aye, if we were not weak—and we aspire
How vainly to be strong !' said Maddalo."
                  SHELLEY, *Julian and Maddalo.*

" Ἀρχαῖον τοῦτο πάθος Ἑλλήνων, οἳ, πρὸς ἀλλήλους
στασιάζοντες ἀεὶ καὶ τοὺς ὑπερέχειν δοκοῦντας
καθαιρεῖν θέλοντες, ἐτρύχωσαν τὴν Ἑλλάδα καὶ τὰ
μὲν ἐκείνων γηράσαντα καὶ παρ' ἀλλήλοις
συντριβέντα, Μακεδόσιν εὐάλωτα καὶ Ῥωμαίοις
δοῦλα γεγένηται."—HERODIAN, iii. 7.

"Et puis si tu savais combien il est devenu difficile de te servir ! . . .
Les Scythes ont conquis le monde . . . De pesants Hyperboréens appellent
legers ceux qui te servent."—ERNEST RENAN, "Prière sur l'Acropole."

PREFACE

I HAVE written this book in the hope that the impending centenary of Byron's death will render such a narrative not wholly superfluous. I am aware, however, that there is some presumption in traversing again the ground which has been so minutely explored by the scholarship of Mr. Richard Edgcumbe. My excuse is that the story is one that can well be told again, and that the material which has become available since the publication of Mr. Edgcumbe's book may justify a younger man in approaching the subject from a slightly different angle.

I have endeavoured, by presenting the facts in narrative form, to tell what I conceive to be the truth with that realism which Byron, of all men, would himself have desired. I have thus discarded the legend that Byron went to Greece inspired solely by Philhellenic enthusiasms, or that his sojourn in Missolonghi was anything but a succession of humiliating failures. For the living fascination of Byron arises from the perpetual conflict between his intelligence and his character, and in the last weeks of his life this conflict is vivified, and finally allayed, by the emergence of that superb physical courage which even his own flickering imagination could not affright. This element can only be apprehended if set against a background (and it is the true background) of diffidence, irresolution, perplexity, and fear. The romantic or dramatic treatment leads only to an insincere and unconvincing presentation. Lord Byron accomplished nothing at Missolonghi except his own suicide; but by that single act of heroism he secured the liberation of Greece. Had Byron, as he was urged, deserted the Hellenic cause in February 1824, there would, I feel convinced, have been no Navarino : the whole history of South-eastern Europe would have developed differently.

In selecting from the vast amount of facts and documents which are available, I have endeavoured to exclude those aspects and passages which are already familiar, and to expand the less familiar circumstances, or those which have become known to me from unpublished material. The little that this book has gained thereby in novelty may not, perhaps, compensate for what it has lost in lucidity and in construction. But here again, if excuse were needed or fitting, my method has been deliberate. For on the one hand Byron himself possessed but little sense of proportion : his mind worked at moments with eagle rapidity, and at other moments loitered in a tangle of detail. And, on the other hand, the whole atmosphere of his last journey was one of confusion and discord, of sudden rushes and prolonged delays. I have attempted to reflect this atmosphere in the narrative itself; it may well be that it was beyond my powers to avoid it; but to those on whom a change of tone and movement grates intolerably, I can at least recommend the omission of my Chapter III.

In Appendix II will be found a list of the more important books and memoirs on which I have based my story. I should wish, however, at the outset to record my gratitude to those who have assisted me personally in the preparation of this volume. Predominantly I desire to thank Mr. John Murray for his generosity in allowing me to read and to make use of the papers and manuscripts bequeathed to him by Lady Dorchester. Whatever value this book may possess is due entirely to the new material which Mr. Murray, with true munificence, has placed at my disposal.

To Mr. S. C. Atchley, also, who during his long residence in Athens has acquired unrivalled knowledge of the details of Lord Byron's two journeys to Greece, and who has himself published in the Greek language a very admirable monograph on the subject, I am indebted for unstinted and indispensable assistance.

PREFACE

M. Gennadius, for so many years Greek Minister in London, has been so good as to allow me free access to his remarkable library; and I am also under various obligations to Mrs. Fraser of Newstead Abbey, to Lady Lovelace, to M. Caclamanos, the present Greek Minister in London, to Count Gamba, to Mr. Montgomery Carmichael, to Mr. H. L. Churchill, to Mr. Eumorphopoulos, to Mr. E. A. Gates, and to Mr. Z. D. Ferriman.

I can only regret that the kindness which these friends have shown me has been so inadequately requited.

H. N.

Finished on October 25, 1923,
at Villa Medici,
Fiesole.

CONTENTS

BYRON : THE LAST JOURNEY

CHAPTER I

LADY BLESSINGTON

April 1—June 3, 1823

I

IT was already dark when Lord and Lady Blessington arrived at Genoa. The narrow street which led to the Albergo della Villa flared suddenly to the lights of their calèche, of the two travelling carriages which followed, and of the large and jumbled fourgon which loomed behind. The bustle of their arrival was stupendous : Italian couriers, British footmen, and French maids emerged in an exhausted and dusty cohort from the several vehicles. Lady Blessington, hidden in shawls and bombazine, swept into the hotel. Lord Blessington, complaisant always, and Count d'Orsay, always immaculate, remained at the entrance. The English tourists gathered in the corridors to gaze with admiration on such an arrival. The proprietor was all attention ; and as the endless succession of trunks and packages streamed up the marble staircase, he conversed with Lord Blessington about the lateness of the spring, and the dust of the road from Forlì, and of how another English milord, Lord William Russell, was at that moment honouring the Albergo della Villa with his presence. Lord Blessington, unfailing in his affability, sent up his card and that of his companion. They were at once admitted. But Lady Blessington, by that time, was in her bath.

When it was all over, she came out into the salone in her dressing-gown. Tired as she excusably was, she grasped her diary and proceeded to the balcony. The lights of the harbour were below her, shining, as she was about to record, " with an effulgence that looked magical." The fanale at the end of the jetty threw a curious red light upon the sails of the passing fishing vessels. Some of them still stabbed the darkness with the tar-flares at their prows. And behind her the salone, palatial in its gilt and damask, gave a comforting sense of that spacious luxury which, since the day when kind Lord Blessington had swum into her ken, had become as natural to her as had once been the squireen existence at Clonmel, Tipperary. She pulled the little table towards her, and opened her diary. " Genoa," she wrote in her flowing hand, and added " March 31st." Then, quite conscientiously, she began the description of the day's journey : of how, from the Voltri road, Genoa had looked like " a fairy city of white marble rising out of the sea " ; of how the waters of that sea were " only one shade deeper than the cerulean sky with which at a distance they seem to mingle " ; of the very odd religious procession which they had encountered in the dusk on passing the city gates ; and of the ghastly image of the Saviour, rocking on a gilded litter, white and bloodstained under the immense wax tapers of the monks. After which she came to the point :—

> " And am I indeed," she wrote, " in the same town with Byron ? And to-morrow I may perhaps behold him ! ! ! I never felt before the same impatient longing to see anyone known to me only by his works. I hope he may not be fat, as Moore described him at Venice : for a *fat poet* is an anomaly in my opinion. Well, well, to-morrow I may know what he is like ; and now to bed to sleep away the fatigues of my journey."

As will have been observed, therefore, the gorgeous

Lady Blessington did not, on that 31st of March, 1823, know Lord Byron. For at the period when the latter had blazed upon London, Lady Blessington, then Mrs. Farmer, was living quite obscurely with a Captain Jenkins in Hampshire. And when, in October 1817, her first husband, Captain Farmer, had fallen out of the third storey window of the Fleet Prison, enabling her by so doing to become, with the willing consent of Captain Jenkins, the second Countess of Blessington, Lord Byron had already fled his outraged country and was an exile in that Italy which, for him at least, was ceasing in a very poignant and galling fashion to be a paradise. Lord Blessington, on the other hand, had known Byron amicably enough in the dazzling year of 1812, and even later in '13 and '14 : at Watier's chiefly, and at the Cocoa Tree, when Byron had envied the then Lord Mountjoy his self-assurance, his enamelled canes and snuff-boxes, his sturdy English manner and, perhaps predominantly, his very large income.

It was thus Lord Blessington who, when they all drove up the next afternoon to Albaro, was sent in to the Casa Saluzzo to call upon Byron. Count d'Orsay, who, for the purposes of Lady Blessington's diary, appears only as a " gentleman of our party," accompanied him. Lady Blessington with her sister, poor Miss Power, remained, rather expectantly, we may suppose, in the carriage. They had not long to wait. But a few minutes had passed before they heard the sound of hurried shambling footsteps on the gravel of the courtyard. And there, lounging towards them, came a pale little man without a hat and with wisps of auburn-grey hair tumbling over the back of his collar. He undulated towards them with that swinging gait which is the mark of those afflicted with the peculiar form of lameness known as Little's disease. " You must have thought me," he drawled, bowing very low to Lady Blessington, " quite as ill-bred and *sauvage* as fame reports, in having permitted Your Ladyship to remain a quarter of an hour at my gate ; but my old

3

friend Lord Blessington is to blame; for I only heard a minute ago that I was so highly honoured. I shall think you do not pardon this apparent rudeness unless you enter my abode, which I entreat you will do."

" Our visit was a long one," records Lady Blessington. It was. They sat in the large, cool room which was Byron's study, the windows of which opened on to the wide balcony, from where, above the lemon trees of the garden, spread the wide prospect of the Mediterranean. The smell of the narcissus which he loved hung heavily in the air, and he spoke to them in his soft sentences of his daughter Ada; of Tom Moore; of Hobhouse; of Douglas Kinnaird and other London friends; of the penalties of fame, and of the tortures of notoriety; of the attacks which were published against him in the English papers by those of his prying countrymen who had pestered him in Pisa and Genoa, and to whom he had refused admittance.

Then they drove back to the Albergo della Villa, and that evening upon the balcony Lady Blessington again took out her diary and made a second entry: " Genoa, April 1st. I have seen Lord Byron : and am disappointed."

II

It must be remembered, in palliation of this remark, that Lady Blessington, from the moment that she had landed at Calais from the steam packet—that novel and most promiscuous vehicle—had been obsessed by the excitement of this ultimate revelation. Throughout her protracted journey she had kept Lord Byron very consistently, and at times quite irrelevantly, in her mind. She had quoted him in the Louvre at Paris. Byron had never been to Paris. Passages from *Childe Harold* had " recurred to her irresistibly " at other moments of her pilgrimage. At Avignon they had been joined by Count d'Orsay, and all through Provence these passages, still irresistible, had recurred. It was to the tune of

Lara that she arrived in Italy and drove up to the Casa Saluzzo. And then through the iron gate she had seen him coming towards her, self-conscious and effeminate, with that " certo leggero e lento dondolare della persona " which had four years ago so acutely disconcerted the Countess Albrizzi. Her disillusion was inevitable. We cannot blame Lady Blessington. She expected something sinister, poignant, and possibly fat : she found something sinuous, appallingly affable, and thin. So thin, in fact, that his tawdry Venice clothes hung round him like a sack, and bulged over his little martyred feet and his little dimpled hands. She had expected something promethean and recondite : she found something soft, sociable, and chatty. " No," she confided to her diary, " the sublime passages in *Childe Harold* and *Manfred* cannot be associated in my mind with the lively, brilliant conversationist that I this day saw. *They* still belong, in my fancy, to the more grave and dignified individual that I had conceived their author to have been : an individual resembling Philips' portrait of Byron, but paler and more thoughtful. I can imagine the man I saw as the author of *Beppo* and *Don Juan*. He is witty, sarcastic, and lively enough for these works ; but he does not look like my preconceived notion of the melancholy poet. Well, I never will again allow myself to form an ideal of any person I desire to see ; for disappointment never fails to ensue."

Or again (for the diary of the " Conversations with Lord Byron " is not quite the same as the diary of the " Idler in Italy ") :—

" The impression of the first few minutes disappointed me, as I had, both from the portraits and descriptions given, conceived a different idea of him. I had fancied him taller, with a more dignified and commanding air ; and I looked in vain for the hero-looking sort of person with whom I had so long identified him in imagination. His appearance is, however, highly prepossessing; his head is finely shaped, and the forehead open, high, and noble; his eyes are grey and full of expression, but one is visibly larger than the other; the nose is large and well shaped, but, from being a little *too thick*, it looks better in profile than in front-face; his mouth is the most remarkable feature in his face : the upper lip of Grecian shortness, and the corners descending; the lips full and finely cut. In speaking, he shows his teeth very much, and they are white and even; but I observed that even in his smile—and he smiles frequently—there is something of a scornful expression in his mouth that is evidently natural, and not, as many suppose, affected. This particularly struck me. His chin is large and well shaped, and finishes well the oval of his face. He is extremely thin, indeed so much so that his figure has almost a boyish air; his face is peculiarly pale, but not the paleness of ill-health, as its character is that of fairness—the fairness of a dark-haired person—and his hair (which is getting rapidly grey) is of a very dark brown, and curls naturally; he uses a good deal of oil in it, which makes it look still darker. His countenance is full of expression, and changes with the subject of conversation; it gains on the beholder the more it is seen, and leaves an agreeable impression. I should say that melancholy was its prevailing character, as I observed that when any observation elicited a smile—and they were many, as the conversation was gay and playful—it appeared to linger but for a moment on his lip, which instantly resumed its former expression of seriousness. His whole appearance is remarkably gentlemanlike, and he owes nothing of this to his toilet, as his coat appears to have been many years made, is much too large, and all his garments convey the idea of having been purchased ready-made, so ill do they fit him. There is a 'gaucherie' in his movements, which evidently proceeds from the perpetual consciousness of his lameness, that appears to haunt him; for he tries to conceal his foot when seated, and when walking has a nervous rapidity in his manner. He is very slightly lame, and the deformity of his foot is so little remarkable that I am not now aware which foot it is. His voice and accent are peculiarly agreeable, but effeminate—clear, harmonious, and so distinct that, though his general tone in speaking is rather low than high, not a word is lost. His manners are as unlike my preconceived notions of them as is his appearance. I had expected to find him a dignified, cold, reserved, and haughty person, resembling those mysterious personages he so loves to paint in his works, and with whom he has been so often identified by the good-natured world; but nothing can be more different; for were I to point out the prominent defect of Lord Byron, I should say it was flippancy, and a total want of that natural self-possession and dignity which ought to characterise a man of birth and education."

III

We are ourselves in a position to discount the romantic prefigurements which Lady Blessington had formed of Byron's personal appearance. We can judge from many a contemporary witness of what he looked like on that 1st of April, 1823. He was not tall—he measured five feet eight inches and a half. The small curly head which had enraptured London in 1812 seemed smaller now that the curls had thinned to the grey-flecked wisps of 1823, which hung darkened to deep auburn by Russian oil and in a most un-English manner from the nape upon the collar. He had lost his looks at Venice in 1817, when young Newton Hanson had found him fat and round-shouldered, with a face " pale, bloated, and sallow." Two

7

years later, when Moore saw him among the lush and
lavish mulberry trees of La Mira, he had not improved ;
and Moore had told Lady Blessington but a few months
ago, while they disported themselves upon the *montagnes
russes* at Paris, what she must expect. We do not know
exactly how much he told her, or whether his remarks
were as cruel as those recorded by d'Israeli. For d'Israeli
had met Moore dining with Murray in Albemarle Street
on November 27, 1822, and the following dialogue had
ensued :—

> " *D'I.* 'Pray, is Lord Byron much altered ? '
> " *M.* 'Yes, his facing has swelled out and he is
> getting fat ; his hair is grey and his countenance
> has lost that " spiritual expression " which he so
> eminently had. His teeth are getting bad, and
> when I saw him he said that if he ever came to
> England it would be to consult Wayte about them.
> . . . I certainly was much struck with an alteration
> for the worse. Besides, he dresses very extra-
> ordinarily.'
> " *D'I.* 'Slovenly ? '
> " *M.* 'Oh, no, no ! He's very dandified and yet
> not an English dandy. When I saw him he was
> dressed in a curious foreign cap, a foreign great-coat
> and had a gold chain round his neck and pushed into
> his waistcoat pocket.' "

Had Moore warned Lady Blessington in this extensive
manner her ultimate disillusionment would have been
less disturbing. For since that day in October 1819
when Byron parted from Moore at Strà, he had taken
drastic if intermittent steps to grow thin again. I say
" intermittent " advisedly, since when Leigh Hunt saw
him at Monte Nero in the summer of 1822 he had swelled
again to almost unrecognisable proportions. Since then
he had redoubled his efforts, and by the spring of 1823
he was actually emaciated. Amazingly so ; to such an
extent that his jacket appeared to be double-breasted,

and that, more than ever before, his nose looked too large for his face, " as if," Leigh Hunt commented unkindly, " it had been grafted on to it." But there was no aspect of Byron which Leigh Hunt in his pert rancour did not seek to distort. We may prefer the romantic charity of Lady Blessington, and to Lady Blessington, as she so fittingly observed in the passage above quoted, his appearance was none the less " highly prepossessing."

IV

On the next day, as they were finishing what Lady Blessington calls, in her fluent way, their " déjeuné à la fourchette," Byron rode down to the Albergo della Villa to return the visit. And two days later he dined with them. The news of his impending presence had spread through the hotel, and the English visitors thronged the vestibule and passages to stare at him as he went by. But he was on his best behaviour : affable and engaging he ambled up the staircase and entered the bedizened apartments which had been reserved for Lord and Lady Blessington. The accomplished Lady Blessington, a little apprehensive even now, was at pains to entertain him : she swayed towards him from her high gilt chair, engaging, voluble, and witty ; the food and wines were lavish ; and for this one evening he abandoned his austerity, and gorged and prattled with an appetite born of long months of physical and conversational starvation.

The intimacy thus established was not slow to ripen. On the 5th the Blessingtons' saddle-horses arrived from Nice, and Byron, having by then recovered from the ill effects of the dinner-party, would join them in their evening rides along the road to Nervi. Very cautiously he would ride beside her, mounted on one of the sorry jades of his Romagna stable, his saddle garish with the gilt upholstery of Venice, his bridle draped with cavesons and martingales, his blue cap glistening with its band of gold. He would ride very cautiously beside her charger "Mameluke," and leer up into her face with some tentative witticism, watching for the effect, sullen as a school-boy if the effect were not immediate, laughing like a school-boy if she smiled. And the volubility of the man ! "Mind you," he would say, "not that I think how Lady Byron. . . ." And then would follow a stream of domestic revelations, of sly indiscretions, ending in dark and wholly unconvincing hints of mysterious and sinister happenings in his past. "Mind you, mind you, my dear lady, I have known what it is, I have known . . ." and the insinuating, gentle voice would continue, echoing in her ears at night time when she sat with her journal upon the balcony : echoing with vivid insistence afterwards, when he was dead.

Lady Blessington, disconcerted and mesmerised, experienced the inevitable human reaction. The unreality of the "beau ideal" which she had imagined stirred in her successive waves of criticism, indignation, and revolt. At the first, St. James's Square loomed larger for her than the give-and-take humanity of Clonmel ; but gradually, for she was on the whole a kindly woman, there emerged the instincts of that protective sympathy which, owing to the insincerity of his relations with other women, Byron had hitherto failed, and most unfortunately, to kindle. She thus awoke to one of the essential secrets of his character. "Poor Byron," the diary begins to exclaim—"poor Byron"; and it is on this note, intensified, as the four weeks of her sojourn drew to an end, that she concludes.

The very real value of Lady Blessington's "Conversations" and her "Idler in Italy" is to be looked for therefore in their reflection of the subtle reactions which the Byron of 1823 stimulated and finally allayed. She passed through those several stages of preconceived admiration, of irritated disapproval, of amused understanding, of profound and poignant sympathy, which we should traverse ourselves. From the first moment she discovered that Lord Byron was not the typical and sinister poet of her imagination. Shortly, very shortly, afterwards she came to the obvious conclusion that he was not in any way the typical English peer. The nobility and gentry who flocked, even if unaccompanied by their wives, to St. James's Square did not discourse either upon their own nobility or upon that of their mistresses. The consciousness of their exaltation and good fortune was felt, but unexpressed. It was not so with Byron. " I never met," she recorded, " anyone with so decided a taste for aristocracy as Lord Byron, and this is shown in a thousand different ways." Or again : " Were he but sensible how much the *Lord* is overlooked in the *Poet* he would be less vain of his rank ; but as it is, this vanity is very prominent, and resembles more the pride of a parvenu than the calm dignity of an ancient aristocrat."

All this was extremely disconcerting; but there was worse to come. Gradually upon the sensitive mind of Lady Blessington there dawned the appalling conviction that Byron, so far from being a typical English peer, was not even a typical English gentleman. Was he, to be frank, a gentleman at all ? His clothes, in the first place : they were of cheap material ; they were nearly ten years out of fashion ; they were over-decorated ; they did not even fit. How could she pause to consider his seven years of exile, or the fact that when he had ordered them at Venice, but a year ago, they had followed becomingly enough every ample line of his figure ? How could she consider that his subsequent shrinkage was the symbol of a triumph, a combative dietetic triumph, over the flesh ? And the colours ! That absurd little green tartan jacket ! What difference did it make that green should be his favourite colour, or that the blue spectacles had been bought at Pisa merely to annoy the English tourist ? The clothes of an English gentleman should be sober, well fitting, and above all expensive. The clothes and accoutrements of Lord Byron fulfilled none of these conditions. In the second place, there was his lack of reticence, his lack of taste. It appeared misplaced, in the circumstances, for him to boast about the six black horses of the Count Guiccioli or of the latter's ducal connexions. What Moore refers to as " that incapacity of retention which was one of his foibles," grated sadly upon the Countess of Blessington. It wasn't English, she felt ; it was foreign. It was the same with everything about him. " I should say," she confided to her diary and subsequently to the world, " that a bad and vulgar taste predominated in all Byron's equipments, whether in dress or in furniture. His bed at Genoa was the most gaudy and vulgar thing I ever saw; the curtains in the worst taste, and the cornice having the family motto ' crede Biron ' surmounted by baronial coronets. His carriages and his liveries were in the same bad taste, having an affectation of finery, but mesquin in the details and tawdry in the *ensemble ;* and it was evident that he piqued himself upon them by the complacency with which they were referred to."

What a chasm was thus opened between the Casa Saluzzo and St. James's Square !

V

During the eight weeks for which the Blessingtons remained at Genoa this chasm, profound as it was, was bridged by a succession of small and intimate incidents which served to establish an increasing community of understanding and sympathy. By the middle of April Byron had introduced them to Count Pietro Gamba, the handsome, fair-skinned brother of the Countess Guiccioli, and by the 22nd he had been allowed to read the manuscript of the memoirs which Alfred d'Orsay had compiled in the manner of Count Hamilton, on his visit to London. Day after day they would go riding together to visit the Lomellini Gardens or the Palazzo Doria. By the end of April an incident occurred which showed Lady

Blessington that under all the apparent assurance and complacency of Byron there lurked something very vulnerable, something which galled him with a perpetual and morbid diffidence. Colonel Montgomery arrived in Genoa; and Colonel Montgomery had been one of the most intimate and active partisans of Lady Byron. The effect of this arrival upon Byron himself is rendered vividly in the entry for April 29th in Lady Blessington's diary :—

> " Rode out with Byron. His pale face flushed crimson when one of our party inadvertently mentioned that Colonel M. was at Genoa. He tried in various ways to discover whether Colonel M. had spoken ill of him to us, and displayed an ingenuity in putting his questions that would have been amusing had it not betrayed the morbid sensibility of his mind. He was restless and unequal in his manner, being at one moment cold and sarcastic, and at the next cordial and easy as usual. He at length confessed to me that, knowing Colonel M. to be not only a friend, but a bigoted partisan of Lady Byron's, and as such an implacable enemy of his, he expected that he would endeavour to prejudice us against him, and finally succeed in depriving him of our friendship."

This sudden drooping of the wing in what had hitherto been the genial flight of Byron's intercourse awoke in Lady Blessington what we can recognise as the first definite reaction in his favour. Already we hear her confessing that she " felt disposed to think much better of this child of genius than most people do," and that very afternoon we find her panting breathlessly after Colonel Montgomery up the steep gravel pathways of the Villetta Dinegro, trying to persuade him " to think less harshly of Byron." Her championship in this instance had its sequel. On the 3rd of May we find the following entry :—

" Byron has asked me to use my influence with Colonel M. to induce him, through the medium of his sister, who is the intimate friend of Lady Byron, to procure a copy of Lady B.'s portrait, which her Lord has long wished to possess. This request has given me an opportunity of telling Byron that Lady Byron was apprehensive that he might claim their daughter, or interfere in some way with her. Byron was greatly moved, and after a few minutes' silence, caused evidently by deep emotion, he declared that he never intended to take any step that could be painful to the feelings of Lady Byron.

" ' She has been too long accustomed to the happiness of a daily, hourly communion with our child,' said he, ' to admit of any interruption to it, without being made wretched ; while I '—and he looked more sad than I had ever observed him to do before—' have never known this blessing, have never heard the sound of Ada's voice, never seen her smile, or felt the pressure of her lip '—his voice became tremulous—' and can therefore better resign a comfort often pined for, but never enjoyed.' "

This conversation, this faint offer of mediation from Lady Blessington in a matter which had never ceased for seven years to be the continual obsession of Byron's inner life, was confirmed by him the next day in a letter which convinced the recipient of the essential sincerity, and even generosity, of his feelings. The letter is reprinted in Lord Ernle's edition as number 1076, and runs as follows :—

" *May* 3, 1823.

" Dear Lady Blessington,

" My request would be for a copy of the miniature of Lady B. which I have seen in possession of the late Lady Noel, as I have no picture, or indeed memorial of any kind of Lady B., as all her letters were in her own possession before I left England, and we have had no correspondence since—at least on her part.

" My message, with regard to the infant, is simply to this effect—that in the event of any accident occurring to the mother, and my remaining the survivor, it would be my wish to have her plans carried into effect, both with regard to the education of the child and the person or persons under whose care Lady B. might be desirous that she should be placed. It is not my intention to interfere with her in any way on the subject during her life; and I presume that it would be some consolation to her to know (if she is in ill health, as I am given to understand) that in *no* case would anything be done, as far as I am concerned, but in strict conformity with Lady B.'s own wishes and intentions—left in what manner she thought proper.

" Believe me,
" Dear Lady B.,
" Your obliged, etc."

The good impression thus created was maintained, for Lady Blessington at least, by the very moving manner in which Byron told her of the " Sheppard " letter, an incident which by then was, in fact, becoming somewhat stale. For it will be remembered how Mrs. Sheppard had, in the summer of 1814, observed Lord Byron scrambling about the cliffs at Hastings, and how she had thereupon written down a prayer that he might " be awakened to a sense of his own danger and led to seek that peace of mind, in a proper sense of religion, which he has found this world's enjoyments unable to procure." Her widower, Mr. John Sheppard of Frome, had found this prayer among her papers seven years afterwards, and had sent it to Byron in November 1821. The latter had replied from Pisa in a letter expressing his appreciation and his thanks; the incident had since become for him cne of the stock texts with which he would convince

15

people of how deep and sincere an effect was produced
upon him by the manifestations of spontaneous and
disinterested virtue. And thus when, in his conversations with Lady Blessington, he came to the part about
the " Sheppard " letter, that lady was very beautifully
and immediately impressed.

> " If," she records, " vanity, selfishness, or mundane
> sentiments are brought in contact with him, every
> arrow in the armoury of ridicule is let fly, and there
> is no shield sufficiently powerful to withstand them.
> If vice approaches, he assails it with the bitterest
> gall of satire; but when goodness appears, and that
> he is assured it is sincere, all the dormant affections
> of his nature are excited, and it is impossible not to
> observe how tender and affectionate a heart his
> must have been, ere circumstances had soured it.
> This was never more displayed than in the impres-
> sion made on him by the prayer of Mrs. Sheppard,
> and the letter of her husband. It is also evident in
> the generous impulses that he betrays on hearing of
> distress or misfortune, which he endeavours to allevi-
> ate; and, unlike the world in general, Byron never
> makes light of the griefs of others, but shows com-
> miseration and kindness. There are days when he
> excites so strong an interest and sympathy, by
> showing such undoubtable proofs of good feeling,
> that every previous impression to his disadvantage
> fades away, and one is vexed with oneself for ever
> having harboured them."

Never assuredly had the Sheppard incident been used
with more immediate or more telling effect.

With the approach of May their relations became if
possible even more constant. We find that d'Orsay has
been much at the Casa Saluzzo, and has been making
sketches of Byron and of the Countess Guiccioli. There
is also in the library at Chatsworth a d'Orsay drawing
which was at one time identified by the present Count

Gamba as that of his great-uncle Pietro, and which, if so, is the only extant portrait of that nebulous, but very sympathetic, character. A few days later we find Byron referring to Count d'Orsay by his Christian name. He is exchanging verses with Lady Blessington and writing to her husband upon foreign and internal politics. But the day of their departure was approaching. Byron looked forward with panic dismay to the moment when this new and very stimulating friendship should cease. He endeavoured by all manner of cajolery to induce them to remain at Genoa, at least until he should have left it himself. He took Lady Blessington to the neighbouring Villa " Il Paradiso " in the hope that she would purchase it, and wrote her some bad but appropriate verses upon the occasion. The stratagem failed ; Lady Blessington by then was already becoming restless ; already she was framing new passages for her diary which would be drawn from the richer local colour of Rome and Naples. " In future times," he said to her, " people will come to see Il Paradiso, where Byron wrote an impromptu on his countrywoman : thus our names will be associated when we have long ceased to exist."

" And Heaven only knows," remarks Lady Blessington in her diary, " to how many commentaries so simple an incident may hereafter give rise."

VI

The Countess of Blessington might have spared herself this anxiety : the incident was too simple to give rise to any commentary ; the relations between Byron, who was ineluctably pledged to the Guiccioli, and Lady Blessington, who was already interested in d'Orsay, were not such as to provoke the scandal which both of them deprecated and desired. The commentary, such as it is, is thus wholly psychological. And Lady Blessington's concluding remarks are not, when we consider her romantic disposition, so very much beside the point.

"How much," she records at one moment, "has Byron to unlearn before he can hope for peace." "Byron's heart," she says again, "is running to waste for want of being allowed to expend itself on his fellow creatures : it is naturally capacious and teeming with affection ; but the worldly wisdom he has acquired has checked its course, and it preys on his own happiness by reminding him continually of the aching void in his breast." And finally, in the last paragraph of her "Conversations," she strikes what to her was the essential, if somewhat posthumous, note with the phrase, "There was that in Byron which would have yet nobly redeemed the errors of his youth, and the misuse of his genius, had length of years been granted him."

And in all this Lady Blessington was neither wholly right nor wholly wrong, as is the fate of all who analyse the character of Byron.

On the 29th of May they had their last dinner together, and on June 2nd he came to say good-bye. Lady Blessington has chronicled the scene as follows :—

"Byron came to take leave of us last night, and a sad parting it was. He seemed to have a conviction that we met for the last time, and yielding to the melancholy caused by this presentiment, made scarcely an effort to check the tears that flowed plentifully down his cheeks. He never appeared to greater advantage in our eyes than while thus resigning himself to the natural impulse of an affectionate heart, and we were all much moved. He presented to each of us some friendly memorial of himself, and asked from us in exchange corresponding 'gages-d'amitié,' which we gave him. Again he reproached me for not remaining at Genoa until he sailed for Greece, and this recollection brought back a portion of the pique he had formerly felt at our refusing to stay ; for he dried his eyes, and, apparently ashamed of his emotion, made some sarcastic observation on his nervousness, although his voice was inarticulate, and his lip quivered while uttering it. Should his presentiment be realised, and we indeed meet no more, I shall never cease to remember him with kindness; the very idea that I shall not see him again overpowers me with sadness, and makes me forget many defects which had often disenchanted me with him. Poor Byron! I will not allow myself to think that we have met for the last time, although he has infected us all by his superstitious forebodings."

The next entry in Lady Blessington's diary is dated from Lucca.

VII

I have in my possession the actual copy of Moore's " Life of Byron " which belonged to John Cam Hobhouse, the most intimate and the most truthful of all Byron's friends. In the wide margins of these two quarto volumes Hobhouse has pencilled a running commentary —approving, at moments, of Moore's flashy conclusions, supplementing them at moments from his own store of reminiscences, but in general contradicting them with the conviction, and sometimes with the asperity, of more intimate and exclusive knowledge. "Admirable," he has scribbled against certain paragraphs; "excellent but too fanciful," he comments at another place; "very possible," he annotates occasionally, or again, "This is the very man." Such confirmatory rubrics are, however, the exception; in most cases, and invariably when Moore has allowed himself the luxury of a too romantic representation, Hobhouse's comments are trenchant and negative: "Most unlikely," he pencils; "I do not believe it;" "This is a lie;" "My dear T. M., you know nothing whatsoever of the true facts;" "Oh, no, Mr. Moore!" And sometimes merely "Oh, no!"

It is this negative attitude which Hobhouse has

adopted towards those moving paragraphs in Moore's Life where he records the visit of Lord and Lady Blessington to Genoa. For the passage in which Moore speaks of Byron's emotion at parting with these new friends is sharply underlined by Hobhouse, and in the margin he has written the words " Very unlike him." We must discount, of course, the tendency of John Cam Hobhouse to regard Byron as his own exclusive speciality, to look upon him with a jealous and protective eye, and to deride with robust realism not only the several portraits of his friend which were the work of others, but also the romantic postures which Byron would himself assume for the proper mystification of his contemporaries and of posterity. It must be admitted, however, that the judgment of Hobhouse, unlike that of other authorities, was disturbed by no undue complexities : to him Byron was simply the " dear fellow " whom he had so much disliked that first year at Trinity, and who had later become the most charming and intimate of all his friends. It was a great pity, in Hobhouse's opinion, that people should talk so much nonsense about Byron ; it was an even greater pity that Byron should talk such arrant nonsense about himself. All this romantic business made no impression whatsoever upon J. C. Hobhouse ; for Hobhouse *knew*. He knew that his friend was irresponsible and kind ; that he was humorous and childish ; that he was infinitely muddle-headed and unspeakably perverse ; that he was irritable sometimes, and generally lazy, and a little mad perhaps, but then so sincere, affectionate, gentle ; and of course appallingly weak ; but then " always so very funny." Hobhouse could never quite get over how very funny Byron always was. " Of all the peculiarities of B.," he has scribbled at the end of Moore's biography, " his laugh is that of which I have the most distinct recollection."

To Hobhouse, therefore, on whom the fame of Byron grated as something fortuitous and wholly regrettable, the character of Byron was in no sense a mystery. He was irritated by the elaboration which other less well informed people attributed to a personality which to him was anything but opaque—was, in fact, perspicuous, lucid, almost childishly transparent. The little blurred bits in Byron's nature were to him merely affectations : it was ridiculous to take them seriously. The dear fellow had, of course, muddled his affairs very considerably; but if he only would trust to his friends, his efficient and reputable friends, the whole thing could easily be re-arranged. It was absurd and self-conscious of Byron to talk of " exile " and " ostracism " ; these things bore no relation to the facts ; they existed only in the imagination of Byron and of those deleterious sycophants by whom he was now surrounded and whose influence it was incumbent upon Hobhouse to destroy. He did his loyal best to contrive this destruction : endless and very outspoken were the letters which he addressed to Genoa, and the purport of them was invariably " Byron s'encanaille."

The latter imagined optimistically that Hobhouse would be propitiated and indeed impressed by the Blessington connexion. After all, Lord Blessington was rich and an Earl, while Lady Blessington, in spite of her past, was legally and absolutely gorgeously a Countess. But Hobhouse was not propitiated. Obviously, his was a high and exacting social standard. For when Moore describes Shelley as " an aristocrat by birth, and, I under-stand, also in appearance and manners," the angry pencil of Hobhouse has scribbled, " Not in the least, unless to be lean and feeble is to be aristocratical." In regard to the Blessingtons he is even more decided. For Thomas Moore, as I have indicated, had laid some stress upon the " sense of refreshment " which the visit of the Blessingtons with its " revival of English associations and habitudes " had provided for Byron. " Not much more reputable," comments Hobhouse, " than the Hunts."

This latter annotation is particularly cruel. For of all the connexions into which Byron, aimless and affable, had drifted, that which drove Hobhouse (and incidentally Byron also) to the verge of frenzy was the connexion with Leigh Hunt.

And thus when, on that June evening, Byron rode back to the Casa Saluzzo after his tear-stained farewell from the Blessingtons, the bitterest of his reflexions was that over there at Albaro in the Casa Negroto there lay in wait for him the most gratuitous of all his many responsibilities—the responsibility for Leigh Hunt, for Mrs. Leigh Hunt, and for Leigh Hunt's six infants.

CHAPTER II

THE CASA SALUZZO

June 3—July 13, 1823

I

LEIGH HUNT was Shelley's fault entirely: Shelley was like that, he let one in for things. One would just mention an idea, and expand it a little, and before one knew what had happened Shelley had shrilled off into another of his enthusiasms. That was the worst of Shelley: he could never see the difference between an idea and a proposal; obviously there was a very great difference. Byron, that hot night at Ravenna when they had sat up together drinking gin and water, had merely suggested that, in certain circumstances, it would be great fun if he and Shelley and Leigh Hunt were all to edit a radical newspaper together from Italy, which could be published by John Hunt in London. Shelley had called it a " generous proposal ": it *wasn't* a proposal, it was only an idea; on second thoughts it was a devilish bad idea. And there was Shelley writing to him from Pisa saying " Poor Hunt is delighted by your *noble* offer." Had Byron ever made an offer? He certainly had never intended to: at least not exactly an offer, only an idea. And then, before he could explain it all away, there was the Hunt family already embarked and well on their way to Italy.

They arrived on July 18th, 1822. Hunt was installed, with his wife, his six children and the goat which they had brought over from England, on the ground floor of Byron's palace at Pisa, the Palazzo Lanfranchi. Shelley sailed up from Lerici to meet them. For two days he remained there, the sparkling optimism of his prominent blue eyes clouded by the altercations which, when it was too late, took place with Byron on the subject of Leigh Hunt's arrival. For the two Hunts had lied about their financial position—it amounted to a lie : they had suppressed the fact that they no longer owned the *Examiner*, and would be dependent solely on the success or failure of this new venture. Then on the second night Shelley took a post-chaise to Leghorn, where Ned Williams was waiting for him with the " Ariel." A few days later they heard that he was drowned. " I underwent," records Leigh Hunt, " one of the sensations which we read of in books, but seldom experience : I was tongue-tied with horror. From that time Italy was a black place to me."

From that time, also, Leigh Hunt was left alone with Byron. And Byron did not, in any convinced or consecutive manner, take to Leigh Hunt. He did not even appreciate his poetry. He would refer to *The Story of Rimini* as " Riminipimini," and he would speak of *Foliage*, quite openly and in his soft patrician way, as " Follage." Nor did he care for Mrs. Hunt : he classed her as " no great things." Irritable, fecund, and consumptive (for had not the great Vaccà himself pronounced her to be in a decline ?), Marianne Hunt was not at her ease in the dark and grated ground floor of the Palazzo Lanfranchi. She would sit about in the garden snipping viciously at little black silhouettes and wishing that she were back in Hampstead. She did not like the Italian wines—a very personal deprivation—or the way they cooked things, or the wide, sun-baked space of the Lung' Arno, or even Lord Byron. Leigh Hunt has left us, in his vivid, egoistic way, a very admirable analysis of the relations which existed between his wife and Lord Byron :—

" My wife," he says, " knew nothing of Italian, and did not care to learn it. Madame Guiccioli could not speak English. They were subsequently introduced to one another during a chance meeting, but that was all. No proposition was made for an intimacy on either side, and the families remained separate. This, however, was perhaps the first local cause of the diminished cordiality of inter-course between Lord Byron and myself. He had been told, what was very true, that Mrs. Hunt, though living in all respects after the fashion of an English wife, was anything but illiberal with regard to others; yet he saw her taking no steps for a farther intimacy. He learnt, what was equally true, that she was destitute, to a remarkable degree, of all care about rank and titles. She had been used to live in a world of her own, and was, and is, I really believe, absolutely unimpressible in that respect. It is possible that her inexperience of any mode of life but her own may have rendered her somewhat jealous in behalf of it, and not willing to be brought into comparison with pretensions, the defects of which she is acute to discern; but her indifference to the nominal and conventional part of their importance is unaffectedly real, and it partakes of that sense of the ludicrous which is so natural to persons to whom they are of no conse-quence, and so provoking to those who regard them otherwise. Finally, Lord Byron, who was as acute as a woman in those respects, very speedily dis-cerned that he did not stand very high in her good graces, and accordingly he set her down to a very humble rank in his own. As I oftener went to his part of the house than he came to mine, he seldom saw her, and when he did, the conversation was awkward on his side and provokingly self-possessed on her's. He said to her one day, 'What do you think, Mrs. Hunt? Trelawny has been speaking against my morals! What do you think of that?' —'It is the first time,' said Mrs. Hunt, 'I ever heard of them.' This, which would have set a man of address upon his wit, completely dashed and reduced him to silence."

Nor were Byron's relations with the younger members of Leigh Hunt's household any more agreeable. He had never had any pronounced weakness for children. "I do not know," he had written to his sister in 1811, "what Scrope Davies meant by telling you that I liked children. I abominate the sight of them so much that I have always had the greatest respect for the character of Herod." This instinctive respect was rapidly confirmed by the number and the behaviour of the Hunt children. "I have a particular dislike," he wrote to Mrs. Shelley, "to anything of Shelley's being within the same walls with Mrs. Hunt's children. They are dirtier and more mischievous than Yahoos." And again : "Poor Hunt with his six little blackguards are coming slowly up. As usual he turned back once—was there ever such a kraal out of the Hottentot country ? "

It is scarcely surprising that this uncongenial promiscuity led to a rapid deterioration in Byron's manners. He could not leave his palace without finding three or four of the Hunt children slobbering round the gateway. He trained his bulldog to growl at them if they ever dared to venture up the staircase, and the result was that the bulldog bit off the ear of Mrs. Leigh Hunt's goat. Byron irritated his tenant by singing snatches from Rossini in the garden "in a swaggering style, though in a voice at once small and veiled." And Hunt for his part irritated Byron by playing the piano.

"He said," Hunt writes in his journal, "that all lovers of music were effeminate. He was not in good humour, and had heard me, that morning, dabbling on a pianoforte. This was to provoke me to be out of humour myself; but I was provoked enough not to oblige him. I was ill, with an internal fever preying upon me, and full of cares of all sorts. He, the objector to effeminacy, was

sitting in health and wealth, with rings on his
fingers and baby-work to his shirt; and he had just
issued, like a sultan, out of his bath. I was nevertheless really more tranquil than he, ill and provoked as I was. I said that the love of music might
be carried to a pitch of effeminacy, like any other
pleasure; but that he would find it difficult to
persuade the world that Alfred and Epaminondas,
and Martin Luther, and Frederick the Second, all
eminent lovers of music, were effeminate men.
" He made no answer."

II

In September they all moved to Genoa, and the
strained propinquity which had characterised their life
at the Palazzo Lanfranchi was at least relieved. Byron
established himself in the Casa Saluzzo at Albaro with
the Guiccioli, her father and her brother. The Hunts,
with Mrs. Shelley, took lodgings near by in the Casa
Negroto. Trelawny hired rooms in Genoa itself, re-
gretting that " the fine spirit that had animated and
held us together was gone"; and that when left to
their own devices they should have " degenerated
apace." Meanwhile the *Liberal*, as they christened the
joint periodical to which Byron had been committed,
had begun to appear in London. The first number was
issued on October 15th, 1822; it provoked an immediate and quite unanimous chorus of indignation. " That
scoundrel-like publication," as the *Courier* called it,
aroused vehement anxiety in the minds of Byron's
friends and tended still further to make him repent the
venture on which he had so gratuitously embarked.
From the very moment of Shelley's death, he had voiced
his own misgivings about the *Liberal*. " Can you give
us anything?" he wrote to Moore on July 12th, 1822.
" He [Leigh Hunt] seems sanguine about the matter,
but (*entre nous*) I am not. I do not, however, like to

put him out of spirits by saying so ; for he is bilious and unwell. Do, pray, answer *this* letter immediately." These early suspicions were reinforced by the shouts of disapproval which, after the first appearance of the *Liberal*, began to reach him from London. He read that the *Liberal* had a taint in it. He realised, to his mortification, that it was not even a *succès de scandale* ; in fact it only maintained a harried existence through four numbers. Hobhouse, as I have said, wrote letter after letter expostulating with his friend for the harm that he would do, and was already doing, to his reputation by associating with the Hunts. Byron himself had already arrived at the same lamentable conviction. For the moment, however, he determined to behave with loyalty and generosity. " I dare say," he wrote to Murray from Genoa in November 1822, " that it is true, and that you mean well. I never courted popularity, and cared little or nothing for the decrease or extinction thereof. As to any other motives, they will, of course, attribute motives of all kinds ; but I shall not abandon a man like H. because he is unfortunate." And a month later he was replying to Murray's criticisms as follows :—

" Now, do you see what you and your friends do by your injudicious rudeness ?—actually cement a sort of connexion which you strove to prevent, and which, had the H.'s *prospered*, would not in all probability have continued. As it is, I will not quit them in their adversity, though it should cost me character, fame, money, and the usual et cetera. . . .

" As to any community of feeling, thought, or opinion, between L. H. and me, there is little or none ; we meet rarely, hardly ever ; but I think him a good-principled and able man, and must do as I would be done by. I do not know what world he has lived in, but I have lived in three or four ; and none of them like his Keats and Kangaroo

' terra incognita.' Alas! poor Shelley! How he
would have laughed had he lived, and how we
used to laugh now and then, at various things,
which are grave in the Suburbs!"

These recriminations and defences were not calculated
to mitigate the increasing embarrassment of their relations. Leigh Hunt would send up to the Casa Saluzzo
little begging letters, conceived in a tone at once peremptory and whining. "I must trouble you," runs one
such intimation, "for another 'cool hundred' of your
crowns, and shall speedily, I fear, come upon you for
one more." At times he would vary these appeals by
introducing a note of jocularity into his communications,
in order, as he himself puts it, to "joke away the consciousness of our position." "You make me affectionate,"
one of these letters concludes, "when you call me
Leigh, and so I feel ladylike, and insist upon your coming
to my house." Another letter, written in the same
appalling strain, runs as follows :—

" *Casa Negroto,*
" *October 25, 1822.*

MY DEAR BYRON,
"Thank you : I will speak to you further on
that subject when I have the pleasure of seeing
you.
"Excuse all this talk, or rather excuse the
excuse; but as something or other seems averse to
my seeing you often, I love to chat with you as
long as possible. Must we not have our ride?
I thought to talk with you of ' Liberals ' and
illiberals, of copy, of subjects, and absolute Johns,
and Boswells and Spencers and all sorts of possible
chattabilities. ' Sir,' as Johnson would say (or
Scrope would say, before he became a fallen Arch-
Davies), ' the world has few things better than
literary inter-chattation ; but Byron, Sir, is milky :
Sir, he is lacteolous, and has gone off to a young

lady.' I think I will be indecent, and try to hold you to your promise, especially as you need not go in about the house, nor need we look at one that day. Our motto shall be ' Observation with extensive View.'

> " Yours sincerely,
> " LEIGH HUNT."

Such letters date from the autumn of 1822. By 1823 even these gestures of cordiality had been abandoned. The letters no longer begin " My dear Byron," they begin " Dear Lord Byron." At first Byron had striven to counter this move by beginning his own letters " Dear Lord Hunt," but after a week or so even this amiability was discarded. The two co-editors ceased, in practice, to meet : the iron gateway of the Casa Saluzzo opened to Leigh Hunt only when he came to receive his weekly doles from Byron's factotum, Lega Zambelli. The quarrel was complete : Byron would sit there grinding his teeth at the lacerating thought that, but for a mischance, he would never even have met the Hunt family ; and Leigh Hunt for his part would spend day after day " walking about the stony alleys of Albaro and thinking of Mr. Shelley."

One should doubtless feel sorry for Leigh Hunt— that little London sparrow beating his wings against the florid pink façade of the Casa Saluzzo. Leigh Hunt, at any rate, felt excessively sorry for himself : after Byron's death he published those venomous volumes which, in spite of their brilliant journalistic qualities, are marred irretrievably by a note of chirpy rancour. They ruined Leigh Hunt's reputation at the time ; they rob him of all meed of sympathy from posterity ; they are meanly inaccurate even in the details of his indebtedness to Byron. For Leigh Hunt, while admitting that he possessed " some peculiar notions on the subject of money," maintains that he received from Byron little more than £320. This is not true. In

February 1822 Byron advanced to him the sum of
£250; within the next six months another sum of
£300 was forthcoming. There were further payments,
even on Leigh Hunt's own showing, of which no record
has come down to us. And finally (a very notable
omission) there were all the copyrights which Byron
surrendered to Leigh Hunt's brother. There was *The
Vision of Judgment, The Age of Bronze*, and eight whole
cantos of *Don Juan*. Of the profits of these publications
Byron took no share for himself; and these profits, as is
shown by the accounts which Byron left behind him at
Missolonghi, were, even by our present standards, little
short of prodigious.

III

By June of 1823 a further complication was introduced
in the shape of Mrs. Shelley. The latter had remained
on in Italy after her husband's death, and was waiting
in the Casa Negroto for the birth of Mrs. Hunt's seventh
child before returning to England. Mrs. Shelley had,
it may be said, no claims on Byron, who had not only
lent Shelley money immediately before his death, but
had refused the legacy of £2000 which the latter had
bequeathed to him. Moreover since those early days
on the lake of Geneva, when Mrs. Shelley would refer
to Byron, at least behind his back, as " dearest Albé,"
their personal relations had been the reverse of cordial.
Mary was jealous of Byron; and Byron, for his part,
was irritated by a certain hardness in her character, by
certain elements therein which appeared to him to be
calculating, disapproving, worldly, and even insincere.
There was perhaps some justification for his view of
Mrs. Shelley: "Mary," wrote Trelawny in his inaccurate and embittered old age, "was the most conventional slave I ever met. She even affected the pious
dodge, such was her yearning for society." The opinions
of Trelawny must in general be discounted; but for this

particular opinion there are some shreds of evidence. We know that Mary Shelley did not like being seen in public with Shelley because his clothes made people stare so; we know that she objected to his bathing at Lerici because the absence of the said clothes made people stare even more; and we know also that while at Pisa she would slip down to the ground floor of the Tre Palazzi and attend Dr. Nott's rendering of the Church of England's service. These things were reported to Byron. They killed in him whatever sympathy may have been awakened by Mrs. Shelley's detestation of their mutual incubus, Claire Clairmont; and they fostered the sensitive hostility which he was always apt to visit upon those who refused either to admire him as a personage, or to joke with him as a man.

Apart from all this, the pose of avarice which he had adopted as an experiment in the only vice which he had as yet not essayed, had by this time become a habit. It had almost ceased to be a pose. It annoyed him excessively to be forced into a position of moral responsibility towards people with whom he had no temperamental affinity, and who should surely have had other closer and more congenial friends on whom to sponge. None the less, if he had been approached tactfully in the matter, he would undoubtedly have assisted Mrs. Shelley to return to England. He was not approached tactfully: he was approached by Leigh Hunt—and at a moment when he was nursing all his resources for his impending departure for Greece. On July 1st, a year after his arrival in Italy, Leigh Hunt addressed to Byron the following abrupt letter on Mrs. Shelley's behalf :—

" *July 1st*, 1823
(a melancholy month).

" Dear Lord Byron,
    " I am sorry to trouble you, but will you have the goodness, by the earliest hour that is convenient to you to-morrow, to let me know your final senti-

ments on this matter, or whether you have any other than what you have stated? As I know that Mary, however against her inclination on account of his own demands upon him for money, will think herself obliged, under certain circumstances, to apply to Trelawney (*sic*), who offered her (I also know) the use of his purse some time back. She is not aware of my saying a word to you on this point.

" Yours in all dutifulness,
" LEIGH HUNT."

This eleventh-hour complication roused Byron to fury, and induced him apparently to write one of those cruel and impulsive rejoinders of which he was sometimes capable. Leigh Hunt at once communicated Byron's letter to Mrs. Shelley, who thereupon decided not to accept the assistance thus ungenerously offered, and applied to Trelawny.

Leigh Hunt, for his part, replied to Byron in a long screed in which, while asking for money for himself, he reviewed their whole past relations. On the receipt of this curious communication, Byron experienced some twinge of remorse, and replied in a conciliatory and amicable manner. But again Leigh Hunt returned, although with less impassioned invective, to the charge.

These were the two last letters which Byron received from Leigh Hunt. They are not, however, the last which the latter addressed to him. I have in my possession a final appeal for money written in the old peremptory manner, which Leigh Hunt sent across to the Casa Saluzzo on the very day that Byron left for Greece, and which was never delivered. This letter runs as follows :—

" *Albaro,*
" *July 13th,* 1823.

" DEAR LORD BYRON,

" Will you oblige me (it will greatly do so) by letting the business of the journey be settled between

ourselves before you go, and 'save me the mortification of the money and the turmoil'? (You know
the passage in Smollett.) I have quite determined
to take the goods; and it is calculated that the
expense of this, and of the journey of a family under
such circumstances as mine, will be barely covered
by £50: some say it will not; but I conclude it
will, with the proper economy. I mention this,
because it is, of course, the pleasantest to myself
to trespass upon you as little as possible—so much
so, that should our calculations turn out to be over-
valued, you will excuse me for adding, that it is
my intention (as a proof of it) to send back the
surplus to your banker at Genoa.

" Yours sincerely,
" LEIGH HUNT."

IV

The sense of vicarious responsibility which Byron
could not but feel for these two provoking encumbrances,
his indignation with Shelley for having died and left him
so uncongenial a legacy, lashed his nerves at moments
into wild and hysterical storms of fury. For Byron, it
must be remembered, was a very irritable man. These
moods of anger would descend upon him between seven
and eight in the evening, when the sedative effect of
the morning's magnesia had subsided. He would lower
at people, as Stendhal has described it, " like Talma in
the part of Nero." There were times when Leigh
Hunt had seen his face " absolutely fester with ill-
temper and all the beauty of it corrugated and made
sore"; when he would not only be irritable, but would
" drain the wine of Passion—Rage "; when his white
and even teeth would flash and clash as those of a panther;
when he would scream aloud in his vexation. And at
such moments even Trelawny was glad to hear the great

doors of the Palazzo Lanfranchi slam behind him, and to find himself safe again upon the sunlit quay.

To some extent, perhaps, these outbursts were but the moods of a man by nature neurasthenic, and by practice actually under-fed. It is true indeed that he did not like scenes : " for I am a quiet man," he explained, " like Candide, though with somewhat of his fortune in being forced to forego my natural meekness now and then." But scenes were continually being thrust upon him, and whole thickets of complications would gather round him over-night. It was then that there would rise in him " the spirit of a bulldog when pinched, or of a bull when pinned." And it was in this spirit that he lunged, a little ruthlessly, perhaps, at those two provoking persons—Leigh Hunt and Mrs. Shelley.

With the Guiccioli it was different. She also was an incubus and a responsibility. But then, to some extent, the Countess Guiccioli was his own fault.

But *was* she his own fault ? There were moments when he doubted it. " I only meant to be a Cavalier Servente, and had no idea it would turn out a romance in the Anglo fashion." He had not wanted, that April night in 1819, to be introduced to her ; it was Countess Benzoni who had insisted. He had not wanted, in the following June, to follow her to Ravenna ; " it depended," says Hoppner, " on the toss-up of a halfpenny whether he should follow her to Ravenna or return to England ; " but then she developed consumption and he went. He had tried at the end of the same year to induce her to rejoin her husband, but once again she had flung herself into a decline. In June of 1820 there came another opportunity, but " the Countess T. G., in despite of all I said and did to prevent it, *would* separate from her husband, and all on account of P. P., clerk of this parish." Then the Pope had chosen pontifically and gratuitously to intervene : he had decreed her separation from her husband, insisting at the same time that she should henceforward live under her father's roof—which meant,

35

in practice, that the arthritic figure of the aged Count
Gamba came to swell the household of Lord Byron.
No wonder that once she and her father had safely left
Ravenna Byron should have remained behind, hoping
that "something would turn up." No wonder, either,
that the Guiccioli should write to Shelley when the
latter was on his visit to Byron, and should beg him,
though he was personally unknown to her, " Non partite
da Ravenna senza milord." It was most provoking, after
one had behaved in so chivalrous and exhausting a manner,
to be told that one had abducted the lady from a convent. " I'd like to know," he expostulated, " who has
been carried off except poor dear me."

Moreover she interrupted him in his work and stood
there apologising at great length when he looked up
impatiently; and she imposed on him a promise not to
continue *Don Juan;* and she was terribly jealous of
his friends—of Lady Blessington and even of that Mrs.
Shelley; and she would cry sometimes at the complications and indignities of her own position :—

> " Liaisons," he said to Lady Blessington, " that
> are not cemented by marriage, must produce un-
> happiness, when there is refinement of mind, and
> that honourable ' fierté ' which accompanies it.
> The humiliations and vexations a woman, under
> such circumstances, is exposed to, cannot fail to
> have a certain effect on her temper and spirits,
> which robs her of the charms that won affection;
> it renders her susceptible and suspicious; her self-
> esteem being diminished, she becomes doubly jealous
> of that of him for whom she lost it, and on whom
> she depends; and if he has feeling to conciliate her,
> he must submit to a slavery much more severe
> than that of marriage, without its respectability.
> Women become ' exigeante ' always in proportion
> to their consciousness of a decrease in the attentions
> they desire; and this very ' exigence ' accelerates

the flight of the blind god, whose approaches, the Greek proverb says, are always made walking, but whose retreat is flying."

And how, and above all *when*, would come the conclusion ? That was the worst of Italian liaisons. "They have," he discovered, "*awful* notions of constancy." His own conception of such relations was wholly different : "Wait not " he had written at Ravenna :—

> "Wait not, fond lover !
> Till years are over,
> And then recover
>   As from a dream.
> While each bewailing
> The other's failing,
> With wrath and railing,
>   All hideous seem—
>
> While first decreasing,
> Yet not quite ceasing,
> Wait not till teasing
>   All passion blight :
> If once diminished
> Love's reign is finished—
> Then part in friendship—and bid good-night."

Such advice had been completely lost upon the Guiccioli : it was already a long time since he had composed that poem ; and Teresa, for her part, was still quite determined to wait. "All this," remarked Byron, "comes of reading Corinne."

He realised, of course, that there was another side to the picture. "I have got the poor girl into a scrape," he confessed, and added (characteristically, I fear), "and as neither her birth nor her rank nor her connexions by birth and marriage are inferior to my own, I am in honour bound to support her through ; besides she is a very pretty woman."

It was kind of Byron to add the latter qualification ; it was not very true. She had fine eyes, doubtless (an all-important feature for Byron), and beautiful yellow hair. But she had but an indifferent figure from all accounts : " chumpy " Cordy Jeaffreson calls it ; " A buxom parlour-boarder," Leigh Hunt exclaimed. And then " she waddled like a duck," and her complexion was like " boiled pork " ; and she spoke with a strong Romagna accent. " A nice pretty girl without pretensions, good-hearted and amiable," is Mary Shelley's description—the most charitable of many definitions. But even the pretensions were, later on, to develop : there are pictures of her when in London in 1832 bawling out Italian songs to the piano ; and still later, when after 1848 she had become the wife of the rich Marquis de Boissy, we catch glimpses of her holding a salon in Paris, and receiving somewhat ostentatiously under the glamour of Byron's portrait upon the wall. " Dieu ! qu'il était beau ! " she would exclaim to the succeeding generation. After which she returned to Florence, where, in spite of the consumptive tendencies already noted, she lived on for years as a wizened and rather fatuous old woman, dying peaceably at the age of seventy-three.

Could Byron in 1823 have foreseen all this eventual wealth and longevity, his troubled conscience would have been allayed. It would have delighted him extremely had he been granted a vision of his successor, the amiable M. de Boissy, beaming introductions at his Parisian guests in the early 'fifties : " Madame la Marquise de Boissy, ma femme, ancienne maîtresse de Lord Byron." Here, had he known it, was the posthumous vindication of his behaviour. So comforting a vision was not, however, vouchsafed. For the moment there was only his poor penniless " piccinina," sobbing under the lemon trees of the Casa Saluzzo. Penniless and ostracised, she had begun as a light-hearted adventure, and was by now a very heavy-hearted complication. " There was no real love on either side," comments the sly and venomous Leigh Hunt. I do not believe it. But it cannot be denied that by the month of May 1823 the Countess Guiccioli had become, and that quite definitely, a burden.

V

In estimating the unhappy, and indeed despairing, mood by which Byron was overwhelmed during those spring months of 1823, the figures of Lady Blessington, of the Leigh Hunts, of Mrs. Shelley, and of the Countess Guiccioli afford, each from a different angle, significant illustrative material. They are the symbols of the very deplorable muddle in which he had become involved; they enhance by little side-lights the essential falsity of the position into which, as usual, he had drifted.

For it must be realised that the life of Byron is not, as has often been imagined, a series of wasted opportunities; rather is it a catalogue of false positions. His brain was male, his character was feminine. He had genius, but it was misunderstood and misdirected; he had beauty, but it was branded by deformity; he had rank, but no position; fortune, but it came too late; fame, but it blazed for him too early. From his childhood the foreground of his life had been out of focus with the background; throughout his career this error in focus marred the sincerity, the completeness, and even the meaning, of the whole.

He might, for he was then sturdy enough, have fitted into the rough and tumble of the grammar school at Aberdeen. After all, he was but a scrubby, chubby little cripple, whose mother dragged her meagre possessions from lodging-house to lodging-house, on an income of some £160 a year. But behind it all there was that pernicious theory that he was different from his fellows; that he was the descendant of Scottish kings; that he would one day (although at his birth there were six lives between himself and the title) become an English peer. This theory, rammed into him persistently, vitiated his attitude towards his early surroundings. The same false focus, though in an inverse sense, marred his career at Cambridge. By then he was the sixth Lord Byron and the owner of Newstead. All this, unfortunately, was very flamboyant ; but in actual fact he was spending his holidays either with his solicitor in Chancery Lane or in constant altercation with an hysterical and, on occasions, drunken mother in the little Manor House at Southwell. Stimulated by the emancipation of his first visit to Greece, he returned to a London in which he found himself more solitary, more unknown, more disregarded, than any nameless orphan ; within a few weeks he awoke more famous than even his rapacious and impatient ambition could have conceived as possible. That in this sudden ferment of unexpected adulation Byron should have been manœuvred into adopting the postures which were expected of him was perhaps inevitable. For how else could this shy young cripple of twenty-four, who knew so few people, who could not dance, who had such difficulty in concealing his Scottish accent, cope with the prominence which London had so miraculously and hysterically thrust upon him ? He would lean against the door of the ballroom acutely aware that all those lovely eyes were turned in his direction. He was little more than an undergraduate, and yet they saw in him

> " The man of loneliness and mystery
> Scarce seen to smile, and seldom heard to sigh."

They had from the first identified him as " pleasure's palled victim " ; they expected him to " stalk apart in joyless reverie " ; they were shocked by the slightest deviation in his " settled ceaseless gloom." If he met their advances with a polite if embarrassed smile, it would be labelled as " an evil smile just bordering on a sneer." If, on the contrary, he frowned at their silly staring faces, they would be enraptured, murmuring to each other :—

> " Yet ofttimes, in his maddest mirthful mood,
> Strange pangs would flash along Childe Harold's brow."

How, in such condition, could any young man be expected to remain natural?

It was not only in society, however, that Byron was placed in a false position by *Childe Harold*. That provoking spectre dogged his every intimate footstep. It was continually landing him in very deleterious perplexities. It thrust upon him the exacting function of being a very dangerous and enterprising man. His slightest civility was interpreted as a seduction; his chance encounters became assignations. They persisted, all of them, in taking him at his word. For a man who, although kindly and sentimental, was only adequately sexed, all this became extremely exhausting. There were thus Lady Caroline Lamb, and Lady Oxford, and Lady Frances Webster. And finally, as an escape, and an ill-chosen one, there was Anne Isabella Milbanke.

During the exile which followed on his marriage he made several successive efforts to achieve some unity of personal impression. He essayed debauchery at Venice, and we have the harlots and the other denizens of the Palazzo Mocenigo; he experimented in politics at Ravenna, and appears for a while as the leader of a section of the Carbonari; at one moment he would drape his self-imposed exile in the purple splendour of martyrdom; at another he would adopt the more garish rôle of the "giovane milord stravagante," and would trundle a vast trail of bedizened carriages, of monkeys, dogs, and peacocks across the dusty plains of the Romagna. By 1823 even these expedients had begun to pall: they convinced no one, least of all himself; they were degenerating into the ridiculous; the Pilgrim of Eternity was becoming merely comic.

For in the first place he had fallen into bad odour with the local authorities. The Carbonari movement at Ravenna had been but an impotent fizzle, but it had led to the expulsion of the Gamba family. The unfortunate affray with Serjeant Masi at Pisa, when Count Taafe had behaved so disconcertingly, and when Shelley, shrill and freckled, had tumbled off his horse, was anything but a creditable performance. It had led to a second expulsion. The squabble between his own servants and the Gamba household, into which Leigh Hunt, fresh from Hampstead, had blundered on the occasion of his first visit to Monte Nero, had again led to friction with the prefettura. His exile from England, self-imposed though it was, might perhaps have possessed something of the magnificent; these police-court proceedings in Italy, at the hands of an authority whom he despised, had become, from any aspect, merely galling and grotesque. And the worst of it was that these shoddy incidents were invariably reported home to England; they would reach the ears of Lady Byron; they would confirm her in her decision to separate him from Ada. He had always, as Moore noted, been surrounded by a " tremulous web of sensitiveness " : even before the separation, Scott had observed the " starts of suspicion " which would twitch across his mobile features. In the years following his exile this conviction of a fixed and general hostility towards himself had attained the dimensions of a persecution mania. " I can't go anywhere," he said to Medwin, " without being persecuted." Nor, when we consider the obloquy which was heaped upon him by the English press, should this obsession surprise us. There had been that terrible party at Lady Jersey's three days before his flight from England; there had been the curious hostile crowds at Dover; the telescopes of the tourists at Sécheron; the English lady-novelist who had fainted when he entered the drawing-room at Coppet; there had been the pamphlets, and the articles, the broad-sheets, and the lampoons; the gaping faces of his countrymen peering up at the windows of the Palazzo Mocenigo, the figures of his countrymen sprinting along the sands of the Lido to intercept him as he entered his gondola, the rows of " damned Englishers " who would lean against the parapet of the Lung' Arno and stare and stare at the ochre frontage of the Palazzo Lanfranchi. Even within the walls of his successive palaces and villas he had not been immune from such inquisition : he had marked the presence, even in his home, of the " staring stranger with his notebook," the " genial confidant and general spy."

In the second place, he was convinced, although mistakenly, that his literary popularity was on the wane. In regard to his poetry he prided himself on possessing no illusions. For him the quill of the writer was but " the mighty instrument of little men." He despised his own romantic manner : *Don Juan* alone appeared to him to possess some claim to immortality. " As long," he said to Shelley, " as I wrote the exaggerated nonsense which has corrupted the public taste, they applauded me to the very echo ; and now that I have composed within these three or four years some things which I ' should not willingly let die,' the whole herd snort and grumble, and return to wallow in their mire." However much he might despise and condemn his own Corsair days, they had been for him none the less a means of power ; and what he really yearned for, though he scarcely realised it, and was too weak and too sensitive to seize it by force, was always power. This means also was now slipping from him. " At present," he wrote to Medwin in May 1823, " I am the most unpopular writer going." And again : " My day is over. Vixi." The affluence of his soul, which had once been to him " a Crœsus of creation," had become clogged by the deposit of hourly vexations, of little daily turpitudes, of persistent sorrow, of unending remorse. He had " outlived himself by many a day," and his literary influence seemed doomed for ever. And, finally and predominantly, he was no longer young. His youth had left him : he was older, far older, than his years.

" It is painful," he said to Lady Blessington, " to find oneself growing old without

" ' That which should accompany old age
As honour, love, obedience, troops of friends.'

I feel this keenly, reckless as I appear." The obsession of his advancing age, of his retreating youth, weighed upon him with a morbid insistence. What was he now but a " hazy widower," a " broken dandy," his body " a little worse for wear,"—his brain—he was afraid to contemplate what would happen, what even then was happening, to his brain. He had "squandered his whole summer while 'twas May," and now—" in short," as he proclaimed, " I must not lead the life I did do." All of which was perhaps excellent prosody, but as a prospect dismal and unbecoming.

For he had loved Fame ; he had not shrunk from notoriety. They had been to him but as a means towards some further end. What was that end ? He did not know ; he hoped only that there was " that within him " which was worthy of a wider horizon and of more compelling deeds. He hoped only that his muddled past, his sordid, petty present, were but the sorry accidents and not the fulfilment of his destiny. He was not very sure about all this, but at least he hoped.

He would sit there in his cool, flower-scented study at the Casa Saluzzo, checking laboriously the household accounts which his steward, Lega Zambelli, would pre-pare for him, coping with provocative and ill-spelt letters from Trelawny, with impudent letters from the captain of his yacht, with jocular and whining letters from Leigh Hunt, with prim and injured letters from Mrs. Shelley, with complicated letters about bills of exchange from his Genoa banker, Mr. Barry, and finally with persistent letters, accurate, reasoned, admirable, and reproving, from his friends in England. And upstairs, the while, a little tearful, doubtless, this morning, were his " picci-nina " and her bilious father—two silent embodiments of reproach. He would sit there staring in front of him at the little miniature of his daughter, thinking of the sound of falling water in the Newstead meadows, of his little green room there with the prints of Cambridge, of " the line of lights, too, up to Charing Cross " ; and of the cloistral, privileged silence of the House of Lords. Was it indeed too late ? Was there indeed no hope of rehabilitation ? "The love of brighter things and better days" was not yet dead within him. Surely it was not his destiny to "roam along, the world's tired denizen," to drag out "a long and snake-like life of dull decay" ? Surely there was still time to break through the trammels of these grotesque and cruel circumstances ?

For the moment, at last, had come for action ; for ruthlessness ; and for escape. And it was in this mood that he turned his thoughts to Greece.

CHAPTER III

I

THE lure of Greece, which, to those whom it has not assailed, appears but as the emotional indulgence of the scholar or the visionary, possesses for its victims a reality which is not temperamental merely, but organic. The sudden pang with which it will assail one on November evenings is in its essence sensuous. It brings with it the remembrance of transparent waves and glittering promontories, the scent of thyme and lavender among the mountains, the lucid shapeliness, from Samothrace to Ithaca, of all her islands. This insistent physical attraction, shared as it may be by other southern sea-girt countries, is vivified in Greece by the stimulus of more compelling associations—by the actual dramatic prospect which, in that amazing atmosphere, the eye is suddenly enabled to embrace. For above those pencilled mountains, or within those violet valleys, stand Helicon and Parnassus, Athens, Salamis, and Marathon; and in one's ears there echoes a glib and garrulous language—the happy bastard of the old Hellenic speech.

It was predominantly this sensuous recollection of reverberating sun and crisp Ægean which remained to Byron during the thirteen years which had elapsed since his first visit. Those redolent, unhampered days when he was twenty-two, and when with Hobhouse he had ridden through the gorges of Epirus or sailed indolently among the clustering Cyclades, would recur to him unfailingly as a mental solace and a spiritual refuge :—

46

" In the year since Jesus died for men,
    Eighteen hundred years and ten,
    We were a gallant company,
    Riding o'er land, and sailing o'er sea.
    Oh, but we went merrily !

' Fresh we woke upon the morrow :
        All our thoughts and words had scope,
        We had health, and we had hope,
    Toil and travel, but no sorrow."

It was on the 19th of September, 1809, that Byron
and Hobhouse had left Malta, and by the 23rd they
awoke between Zante and Cephallonia with the calm
clear outline of the Morea before them.

They had visited Patras and Prevesa, Janina and
Tepelene; they had been received by Ali Pasha, and
had suffered adventures and exposure by land and sea;
on November 21st they were at Missolonghi, from which
dank, ill-omened village they had passed on to Salona,
Chaeronea, and Thebes; by Christmas day they were in
Athens, and lodged under the shadow of the Acropolis
with Mme. Theodora Macri, mother of the plain but
romantic Teresa, subsequently Mrs. Black, but persistently, and till she died in 1875, " The Maid of
Athens."

In March 1810 they left Athens for Smyrna and
Ephesus, and then in the " Salsette " frigate proceeded
to the Dardanelles and Constantinople. In July, again
in the " Salsette," under Captain Bathurst, they re-
passed the Dardanelles on their homeward journey, and
on the 17th of that month the frigate stopped at Kea
to disembark Lord Byron. Hobhouse continued his
journey alone to Malta and to England.

On this second visit to Athens Byron lodged not with
the Maid of Athens, but in the Capuchin Convent,
using the choragic Monument of Lysicrates as his study.
Eleven more months he remained in the country, and
of his doings during this period there is but little record.
He met Lord Sligo and travelled with him in the Morea;

he met Lady Hester Stanhope; he nearly died of fever at Patras; and he learnt Italian and some smatterings of Greek from a young Frenchman called Nicolo Giraud. The mystery of his proceedings during this period produced in subsequent years a crop of legends which represent him as having joined a pirates' gang and having cruised with the prototypes of his own corsair in the Ægean. These legends, together with much circumstantial and wholly imaginative detail, figure largely in what is the worst of all the earlier biographies—the Life produced in 1825 " by an English gentleman in the Greek Military Service." Byron, had he lived to see it, would have been overjoyed by this sinister biography; he had himself heard the legend, and, as was his wont, had denied it at first vehemently to Galignani, and on second thoughts only with half-hints and mysterious insinuations. One thing alone is certain, namely, that for more than eight months he lived intimately among the Greeks, learning a little of their language and a great deal of their topography and character. And that when, on April 11th, 1811, he and Nicolo Giraud rode down to the Piræus and set sail for Malta, he had acquired a vivid personal knowledge of the country which ought to have proved, and perhaps did prove, of incalculable benefit to him upon his second Odyssey.

II

The immediate use which he thereafter made of the knowledge thus acquired is familiar to us from the pages of *Childe Harold* and the romantic poems in which he employed the Hellenic background. It is not my purpose to quote the coloured rhetoric in which Byron thereafter reproached the Greeks for their subservience to the Turkish yoke and urged them to strike their blow for freedom. The long and impassioned diatribe which concludes the second Canto of *Childe Harold*, the well-worn passages about Thermopylæ, Thrasybulus, and the rest, the oft-quoted threnodies over the corpse of what had once been the home and centre of liberty which found their diapason in the opening stanzas of the *Giaour*, had already by 1820 done more than all the intricate energies of the Greek intellectuals such as Korais, or the intrigues of the Phanariots such as Ypsilanti, to awaken European opinion to the existence of a Greek question, and to prepare men's minds for the upheaval which was so shortly to come. The trumpet call which Byron sounded, irresponsibly perhaps, and with no real conception of the consequences, echoed through England and through France, through Germany and Russia; it was taken up at Jena, at Göttingen, and at Zürich; it became the literary stimulus of the Philhellenic movement in Europe.

It must be realised that the virulent abuse which Byron showered upon the Greek nation was not the superficial contempt of the healthy English wayfarer, but the determined incitation of an angered, intelligent, but sympathetic friend. His cool political instinct, that phenomenon which contrasts so curiously with the plush and tawdriness of his more superficial manifestations, and which stands out so clearly from the vapid and woolly-headed comments of his contemporaries, led him deliberately to recognise and to upbraid what at that time were the essential weaknesses of the Greek national character. For the Hellenes had acquired the habits of slavery; they had inherited this status of bondage. They had forgotten the past; they endeavoured only to compromise with the present. They did not realise the humiliation of their position; they met the physical force of the Turkish tyrant with the subtler weapons of intellect and commerce; they had degenerated into slaves, whose one endeavour was not to break the shackles that bound them, but to manœuvre cunningly in such a manner as to become all but unconscious of the irons that for centuries had galled their flesh. It was his sincere conviction that, although the vestiges of the

E

old glory still lingered in the contours and ruins of that amazing country, and although the old intellectual power still bubbled frothily in the pliant romaic brain, yet the soul of liberty, the fire of patriotism, was dead for ever. In this he was mistaken. His judgment had been influenced, doubtless, by the circumstances of the abortive risings in 1770 and 1771, when, under the instigation of Catherine II, and in the hope of effective assistance from Russia, the tribes in the Morea had risen against their oppressors and driven the Turkish garrisons to the towns. A Russian expeditionary force under the brothers Orloff did in fact reach the Morea, and began to disembark; but they were almost at once recalled by their capricious mistress at St. Petersburg, and the Greeks, thus abandoned, submitted impotently to the massacres and reprisals by which the Turks re-established their authority.

The tragic failure of this early insurrection, the cynical treachery of Russia, influenced the destiny of Greece to an extent which, though not superficially apparent, was in effect decisive. Until that moment the Greek people and the Greek intellectuals had looked to Russia, and to Russia alone, for their redemption. It was not of Hellas they had thought till then; it was of the Byzantine Empire. They had been born to the conviction that the Orthodox Church, which had been at once the symbol and the womb of their national consciousness, could only be freed from Islam by the protagonist of the orthodox religion; but from the day when the forces of Prince Orloff had sailed irresponsibly away and left them helpless among their smoking olive orchards the glamour of Panslavism began to wane. From that day another watchword was needed, and it was found for them in the forgotten memories of Hellas.

III

It is much to the credit of the early Greek intellectuals that they should so clearly have realised, and so prudently have combated, the tendency of their compatriots towards an excessive dependence upon Russia. They realised that liberation secured by Russian intervention, and under the stimulus of the orthodox religion alone, would end in Greece exchanging the intermittent brutalities of Constantinople for the no less galling and perhaps more efficient protectorate of St. Petersburg. They realised that the national vitality of Greece, that persistent element in modern Europe, could only be fed by the fuel of racial, and not of sentimental ideals; and they concentrated therefore upon awakening the sense of race-consciousness which had been dormant since the days of Philip of Macedon. The results of their endeavours, the rapidity with which they achieved their objective, form a remarkable chapter in the history of the early nineteenth century.

So early as 1793 the Koutzo-Vlach Rhigas, the first martyr of Greek independence, who had been educated in France and impregnated with the principles of the French Revolution, had circulated his translation of the Marseillaise, and had founded a Philhellenic society in Vienna. From there he had entered into correspondence with Bernadotte, and even with Buonaparte himself, urging their intervention in the cause of Greece. This correspondence was intercepted by Austrian agents, who thereupon delivered Rhigas to the Turks. He was at once executed by order of the Pasha at Belgrade. "Look," he exclaimed as he faced the Turkish muskets; "this is how a Hellene dies. I have sown the seed within the furrow; the hour is near when my country will gather the harvest."

The secret society founded by Rhigas did not survive his execution; another was formed between 1806 and

1814 at Turin, but exercised comparatively little influence. In 1814 the society of the " Philomuses," which claimed, on somewhat slender grounds, to be the direct descendant of the society formed at Vienna by Rhigas, was established at Athens. Its avowed purpose was to protect the ancient monuments which were being despoiled by a horde of English, French, and German collectors ; its activities were also cultural, and schools were established in favourable centres such as Athens and Janina, where the new generation of Greeks were taught their own literature. It must be admitted that the subsequent operations of the Philomuses tended towards the incidentals rather than towards the essentials of Hellenism. They chose as their President a foolish but quite distinguished Englishman, Frederick North, Lord Guilford. Although this gentleman devoted his life and fortune to the cause of Hellenic education, yet his enthusiasm was peculiarly ill-directed. Arrayed in what he imagined to have been the garb of Plato, his hair bound in a golden fillet, he would recite Pindaric odes to the sons of Epirot chieftains, who would sit around him in an embarrassed circle, clad, for their part, in petasos and chlamys. The stories of these academic performances did much to render the cause of Philhellenism ridiculous in Europe. They enraged Byron. " That charlatan Fred North," he called him ; and again " the most illustrious humbug of his age and country."

Far more important were the activities of Adamantios Korais, who devoted his immense energies to constructing for Greece a language which, while almost intelligible to the modern Greek, should in all essentials recall and perpetuate the ancient Attic. " What Luther's Bible," says Mr. Alison Phillips, " had done for Germany, Korais' editions of the Classics, with their prefaces in modern Greek, were to do for Greece."

In 1815 the most important of all these Hellenic societies, the Hetairia Philiké, was established in Odessa.

The headquarters of this society, which were in 1816 moved to Moscow, acted at first under the direct stimulus and control of the Russian Government; at the same time the hetairists were able, by means of the innumerable emissaries whom they sent to Greece, to establish a network of communications all over the country, to found secret organisations in every province, and even to supply these organisations with stocks of arms and ammunition. By 1820 the membership of this society had reached 80,000. The train was laid; it needed but the word to provoke the explosion.

IV

The internal conditions and organisation of Greece under Turkish sovereignty were not unfavourable to the outburst of some sudden and extensive upheaval. There had been no fusion between the conquered and the conquerors. Encamped in Europe as a predatory horde, the Turks had retained in their methods of government the principles of a military occupation; so long as the occupation itself was not endangered, so long as the fact of conquest was not forgotten, so long as the accustomed tribute was paid to Constantinople the subject races were left, except for spasmodic outbursts of authority, almost completely to themselves.

For the arts of settled government are alien and obnoxious to the Turkish genius; it is difficult for them either to conciliate or even, perhaps, to crush; they can neither construct nor maintain; the word " preservation " does not, in fact, exist in their ungainly language. The earlier Sultans had been fully conscious of this defect in the Turkish character. They had left to the Byzantine Greeks their religion, their ecclesiastical organisation, and even, in some cases, their personal liberty. They had encouraged the wealthier Byzantines of the Phanar quarter of Stamboul to enter the Ottoman service, to enrich themselves by commerce, and even to serve as Viceroys in the Rumanian principalities. It was thus that the great Phanariot families of Ypsilanti, Mavrocordato, Kallimachi, and Cantacuzene attained to precarious riches and influence, and could now and then purchase from the Sublime Porte their appointments as Hospodars in Wallachia or Moldavia. And for all this indolent and cynical exploitation, the Sultans have, by the indulgent historian, been accorded a tribute of enlightenment.

The policy pursued in Greece itself was not dissimilar. Apart from the very liberal measure of autonomy allowed to the Greek Church and clergy, who depended almost solely upon the Patriarchate at Constantinople, the Sultans had, partly from indolence and partly from a recognition of their own incompetence, allowed the local Greeks to retain much of their social organisation. The Sultan, it is true, was represented by his Pashas, his Ayans, his Voivodes, and his Aghas, whose authority was enforced by the scattered garrisons maintained throughout the country. But the real administration of the country was conducted through the Codja-bashis, or primates, who were, in fact, Greeks nominated by the demogeronts of the several provinces, who in their turn had been elected by the village communes themselves. The position of primate had in practice become almost hereditary, and had given birth to what approximated to a governing Greek caste, or at least to a caste possessing some experience of the details of administration and the organisation and fiscal capacity of their own provinces.

Not only, however, had the methods of Ottoman administration called into being the nucleus of a native Greek civil service ; the Turks had also in their nonchalant way created the nucleus of a native Greek army. The old Byzantine militia, the Armatoles, had, in some of the wilder districts of the Pindus and of Macedonia, been retained as a species of locally recruited gendarmerie.

They were employed by the Turkish Pashas to control the brigand bands which infested the mountains, and were recruited partly from the Greek population and partly from the Epirot Albanians. The relations between this gendarmerie and the provincial brigands became increasingly cordial. The brigands, or Klephts as they were called, were regarded by the Greek population as national heroes, and a whole ballad literature, curiously analogous to our own Robin Hood cycle, sprang up around them. The effect of this national hero-worship upon the morale of the Armatoles was, to say the least, disintegrating. A successful Klepht captain would, in winter, join the local Armatole brigade, and in summer many an Armatole would take to the cooler air of the hills and enrol himself in the band of one or other of the Klepht capitani. By the first decades of the nineteenth century the Armatole organisation had become, as it were, but the staff college of the Klepht leaders. Nor was this all : in certain of the remoter districts of the south and north there existed semi-independent clans who had never been permanently subjected to Turkish authority. In the central peninsula of Messenia, in the arid prong of Maina running out to Cape Matapan, there existed the armed clan of the Mavromichaelis under their chief, Petro Bey. In the north there was the fierce Albanian tribe of the Souliots, whose resistance to Ali Pasha had already become legendary, and whose subsequent connexion with Byron was to prove the most harassing of his many complexities at Missolonghi. In this tribal organisation existed the material, if not for offensive operations, at least for defensive resistance. And upon all these disturbing phenomena, as upon the general fermentation of their Rayah provinces, the Turkish authorities gazed with inane, contemptuous, and fatalistic eyes.

A third element, which proved of the greatest value to the Greek insurgents, was the naval prowess of the Ægean islanders. The Turks, as a race, are anything but marine. Their caravels had from the first been manned by Greek sailors, or by the captives which they would from time to time obtain from the Adriatic seaboard. In the year 1774, by the Treaty of Kutchuk Kainardji, the Greeks obtained the right to navigate their own vessels under the Russian flag; the result was a great outburst of mercantile activity in the islands, and by the time of the revolution the islands of Hydra, Psara, and Spetsai possessed between them an important mercantile marine, owned by native capitalists, manned by native sailors adept in the navigation of those intricate waters and in the more adventurous pursuits of active piracy.

By the year 1821, therefore, the Greeks possessed the nucleus of a civil administration, as represented by the primates, the demogeronts, and the village communes; the nucleus of an army, as represented by the Armatoles, the Klephts, and the separate clan organisations in the north and south; and the nucleus of a navy, as represented by the merchants and pirates of the Ægean Islands. As a liaison between these scattered elements there were the priests and monks, who could pass unnoticed from village to village and from cape to island.

From the outset, therefore, the rank and file of the nation were thus perfectly aware of what was impending, and each individual knew in advance what was his immediate station and function. This advantage was counterbalanced, however, by one essential omission: there was no individual or group of individuals who could claim the undisputed right to direct the movement. This absence of leadership, this lack of direction, would in any popular movement have proved dangerous; with a race of passionate and hysterical individualists like the Greeks the result was fatal. The unexpected rapidity of their success left them for the moment without an immediate national objective, and in the ensuing interval of optimism and self-sufficiency they surrendered to their hereditary vice of dissension. The detached elements of their organisation claimed for themselves alone the credit and the spoils of victory; the capitani would not obey the primates; the civilians were determined not to submit to the dictation of the military; the sailors of Hydra and Spetsai thought only of their islands and their booty; the wild chieftains of the south and north considered only the interests of their own clansmen. Hellas was forgotten. And it was for this reason that the Greek War of Independence lasted calamitously for eleven years.

V

The lack of direction and accepted leadership, which was to delay and almost to destroy the fruition of Greek emancipation, was emphasised from the outset of the movement by the unfortunate and abortive rising organised by Prince Alexander Ypsilanti in the Rumanian principalities.

This curious and regrettable reversion to the old Russophile and Byzantine theory, to the old traditions of the Phanar, was the fault, in the first place, of the Odessa Hetairia, which was by then established in Moscow. Realising that the main body of the Turkish army in Europe was at the moment fully occupied under Kurshid Pasha in an endeavour to subdue the recalcitrant Ali Pasha of Janina, the Greek colonies in Russia decided that a delightful opportunity had at last arrived to drive the Turk from Europe. They approached their compatriot Capo d'Istrias, who was then the Emperor Alexander's Foreign Minister, with a request that he would head the march on Constantinople. He replied, as is not surprising, that the moment was highly inopportune. They then turned, in their irresponsible way, to a Prince Alexander Ypsilanti, the scion of a leading Phanariot family, who had served in the Russian army against Napoleon, had figured garishly at the Congress of Vienna, and was at that time one of the most elegant of the Tsar's personal aides-de-camp. Their choice was singularly ill-advised :—

"Alexandre Hypsilanti," records Pouqueville, "officier dépourvu de talents positifs, ignorait, avant tout, 'que les dieux ne laissent rien concevoir de grand que ce qu'ils inspirent.' Élevé, suivant l'usage des soi-disant princes du Phanal, par des précepteurs qui lui avaient appris à parler correctement plusieurs langues, il était savant, sans cette instruction mâle qui est le résultat des études classiques ; poète, sans feu sacré ; aimable, sans urbanité ; soldat, sans être militaire ; quoiqu'il eût perdu le bras droit à l'affaire de Culm, on ne pouvait guère dire, à cause de cela, qu'il était brave. Mais ce qui caractérisait spécialement Alexandre Hypsilanti, c'était la vanité ordinaire aux Phanariotes, leur esprit d'intrigue, dont le terme ambitieux se bornait à devenir hospodar des peuples abrutis de l'antique Dacie, et une faiblesse de caractère telle, qu'il se laissait dominer par des personnes indignes de l'approcher."

The proceedings of Ypsilanti fully confirm this unfavourable opinion. Instead of transporting his heterogeneous collection of Philhellenes to Greece itself, he determined upon making a dash to Constantinople through Rumania and Eastern Thrace. He imagined apparently that the Rumanian peasants would rise to his support. In this assumption he was mistaken. The Rumanian peasantry had too vivid a recollection of the methods of the Greek Hospodars to support any scion of a Phanariot family ; they were, moreover, occupied with a little jacquerie of their own under the leadership of a certain Vladimiresco. The expedition of Alexander Ypsilanti rapidly degenerated into a most egregious fiasco. He crossed the Pruth in March 1821, and pushed on to Jassy. From there he issued a proclamation claiming, on the strength merely of some spiritualistic generalities which the Emperor had let fall one morning as they walked together in the sanded alleys of the Summer Garden, that he had the support of Russia—that a Russian army was, in fact, prepared to follow in his wake. The Emperor Alexander was at that moment at Laibach; it was with little difficulty that Metternich extracted from that affable sovereign a repudiation of Ypsilanti, of his actions and his pronouncements. This intimation reached the liberator at Bucharest, where he was holding a court and dispensing decorations. He explained it away: the Emperor, he explained, did not and could not really mean it; the message from Laibach was but a device to gain time for the passage of the Pruth by the Russian armies. He thus remained at Bucharest enjoying a few weeks of precarious but very ostentatious sovereignty. By May 1821 the Turkish Pashas of Widdin, Silistria, and Braila crossed the Danube, and came upon Ypsilanti on June 19th in the neighbourhood of Dragatschani. He was completely defeated. Abandoning the Greek Volunteers whom he had induced to leave Russia, he escaped to Austrian territory, and was imprisoned by the Austrians in the castle of Munkacz, where he remained six years, only to die miserably in Vienna upon his ultimate release. His followers retreated with difficulty to the Pruth, where, after an heroic resistance, they were annihilated by the Turkish armies.

With a sigh of relief the chanceries of Europe proclaimed that the Hellenic movement was crushed for ever, and that peace had been maintained. The cause of legitimacy had again, and with the marked support of Providence, emerged triumphant.

But while their eyes had been turned anxiously upon the short and pitiful comedy played by Ypsilanti in the north-eastern corner of Turkey in Europe, the little western province, which had once been known as Greece, had suddenly, blatantly, atrociously, and behind their backs, achieved its independence.

VI

In the diary which Mrs. Shelley kept while at Pisa we find the following entry for Sunday, April 1st, 1821 : "Read Greek. Alexander Mavrocordato calls with news about Greece. He is as gay as a caged eagle just free." On the 24th of that month there is another entry : "Alex. calls in the evening with good news from Greece. The Morea is free." And thus for Mrs. Shelley there was an end to those delightful and improving lessons in the Classics from "a real Greek Prince"; and for that fat little Mavrocordato, three times Prime Minister of liberated Greece, who was certainly not a Prince, and only questionably Achæan, there opened a period of misunderstood but splendid activity, of passionate disappointments, of fierce misrepresentation and of triumphant, if vicarious, success.

The rising in the Morea, as has already been indicated, had been prepared by the incitations of the apostles sent to the country by the Hetairia of Odessa. By the beginning of 1821 Salik Aga, the unfortunate Kaimakam of Tripolitza, at last awakened to the fact that the Rayahs were contemplating a very impudent but definite attack upon the Turkish population, officials, and garrisons. He issued a proclamation ordering the Christians to surrender their arms, and he invited the several provincial primates, as well as the heads of the Church, to meet him at a conference at Tripolitza. The long-ingrained habit of obedience induced some of the latter to set out upon their journey to the provincial capital. Archbishop Germanos, of Patras, refused. He took refuge in the convent of St. Laura, raised the standard of the cross, and on April 2nd occupied Kalavryta. Accompanied by the local primates, the Archbishop marched with a mixed rabble, armed with old muskets, scythes, and ploughshares, upon the town of Patras, which was captured on April 4th. Within eleven days the Turkish forces, under Youssuf Pasha, reoccupied the

city, and proceeded to exact reprisals. The French
Consul was able, on that occasion, to rescue some of
the Greeks. The English Consul, Mr. Green, behaved,
on the other hand, with dastardly Anglo-Levantine
neutrality.

By then, however, the insurrection had become
general. The peasants throughout the Morea rushed to
arms, and massacred the Turkish settlers in their neighbourhood. In the south Petro Bey of Maina, assisted
by Theodore Colocotronis, marched upon Kalamata,
and entered the town on the 4th of April. From there
they invested Tripolitza, and defeated the column which
Kurshid Pasha had sent to its relief. In the north the
whole of Attica and Bœotia had already risen in revolt;
by the beginning of May the Turks of Athens were
forced to take refuge in the Acropolis; and a few days
later the garrison of Corinth surrendered to the insurgents. In the Ægean meanwhile all the islands
with the exception of Rhodes, Lesbos, and Chios, joined
the movement, and collected their mercantile marine
of one hundred and seventy-five sail under the command of Admiral Miaoulis. By the end of 1821 the
insurgents were thus everywhere triumphant. The whole
of Greece south of the Thessalian border had been cleared
of the Turks, and there remained only the beleaguered
Ottoman garrisons in the Acropolis at Athens, on the
island of Eubœa, and in the fortresses of Lepanto,
Nauplia, Coron, Modon, and Patras.

Jubilant at these unexpected successes, the insurgents
turned gaily to the congenial task of forming a Government of Independent Greece. From that moment the
unity of the nation was destroyed. To the natural
rivalry between the civilian and the military parties had
been added certain other elements of discord. From
Russia there had arrived the brother of Alexander
Ypsilanti, Prince Demetrius, who was supported by the
Hetairists, and who represented the original Phanariot
conception of a revival of Byzantine Greece. From the

west, and in fact from Mrs. Shelley's boudoir, there arrived the plump little figure of Alexander Mavrocordato, with his gold spectacles and his European clothes, who was opposed to any dependence upon Russia, and who aimed at creating a new Hellas, national and self-sufficing, which should look only to the Western Powers, and particularly to England, for support.

The result was that within a year Greece was split up into three main divisions. There was western Greece under Mavrocordato; there was eastern Greece under a certain Negris; and there was the Morea which was torn between the civilian party, the military party, and the party of Demetrius Ypsilanti. After endless negotiations between these several bodies, and largely owing to the moderate and statesmanlike persuasion of Mavrocordato, it was decided in January 1822 to hold a constituent assembly at Epidaurus. The fierce antagonisms which all but shattered this assembly were allayed by the conciliation of Mavrocordato, reinforced by the news that a vast Turkish army was about to invade Continental Greece and to subjugate the Morea. The proceedings of the Assembly of Epidaurus were thus abruptly terminated. Mavrocordato was able for the moment to impose his influence and to combine with Negris to establish what, on paper at least, was a strong centralised Government. The assembly then proceeded to publish a declaration of Greek independence and to promulgate the constitution of the new Greece. The old black flag of the Hetairists was replaced by the blue and white ensign of modern Greece, and of all the acts of the Assembly of Epidaurus this act alone was destined to have any permanence.

The threatened Turkish invasion, which had in this manner cut short the interminable discussions at Epidaurus, did not, in fact, mature until the summer of 1822, by which time Kurshid Pasha had captured and disposed of Ali Pasha of Janina, thereby releasing his army for operations against Greece. The Turkish expeditionary force was divided into two bodies : one under Reshid Pasha which was to subjugate western Greece, and the other under Drama Ali which was to pass through eastern Greece and on to the conquest of the Morea. Mavrocordato himself hastened to Missolonghi for the purpose of organising the defence of that strategic point against the army of Reshid. He obtained the services of Marco Botzaris, one of the Souliot chieftains, and he collected and organised a legion of European Phil-hellenes from among those foreigners who at the first news of the movement had flocked to Greece. Instead, however, of remaining on the defensive, he divided his forces into two : he sent Marco Botzaris to the relief of Souli, and detached the rest of his forces on a vague offensive operation against the bulk of Reshid Pasha's army. The utter defeat of this contingent at the Battle of Peta was a terrible blow, not only to the prestige of Mavrocordato himself, but to that of the legion of European Philhellenes who were decimated at the first serious encounter. The Souliots for their part were forced to surrender, and Marco Botzaris was obliged to retire on Missolonghi, where he was shortly joined by Mavrocordato.

His conduct of the ensuing siege of Missolonghi, the first of three such sieges, did something to restore the shattered prestige of Mavrocordato. With four hundred men he was able throughout the summer and autumn to resist the assaults of the Turkish army, and, with the assistance of the fleet from Hydra, to maintain the defence until, on January 12, 1823, the Turkish commander, in a fit of petulance, abandoned the siege and withdrew his army to Albania.

Thus western Greece was, by the beginning of 1823, again recovered, and the defeat of Peta was avenged.

An even greater victory for the Greek insurgents marked the campaign of 1822 in eastern Greece and the Morea. On July 11th of that year the army of Drama Ali, 30,000 strong, began their invasion. The isthmus of Corinth was reached without opposition, and in quick succession Nauplia and Argos fell to the invaders. The Turkish army then advanced on Tripolitza, but with their lengthening communications and with the devastation wrought on the Turkish fleet by the brigs of the Ægean islanders, Drama Ali soon found it almost impossible to maintain his army in the centre of the Peloponnese. By August the cumbrous Turkish columns had begun to retreat towards Corinth, where it was hoped that supplies would be available. But Colocotronis, who had been hanging with his bands upon their line of communications, descended from the mountains upon the retreating armies, and only a shattered remnant eventually reached their base.

The Turkish campaign of 1822 had thus ended in complete and devastating failure.

VII

The successes of the Greek insurgents produced upon the Continent of Europe a flame of sympathy and excitement equal only to that which had been kindled by the American War of Independence. In Germany, in Switzerland, and in France committees were formed to collect funds for the Greek cause and to succour the unfortunate Greek patriots who, by the orders of Metternich, were expelled from Russia and Austria as a protest against the escapade of Ypsilanti. By the early summer of 1821, a motley assortment of Napoleonic veterans, of Jena students, of Russian mystics, and of disappointed Carbonari, flocked under the generic title of Philhellenes to the shores of liberated Hellas. Within a few weeks the greater number drifted home again, discouraged and indignant. Of those that persevered, the greater number were subsequently annihilated at the disastrous Battle of Peta. A few, impoverished or obstinate, remained.

In England the interest shown in the Greek insurrection was from the outset less hysterical. The great wars were over, and English public opinion desired only peace, splendid isolation, and no income tax. " The affairs of Greece," remarked the *News*, " partake in some measure of the effects of a dead calm in politics : nothing can again rouse us but a spirit of hostility manifested towards this country in some shape or another; and the nation would then once more turn the focus of its attention on foreign affairs. . . . The approaching fight between Spring and Langham will employ some hundred expresses to record the single event of that fight : when it is doubtful whether the immolation of the whole Royal Family of Portugal would be deemed as intelligence of sufficient moment to warrant the expense of a post letter from one newspaper office in town to another in the country."

This magnificent indifference was disturbed, if disturbed at all, by the problem of Russia : the apprehension felt by the mass of British opinion regarding the designs of that amorphous country was seized upon by the extreme Tories, and by those interested in the trade of the Levant, to revive the formula of the integrity of the Turkish Empire. It is probable indeed that this lack of sympathy with, or even of interest in, the Greek cause would have continued, had not the complacency of British public opinion been ruffled by the very indiscreet manner in which the Turks revenged themselves upon those Greeks who remained within their power. On April 21st, 1821, the Patriarch of Constantinople, the octogenarian Gregorios, was seized as he was leaving the Easter Mass, and hanged in full vestments upon a public gallows. A still more gratuitous error of judgment was committed by the Sultan in April of 1822. The island of Chios had been one of the last to declare for the Greek cause, and had only done so under pressure from the neighbouring patriots of Samos. The defection of Chios, which provided the chewing-gum for the ladies of the Sultan's harem, was taken as a personal affront, and one which the Seraglio could not afford to overlook. The Capitan Pasha at once put to sea with forty-six ships and 7000 men, and within a few days 23,000 Chians had been massacred and the whole island burnt and pillaged.

The effect of this incident upon European opinion was galvanic: even in England accounts of the massacre appeared in some of the more liberal newspapers. The Philhellenes took heart. Sir James Mackintosh asked a question in Parliament, to which Lord Castlereagh replied that atrocities had been committed on both sides, and that " the *transactions* complained of " had been caused by similar massacres on the part of the Greeks at Tripolitza and elsewhere. The Rev. Thomas Smart Hughes of Cambridge, the author of an admirable book of travels in Sicily and the Levant, published in pamphlet form his " Address to the People of England on the Cause of the Greeks," in which he referred in bitter but measured terms to the very Parliamentary nature of Lord Castlereagh's statement. A few weeks later Mr. Edmund Barker of Thetford, and also of Cambridge, published his " Letter to the Rev. T. S. Hughes of Emmanuel College, Cambridge, occasioned by the perusal of his Address to the People of England." " The British Government," Mr. Barker wrote, " discountenances the Greek insurrection on the ground that, if it succeeds, Russia would have entire command of Greece and the Balance of Power would be endangered. . . . But if by our aid Greece emerges more than conqueror, she will adhere rather to England than Russia, which for fifty years plentifully fed her with hopes and in the hour of need has treacherously and cruelly deserted her. . . . I trust that but few days will be suffered to elapse before some high-spirited individual will have the courage to call a general meeting at the London Tavern, or some similar place, for the purpose of consulting on the best means of aiding the Greek insurrection."

Mr. Barker's confidence was not misplaced. Within

a few weeks of the publication of his letter, on August 21st, 1822, a meeting took place in the Merchants' Hall at Edinburgh under the chairmanship of Mr. Stewart Monteith. Similar meetings followed at Ipswich, Norwich, and Cambridge. But for the moment at least the metropolis lagged behind.

In July 1822 appeared Lord Erskine's "Letter to the Earl of Liverpool," in which the Greek policy of Lord Castlereagh in Downing Street, and Lord Strangford in Constantinople, was authoritatively assailed. From that moment the cause of Greece became the cause of the left wing of the Whig Opposition, and the protagonists thereof, Sir F. Burdett and Byron's candid and aspiring friend, John Cam Hobhouse. Jeremy Bentham accepted the post of Nestor of the movement. Owing to the uncertainty caused by the suicide of Lord Castlereagh on August 12th, the Greek Committee in London was not actually formed until January 1823, when Andreas Luriottis arrived in England to plead the cause of the Greeks. The Committee held its first meeting at the "Crown and Anchor Tavern" on February 28th, 1823, under the presidency of Lord Erskine, when it was decided to instruct Edward Blaquière, who had already published certain lucid and instructive works upon the revolution in Spain, to proceed to Greece with Luriottis and to report to the Committee upon the requirements of the country.

By the spring of 1823, therefore, opinion in England was divided into three main categories. There was a Whig minority, who believed in the Greek cause, and who were active in its furtherance; there was a Tory minority, who were convinced of the expediency of the *status quo*, and who laboured with equal ardour in the cause of Turkish legitimacy; and in the third place there was a vast majority, who knew nothing whatsoever about the question. This latter category had at first rallied, with sturdy conviction, to what appeared to be the winning side of Turkey. That they should,

so soon afterwards, have hesitated in this allegiance,
may strike us to-day as strange, and somewhat sentimental. The massacre at Chios produced upon them
an impression which can only be described as painful.
It was in vain that the British merchants of the Levant
and other well-informed Turcophiles explained that the
incidents at Chios had been caused by the wilful behaviour of the victims. The sentimentalists of the early
nineteenth century were not convinced. Nor can we
wholly blame them; for it must be admitted that the
limpid stream of Turcophilism was at that date clouded
by certain rather materialistic ingredients. On the
practical side it was confused by the propaganda of the
Levant Company, who, in their excess of zeal, allowed
it to become a little too apparent that they were fighting
for their own monopoly against the filthy menace of
Hellenic competition. On the moral side, the friends of
Turkey were disconcerted by the persistent manner in
which the Turks would, so to speak, let them down.
On the political side, the cause of Turkey was, perhaps
unduly, identified with that of legitimacy, with that of
the Holy Alliance, with that, in a word, of Castlereagh.
So that the waters of their conviction became, as I have
said, somewhat discoloured.

The stream of Philhellenism, on the other hand, though
at first more tenuous, was from the first more unsullied,
and, in the circumstances of the time, more national.
It represented the reaction against the Holy Alliance—
the reaction, that is, against a foreign policy dictated from
Vienna. The success which the Greeks by their unaided
efforts had already achieved did much to dispel the
bogey of a Russian protectorate. There were several
people who began to feel that Greece, after all, and at
the end of all, might prove the winning side. The advent
of Canning, moderate, British, and convinced, provided
a rallying point for the ignorant and the uncertain.
The British press, although both supercilious and violent,
was at that date almost unanimously Anglophile. The

editors and proprietors of the leading journals took a positively jingo pleasure in maintaining that England and her Foreign Minister might, after all, be in the right.

And finally the adhesion of Byron lifted the cause from the muddied by-ways of party politics, and rendered it at once an enterprise, a novelty, an excitement, and a very emotional romance.

CHAPTER IV

February—July 1823

I

HOWEVER indifferent the great mass of public opinion in England may at first have been to the cause of Greece, however much Hobhouse and Burdett may have seen in it a convenient and dramatic move in the game of party politics, to Byron the Greek cause glimmered with increasing illumination as a great personal opportunity, as a providential chance of escape.

The mood of restlessness and dissatisfaction which culminated in 1823 and which, fusing with his passionate desire for rehabilitation, had by then assumed the form of a determination to break, if need be ruthlessly, with his present associations, had been germinating in his mind ever since he had come to tire of the debauchery at Venice, and to realise that, even on the continent, his reputation was almost irretrievably besmirched. The bitter reactions against Venice, the fierce hatred of that " Sea-Sodom " which those listless days and hectic nights had left behind them, stirred within him as early as July 1818 the desire, nebulous it is true, but persistent, to emigrate to the United States. The *Ode to Venice*, which he composed in that month, concluded with the announcement of some such intention, but his enthusiasm for the new Republic was subsequently chilled by the abuse which was showered upon him in the American papers. In 1819 therefore we find him writing to Hobhouse and informing him quite seriously of his wish to settle in Venezuela. At other times vague plans occurred to him of buying a province in Chili, in Peru, or even in Mexico. "I want," he wrote, "a country and a home, and, if possible, a free one."

These projects were not taken very seriously by his friends in London. They doubted whether Byron was physically, as distinct from imaginatively, capable of anything so drastic. "The undercurrent of his mind," writes Trelawny, "was always drifting towards the East. He envied the free and independent manner in which Lady Hester Stanhope lived in Syria, and often reverted to it. He said he would have gone there if she had not forestalled him. Then his thoughts veered round to his early love—the Isles of Greece and the revolution in that country. For before that time he never dreamt of donning the warrior's plume, though the peace-loving Shelley had suggested it, and I urged it. He asked me to get him any information I could amongst my friends at Leghorn on the state of Greece; but as it was a common practice of his to make such inquiries without any serious object, I took little heed of his request."

I have already indicated that, ever since his return to England in 1811, the attraction of the Greek islands had persisted. In December of that year he had written to Hodgson: "I have no plans; sometimes I think of the East again and dearly beloved Greece." All through his life, whenever perplexities or embarrassments began to shackle him, his heart would veer towards the Levant and the two happy years that he had spent there. We find him considering the purchase of some Greek island; of Naxos at one moment, of Ithaca at another, of Anti-Paros; and at one period even of Zante. His conception of Greece as being for him the last resource, the ultimate asylum, is vividly illustrated in a letter which he wrote to Moore in January 1816, at a time when his domestic difficulties were reaching a climax :—

"This is but a dull scrawl, and I am but a dull fellow. Just at present, I am absorbed in 500

71

contradictory contemplations, though with but one object in view—which will probably end in nothing, as most things we wish do. But never mind—as somebody says—'for the blue sky bends over all.' I only could be glad if it bent over me where it is a little bluer, like the 'skyish top of blue Olympus,' which, by the way, looked very white when I last saw it."

Nor is Moore's comment upon this passage less illuminating than the passage itself :—

"On reading over the foregoing letter, I was much struck by the tone of melancholy that pervaded it ; and well knowing it to be the habit of the writer's mind to seek relief, when under the pressure of any disquiet or disgust, in that sense of freedom which told him that there were homes for him elsewhere, I could perceive, I thought, in his recollections of the 'blue Olympus,' some return of the restless and roving spirit which unhappiness or impatience always called up in his mind."

The memory of those sunlit days when he had sailed spell-bound among the Cyclades, had thus left an indelible mark upon his feelings and his character. The Greek climate and the glittering contours of the Greek promontories had formed the perpetual background of his most inspired verses. Nor did he, for one moment, forget how in the first bloom of his youth and freedom he had sailed below

> " The Acroceraunian Mountains of old name :
> And on Parnassus seen the eagles fly."

Until the spring of 1821 this warm and ever-kindled affection for the shores and seas of Greece had been but the sentimental love for something essentially inanimate and soulless. He felt for Greece the sad regret " of lovers o'er the dust they loved," and he bent over her sufferings as over the body of some cherished being. With the outbreak of the Greek War of Independence in the spring of 1821, his old affection was kindled to a more living and dynamic interest. On June 4th of that year he had concluded a letter to Moore with the words : " The Greeks ! What think you ? They are my old acquaintances—but what to think I know not. Let us hope, howsomever." In September of that year, when deeply involved in the Carbonari movement and with the Countess Guiccioli, he interpolates a sudden query in a letter to Murray : " What thinkest thou of Greece ? " And only a fortnight later there is a passage in a letter to Moore which shows that, had it not been for his responsibilities towards the Countess Guiccioli, he would have already joined the movement in the autumn of its first year. " It is awful work," he wrote, " this love, and prevents all a man's projects of good or glory. I wanted to go to Greece lately (as everything seems up here) with her brother, who is a very fine, brave fellow (I have seen him put to the proof), and wild about liberty. But the tears of a woman who has left her husband for a man, and the weakness of one's own heart, are paramount to these projects, and I can hardly indulge them." And by November of that year he stated definitely to Medwin : " I mean to return to Greece, and shall in all probability die there."

" Lord Byron," says Pietro Gamba in his excellent narrative of the last journey, " had once intended fixing his residence in Italy, but the political state of that country gave rise to feelings of disgust. He likewise had some thoughts of going to the United States of America, where he was known and esteemed. I once saw him nearly on the point of departure. . . . He often felt the want of some other occupation than that of writing, and frequently said that the public must be tired of his compositions, and that he was certainly more so."

" And thus," concludes Gamba, " towards the end of February, 1823, he turned his thoughts towards Greece."

"It was long my great object," wrote Trelawny to Hobhouse from Missolonghi on April 30th, 1824, "to get him out of Italy, and he was wearied of staying there. Exercise and excitement seemed necessary for both his body and mind, and both seemed declining in his long inactive and secluded way of living in the south. He became peevish, sickly and indifferent, and discontented with everything. He acknowledged this, and I continually urged him with new plans. I built him a yacht, for he was always fond of the sea. He got wearied of that. He would then go to South America, and took some ship for that purpose. Then he turned to North America, and from repeated and pressing invitations from them he seemed determined to go there. He got everything prepared, though this was much against my wishes, as I believed it was the country least suited to him. After much delay, the Greeks gaining ground, and his strong partiality to Greece—the interest everyone seems to feel for its fate—and lastly the letters of his friends in England decided him to go there. You know what followed."

II

In the letters which Byron had been writing to Hobhouse in the early weeks of February he had shown his excitement about the affairs of Greece, and had hinted that in certain circumstances he would be willing to go to that country and devote his services to the cause. This was at once passed on by Hobhouse to the Greek Committee. Mr. John Bowring and other members of the Greek Committee, which had at that date been only informally constituted, wrote to Genoa expressing their gratification at Byron's decision. A prolonged silence followed on the part of the Crown and Anchor, although towards the end of March Byron received a letter from Edward Blaquière, then on his way to Greece with the

Greek delegate Luriottis. Blaquière proposed to visit Byron on his way through Genoa and to explain to him the aims and purposes of the Greek Committee and the funds which they could at that moment command. " I shall be delighted," Byron replied, " to see you and your Greek friend, and the earlier the better. I have been expecting you for some time—you will find me at home. I cannot express to you how much I feel interested in the cause, and nothing but the hopes I entertained of witnessing the liberation of Italy itself prevented me from returning to do what little I could as an individual in the land which it is an honour even to have visited."

It was not, however, till April 7th, 1823, that the following note was brought to the Casa Saluzzo :—

> " *Saturday, April 7th*,
> " *Hotel des Quatre Nations,*
> " *Genoa.*

> " My Lord,
> " Having reached this place last night on my way to Greece, I could not pass through Genoa without taking the liberty of communicating with your Lordship and offering you my best services in a country which your powerful pen has rendered doubly dear to the friends of freedom and humanity. . . ."

Edward Blaquière had arrived. The interview took place that afternoon in the Casa Saluzzo, and stimulated by the calm optimism of Blaquière and the eloquent incitations of Luriottis, Byron at once reaffirmed his offer and expressed his immediate readiness to proceed to Greece. " He then," writes Gamba, " decided on as early a departure as possible. Mr. Blaquière was to send information, and we were to be ready on the receipt of his letter."

From the London Committee, however, no official acceptance of his services had been forthcoming, and Byron began to fret at receiving no acknowledgment of the offer which he had made to them unofficially through Hobhouse. Writing to Lord Blessington on April 23rd he complained of the neglect to which he had been subjected :—

> "What the Honourable Dug (Kinnaird) and his Committee may decide, I do not know, and still less what I may decide (for I am not famous for decision) for myself; but if I could do any good in any way, I should be happy to contribute thereto, and without éclat. I have seen enough of that in my time to rate it at its value. I wish *you* were upon that Committee, for I think you would set them going one way or the other; at present they seem a little dormant."

"I conceive," he wrote later, "that I have already been grossly ill-treated by the Committee," and in a burst of petulant susceptibility he decided for the moment to withdraw his offer. "He would hover," records Leigh Hunt, "on the borders of his inclination for Greece."

The silence on the part of the Committee was not intentional. On March 14th their honorary secretary, Mr. John Bowring, had forwarded to Byron a copy of the circular which had been drafted at the inaugural meeting, and had enclosed it in the following letter :—

> "I cannot," he wrote, "send on the accompanying circular without adding a few lines. Mr. Hobhouse has apprised our Committee that we may hope for your kind and cordial support in the good cause. And as you, more than any living being, have been instrumental in awakening that sympathy which, I hope, will become an effective sympathy, we trust that you will lend us your talents and your influence to give our operations more certain success."

On April 26th, relying on further assurances given them by Hobhouse on the authority of a private letter from Byron, the Committee had passed the following resolution :—

"That the thanks of the Committee be communicated to Lord Byron for his generous offer in service of the Greeks, and that he be requested to favour us with any suggestions or communications likely to advance the cause."

Owing to a misunderstanding, due to a notice which was published in the London papers to the effect that Byron had already left Genoa for Paris and London, this resolution and the previous letter had both been addressed to Calais in the hope of intercepting him upon his journey. They were eventually forwarded to Genoa, where they only arrived towards the middle of May. The vote of thanks reached Byron a week sooner than the previous letter, and he acknowledged it as follows :—

> "*Genoa,*
> "*May 12, 1823.*

"SIR,
"I have great pleasure in acknowledging your letter, and the honour which the Committee have done me. I shall endeavour to deserve their confidence by every means in my power. My first wish is to go up into the Levant in person, where I might be enabled to advance, if not the cause, at least the means of obtaining information which the Committee might be desirous of acting upon; and my former residence in the country, my familiarity with the Italian language (which is there universally spoken, or at least to the same extent as French in the more polished parts of the Continent), and my *not* total ignorance of the Romaic, would afford me some advantages of experience. To this project the only objection is of a domestic nature, and I shall try to get over it : if I fail in this, I must do

what I can where I am; but it will be always a
source of regret to me to think that I might perhaps
have done more for the cause on the spot. . . .

"The principal material wanted by the Greeks
appears to be, first, a park of field artillery—light,
and fit for mountain-service; secondly, gunpowder;
thirdly, hospital or medical stores. The readiest
mode of transmission is, I hear, by Idra, addressed
to Mr. Negri, the minister. I meant to send up a
certain quantity of the two latter—no great deal,
but enough for an individual to show his good
wishes for the Greek success, but am pausing because,
in case I should go myself, I can take them with me.
I do not want to limit my own contribution to this
merely, but more especially, if I can get to Greece
myself, I should devote whatever resources I can
muster of my own to advancing the great object. I
am in correspondence with Signor Nicolas Karrellas
(well known to Mr. Hobhouse), who is now at Pisa;
but his latest advice merely stated that the Greeks
are at present employed in organising their *internal*
government and the details of its administration;
this would seem to indicate *security*, but the war
is, however, far from being terminated.

"The Turks are an obstinate race, as all former
wars have proved them, and will return to the charge
for years to come, even if beaten, as it is to be hoped
they will be. But in no case can the labours of the
Committee be said to be in vain; for in the event
even of the Greeks being subdued and dispersed, the
funds which could be employed in succouring and
gathering together the remnant, so as to alleviate in
part their distresses, and enable them to find or make
a country (as so many emigrants of other nations
have been compelled to do), would 'bless both
those who gave and those who took,' as the bounty
both of justice and of mercy.

"With regard to the formation of a brigade

(which Mr. Hobhouse hints at in his short letter of this day's receipt, enclosing the one to which I have the honour to reply), I would presume to suggest—but merely as an opinion, resulting rather from the melancholy experience of the brigades embarked in the Columbian service than from any experiment yet fairly tried in Greece—that the attention of the Committee had better perhaps be directed to the employment of *officers* of experience than the enrolment of *raw British* soldiers, which latter are apt to be unruly, and not very serviceable, in irregular warfare, by the side of foreigners. A small body of good officers, especially artillery; an engineer, with a quantity (such as the Committee might deem requisite) of stores of the nature which Captain Blaquière indicated as most wanted, would, I should conceive, be a highly useful accession. Officers, also, who had previously served in the Mediterranean would be preferable, as some knowledge of Italian is nearly indispensable.

"It would also be as well that they should be aware that they are not going to ' rough it on a beefsteak and bottle of port,' but that Greece—never, of late years, very plentifully stocked for a *mess*—is at present the country of all kinds of *privations*. This remark may seem superfluous; but I have been led to it by observing that many *foreign* officers, Italian, French, and even Germans (but fewer of the *latter*), have returned in disgust, imagining either that they were going up to make a party of pleasure, or to enjoy full pay, speedy promotion, and a very moderate degree of duty. They complain, too, of having been ill received by the Government or inhabitants; but numbers of these complainers were mere adventurers, attracted by a hope of command and plunder, and disappointed of both. Those Greeks I have seen strenuously deny the charge of inhospitality, and declare that they shared their pittance to the last crumb with their foreign volunteers. . . .

"I beg that the Committee will command me in any and every way. If I am favoured with any instructions, I shall endeavour to obey them to the letter, whether conformable to my own private opinion or not. I beg leave to add, personally, my respect for the gentlemen whom I have the honour of addressing."

Such a letter should have convinced the London Committee of the sanity and experience which Lord Byron would be able to contribute. They were not convinced : Hobhouse, for his part, doubted whether Byron would ever execute his engagements, or whether he would have the strength of character to remain there once he had arrived. For Hobhouse was by then a little out of touch with Byron's circumstances and condition : he did not realise that for Byron this Greek venture was the last chance; that there was really nothing else for him to do. It would be great fun, of course, for the dear fellow to revisit the Ægean and to have some active employment. Hobhouse, sceptical, prosaic, and a little jealous, was incapable of visualising the enterprise in its wider and more tragic contours. He was so fully occupied himself with party business, and the views of Mr. Bentham, and the fate of the South American republics, and the future of J. C. Hobhouse, that he could pay but a superficial, although an affectionate and very tolerant, attention to the actions of Byron.

And the latter, meanwhile, mortified but undeterred, proceeded with the detailed preparations for his departure.

III

Trelawny had disappeared : he had wandered off to shoot ducks in the Maremma; he had contracted fever; he had proceeded to Rome, occupying himself with the disposal of Shelley's ashes and the composition of ill-spelt love-letters to Claire Clairmont. Early in May he had reached Florence, and it was only then that Byron was able to communicate with him.

The preparations meanwhile had been left to Pietro Gamba, a youth of infinite charm and enthusiasm, but of great ill-fortune in the conduct of affairs. For the arrangements made by Pietro Gamba were apt to become involved and to miscarry: he would grapple earnestly and conscientiously with some problem, he would write it all down in the most exact and careful of memoranda, each illegible page beginning in the fashion of Bologna University, with the word "Considerando." And then it would all go wrong. He would come to Byron and explain that there had been a confusion, a slight "malinteso," and he would stand there, his white eyelashes flickering and a modest blush upon his boyish phthisic cheeks. "Mio caro Bairon," he would explain . . . and even Byron could not bring himself to be annoyed.

A more efficient assistant was Charles Barry, partner in the firm of Webb & Co., English bankers of Genoa and Leghorn. Not that Charles Barry had any enthusiasm for the cause of the Hellenes; they were a set of dirty and unscrupulous rebels; they had disturbed the trade of the Levant; they had turned the Ægean into a nest of pirates; they had even seized a consignment which the house of Webb & Co. had financed. It was ridiculous that a man of Lord Byron's position and good sense should risk his fortune and his life in a cause both unprofitable and deleterious. But then Lord Byron was a man of rank and genius; a man so cordial, so whimsical and so kind: there was "something about him," Mr. Barry decided; there was something which induced Mr. Barry to do all manner of things which he would not have done for any other client, however rich and noble; there was something which induced Mr. Barry each day to climb the steep and dusty lane which led to the Casa Saluzzo and to spend hours in those cool, empty rooms, drawn by an attraction which he could not " for the life of him " explain.

And finally there was Henry Dunn of Leghorn, the man who kept the English shop in the Via Ferdinanda, to-day the Via Vittorio Emanuele, but then, as now, known as the Via Grande. Dunn could provide all manner of things, from gunpowder to the last copy of the *Quarterly*; incidentally he was a very acute man of business, and so was Byron. There was thus little cordiality between them, and much haggling, and in the end, even at Missolonghi, there was some acrid correspondence about a disputed bill. And Mr. Dunn lived on till 1867, and would recount to subsequent tourists how intimate had been his relations with the late Lord Byron, and how the latter had been reading *Galignani's Messenger* in the back room of the shop at Leghorn when the news arrived of the discovery of Shelley's body. All of which may, or may not, have actually happened.

Aided in this manner by Dunn and Barry, Byron could evade the " mal occhio " of Gamba, and press forward his preparations. Letters were addressed to the Greek refugees at Leghorn, inviting their opinion as to the most suitable centre from which Byron could exercise his influence in the cause of the insurgents. Mr. Dunn was to keep his eyes open for a suitable vessel, not too expensive, to convey Lord Byron to the Morea or elsewhere. Mr. Barry was to consider the question of finance, and such complicated details as letters of credit and exchange. The famous Pisan surgeon, Andrea Vaccà, was asked to recommend a young doctor who would be prepared for £100 to proceed as personal physician to Lord Byron and his staff. And last, but not least, Lord Byron gave his personal attention to the design of the uniform and helmets in which he and his immediate staff were to land resplendently upon the shores of Hellas. The uniforms were to be of scarlet and gold. The three helmets, however, were not all of the same design and manufacture. For Gamba he had proposed a polygon of green cloth rising in the shape of a Uhlan's shako from a base of brass and black leather, bearing in the front an inadequate and rather startled semblance of Athene. For himself, however, and for Trelawny (he counted on Trelawny) he designed two helmets of homeric proportions, and on the lines of that which, in the sixth book of the *Iliad*, had so dismayed the infant Astyanax. Below the nodding plume figured his own coat of arms, and the motto " crede Biron," while the whole was secured by a wide chin-strap of a very menacing aspect. These helmets were the work of Giacomo Aspe of Genoa. Byron was delighted with the one he himself had chosen : he allowed a local artist to take a little scratchy portrait of him thus arrayed ; but Trelawny, when he arrived, refused vehemently to put his on. Byron, disconcerted by this refusal, began to have doubts as to the propriety of his own helmet ; so that they were all put back in their pink cardboard boxes and did not in the end figure in the disembarkation at Missolonghi ; and the order for the three scarlet uniforms was countermanded.

Meanwhile early in May a letter had been received from Edward Blaquière dated from Zante, in which he advised Byron to proceed in the first instance to one of the Ionian islands, where he would be able to obtain first-hand information from Greece, before committing himself to any one of the several parties between which the direction of the movement was at that time being disputed. Blaquière promised to await Byron's arrival, or, failing that, to meet him in the Morea. He undertook, so soon as he had reached Tripolitza, to report on the condition of the country, and he advised them not to leave Genoa until this information had been received.

The importance of avoiding any precipitate action was emphasised in the first week of May, when, on riding one afternoon in the outskirts of Genoa, they encountered two figures limping along the road in rags, whose general appearance showed that they were not natives of the

country, and that their unfortunate plight arose from
causes other than that of voluntary vagabondage. Two
days later these unfortunate people called at the Casa
Saluzzo and asked for assistance. They turned out to
be two young Germans, who had escaped from the Battle
of Peta when the legion of Philhellenes, commanded by
General Normann, had been decimated by the Turks.
From Trieste, where they had landed, they had been
driven out by the Austrian authorities, and had walked
on to Leghorn and to Genoa in the most deplorable
condition, barefooted and penniless. One of them was
a Bavarian and the other a native of Wurtemberg, and
although they accepted their unfortunate condition with
practical philosophy, the account they gave of conditions
in Greece was not encouraging. They laid great stress
upon the need of a few regular troops, and added that what
the Greeks required above all was not arms and ammunition, but food, hospital stores and money. "The
Bavarian," Byron wrote to John Bowring, "wonders a
little that the Greeks are not quite the same with them
of the time of Themistocles (they were not then very
tractable, by the by), and at the difficulty of disciplining
them . . . the other seems to wonder at nothing." In
contradiction to this account, the newspapers had
announced that the Greeks had settled their difficulties,
had formed a central government, and were prepared for
a vigorous defence. Byron became impatient on the
receipt of this intelligence. "What need," he exclaimed
to Gamba, "have they for the assistance of a stranger?"
And he began to "expedite his preparations, fearing that
he would arrive too late."

Another difficulty, and one of a more delicate and
domestic nature, was to arise before Byron could leave
Genoa. On May 10th Mrs. Shelley wrote to Trelawny
as follows: "Do you come to Greece? Lord Byron
continues in the same mind. The Guiccioli is an
obstacle, and certainly her situation is a rather difficult
one. But he does not seem disposed to make a mountain

of her resistance, and he is far more able to take a decided than a petty step in contradiction to the wishes of those about him."

On May 24th we find Byron himself writing to Lord Blessington as follows :—

" May 24th, 1823.

" MY DEAR LORD,

"I find that I was elected a Member of the Greek Committee in March, but did not receive the Chairman's notice till yesterday, and this by mere chance, and through a private hand. I am doing all I can to get away, and the Committee and my friends in England seem both to approve of my going up into Greece ; but I meet here with obstacles, which have hampered and put me out of spirits, and still keep me in a vexatious state of uncertainty."

One thing alone was certain, and that was the determination to leave Genoa, and to break with the complications of his existence at the Casa Saluzzo. " If we do not go to Greece," he said to Captain Roberts, " I am determined to go somewhere, as I am tired of this place, the shore and all the people on it." It was with relief, therefore, that early in June he received the following letter from Trelawny :—

" Florence,
" June 10th, 1823.

" The various rumours reached me of your having seriously turned your thoughts towards Greece, I purported writing to say how happy I should be in accompanying you, but was delayed by the fear you might think me officious or at least premature. But as Mary Shelley assures me that your purpose holds good, and (that should nothing intervene to deter you) that your mind is made up on going, I hastened to express my readiness to join issue with you, in whatever may be your definitive object in

going—either on sea or shore. The most independent and pleasant way will be to have a fast-
sailing armed vessel, as the Archipelago is all alive
with Turks and mirauders (*sic*).

" The Greeks seem to be slowly but progressively
advancing their cause, and the supineness with which
the legitimate government look on augurs favourably,
as there are hopes they will not interfere. There is
a panegyrical paragraph in the French and other
papers asserting that you have offered your services
and fortune to the Greeks. . . . I think of going
there (to Leghorn) to await your definitive determination. In the meantime I can, if you wish it,
keep a sharp look-out on vessels for sale."

This letter crossed one which Byron had already
addressed to Trelawny at Florence. " You must have
heard," he wrote, " that I am going to Greece. Why do
you not come to me ? I want your aid, and am exceedingly anxious to see you. Pray come, for I am at last
determined to go to Greece ; it is the only place I was
ever contented in. I am serious, and did not write
before, as I might have given you a journey for nothing ;
they all say I can be of use in Greece. I do not know
how, nor do they ; but at all events let us go."

Within a few days from the date of this letter Mr.
Dunn and Captain Roberts between them had found
what they considered a suitable vessel to convey the party
to Greece. She was a British brig of 120 tons, called
the " Hercules." Her captain and owner, John Scott,
at once placed himself at the disposal of Lord Byron,
and proceeded to Leghorn to pick up the stores which
Mr. Dunn had been ordered to prepare. Trelawny,
who fancied himself exceedingly in all matters connected
with the sea, did not approve of the " Hercules." " A
collier-built tub," he called her, " built on the lines of a
baby's cradle—she would do anything but go ahead."
But Trelawny was temperamentally addicted to such

criticisms of all decisions for which he had not himself
been made responsible.

Meanwhile the inquiries addressed to the Greek
refugees at Leghorn were producing replies of the most
contradictory nature. The least uninteresting of these
letters was that addressed to Byron from Pisa by the
metropolitan Ignatius, and which I transcribe as
follows :—

> "*le 21 juin/3 juillet,*
> "*1823, Pise.*

" My Lord,

"Mes compatriotes de Livourne m'ont com-
muniqué les lettres, que votre Seigneurie leur a
écrites pour leur annoncer votre départ pour la
Grèce ma patrie. Votre résolution, My Lord, me
fait connaître les nobles sentiments de votre cœur.

" Je vous souhaite un heureux voyage et l'accom-
plissement de vos desirs, qui ne peuvent certaine-
ment être que pour le bien-être et la prospérité de
cette belle, mais malheureuse contrée. . . . La
terre que vous allez visiter, My Lord, dans ce
moment, vous la trouverez encore plus dévastée de
ce qu'elle était lors de votre premier voyage en
Grèce, mais en revanche vous connaîtrez dans ses
habitans des dignes fils de leurs ancêtres et encore
plus dignes de porter le nom des fils de la Grèce.
Les Grecs attendaient le moment pour faire connaître que le sang de leurs pères coulait encore dans
leurs veines ; et lorsque ce moment est arrivé ils
nous ont fait voir que leurs explois sont aussi
sublimes, aussi nobles, aussi grands, que ceux de ces
héros, qui furent conduits par les Thémistocles, les
Miltiades, et les Léonidas. Au milieu de ces vertus,
vous trouverez, My Lord, aussi de la confusion et
du désordre ; mais votre bonté saura les excuser et
en attribuer la cause, partie à l'ignorance, partie
cet esprit d'indépendance personelle propre au
caractère du Grec, et partie enfin à la nouveauté de

leur état. Mais l'ordre dans les sociétés ne se forme que par le tems, et c'est au tems que nous devons confier l'établissement de l'ordre.

" Vous aurez l'occasion, My Lord, de voir notre marine, qui, comme je l'espère, attirera votre attention, et parmi nos héros je dois vous recommender particulièrement le brave Marco Botzaris et ses Souliotes.

" Je ne puis achever ma lettre sans vous renouveler mes souhaits pour votre heureux voyage et vous assurer de ma haute estime et de ma parfaite considération."

Another letter was from Constantine Mavrocordato, a brother of Alexander, which, while indulging in the usual generalities regarding " Nostra desolata patria," is interesting in that it advised Byron to establish himself at Missolonghi. I translate the relevant passage of this letter as follows :—

" In reply to the request made to me by Mr. Barry . . . my opinion is that on your arrival in the Ionian islands the best place for you to establish yourself would be Missolonghi in Ætolia, a place which would be very well adapted to serve as a base for your purposes, as it is the one point in our dear fatherland which is the most threatened by the enemy, and the weakest and most in need in present circumstances. In this place your Excellency could get into touch with General Marco Botzaris, captain of the brave Souliots, who, being honoured by your presence and assistance, could with greater facility increase their numbers, and put themselves in a state to take the offensive against Epirus. . . .

" The above-mentioned Marco Botzaris is one of the bravest and most honest of the Greek captains, and if he could secure your friendship and assistance you would see by the result what advantageous operations he will be capable of. . . ."

PREPARATIONS

These letters were helpful enough, but they did not in Byron's opinion in any way compensate for the absence of all news from Blaquière. Finally in the first week of July Blaquière's first letter arrived from Greece. It informed Byron that the Greek Government were expecting him; it counselled him, however, to await further letters before leaving Genoa. These further letters missed Byron at Genoa, and were not delivered to him until several months afterwards, when he was already established at Missolonghi. There was one dated in May from Tripolitza, in which Blaquière described the conditions of the country, and warned Byron of the discomforts with which he would have to cope. On his arrival at the capital of the Morea, he had found that there were no facilities and no accommodation, and even Mavrocordato himself was obliged to lie upon the floor wrapped only in a great-coat. In a subsequent letter, dated July 9th, and addressed to Byron at Genoa, Blaquière expressed the opinion that the present moment was most inopportune for his arrival, and urged him to postpone his departure indefinitely. By the end of June, however, Byron had determined that he could wait no longer, and it may be doubted whether, once his decision had been taken and the resistance of the Countess Guiccioli had been overcome, he would in any case have followed the advice of Edward Blaquière.

By the beginning of July the die was cast, and on the 13th of that month Byron embarked in Genoa harbour upon the " Hercules."

CHAPTER V

THE BRIG " HERCULES "

July 13—*August* 3, 1823

I

I⊤ would be idle to pretend that Byron set out upon
this his last journey with any very spirited enthusiasm,
either for the cause which he was embracing or for the
particular functions which he would be called upon to
fulfil. Nor would it be honest to portray as some
reckless Elizabethan, intent upon the gain and glory of
a new endurance, the irresolute and dyspeptic little man
who, on that July evening, limped gloomily up the gangway of the " Hercules." For when it had come to
packing up, and destroying old letters, and explaining to
Barry what was to be done with the books, and totting
up the accounts, and sending the horses down to the
harbour, and finding everything at the Casa Saluzzo
hourly more disintegrated and uncomfortable, he began,
definitely and indignantly, to curse the whole undertaking. It was always like that : people never left one
alone ; there he was, good-natured and kindly, and they
came along and took advantage of him, and extracted
promises, and imposed upon him generally. Once
again he had been caught in a chain of circumstances :
there had been his first visit to Greece, and *Childe Harold*,
and *The Corsair*, and that silly passage about the
" hereditary bondsmen " ; and there had been Hobhouse
(damn Hobhouse !), and that egregious ass Trelawny.
And as a result here was he, who had never done any harm
to anyone, sitting alone in the Casa Saluzzo, with his
household gods once again dismantled around him, and

his bulldog growling now and then at the distant voice of Trelawny thundering orders to the servants.

Of all forms of cant, this cant of romanticism was the most insufferable. There was Trelawny, for instance, trying to look like Lara, with his sham eagle eyes, his sham disordered hair, his sham abrupt manners. Why couldn't Trelawny behave quietly and like a man of decent breeding? Surely, if they were committed to this Greek scrape it would be better to take the thing soberly and calmly, instead of all this dust and bustle, of all this cant about Causes, and Liberty, and Adventure. How he *loathed* adventures! At the mere word he ground his teeth in fury.

This petulant reaction against his own decisions had been growing upon him ever since he found himself committed to the undertaking. "It is not pleasant," he had remarked to Lady Blessington, "that my eyes should never open to the folly of the undertakings passion prompts me to engage in, until I am so far embarked that retreat (at least with honour) is impossible, and my 'mal à propos sagesse' arrives, to scare away the enthusiasm that led to the undertaking, and which is so requisite to carry it on. It is all an uphill affair with me afterwards: I cannot for my life 'échauffer' my imagination again; and my position excites such ludicrous images and thoughts in my own mind, that the whole subject, which, seen through the veil of passion, looked fit for a sublime epic, and I one of its heroes, examined now through reason's glass appears fit only for a travestie, and my poor self a Major Sturgeon, marching and counter-marching, not from Acton to Ealing, or from Ealing to Acton, but from Corinth to Athens, and from Athens to Corinth. Yet, hang it," continued he, "these very names ought to chase away every idea of the ludicrous; but the laughing devils will return, and make a mockery of everything, as with me there is, as Napoleon said, but one step between the sublime and the ridiculous. Well, *if I do* (and this *if* is a grand *peut-être* in my future history) outlive the campaign, I shall write two poems on the subject—one an epic, and the other a burlesque, in which none shall be spared, and myself least of all."

The waves of indignation which surged up in him as the moment actually approached for his departure are not, however, to be explained solely by this superficial ruffling of his amazingly fluid character. It was not merely the irritating turmoil of the last preparations, the difficulty which he had always experienced in wresting himself away from any place where he had taken root. It was not merely the vivid realisation of the difficulties which would assail him in Greece, a realisation which contrasted so jarringly with the vapid optimism of his companions. It was a deep and superstitious impression that the chapter which was opening would be the final chapter; it was an abiding presentiment that he would not return alive. " You will think me," he had said to Lady Blessington, " more superstitious than ever, when I tell you that I have a presentiment that I shall die in Greece. I hope it may be in action, for that would be a good finish to a very ' triste ' existence, and I have a horror of death-bed scenes; but as I have not been famous for my luck in life, most probably I shall not have more in the manner of my death, and that I may draw my last sigh, not on the field of glory, but on the bed of disease. I very nearly died when I was in Greece in my youth; perhaps as things have turned out it would have been well if I had; I should have lost nothing, and the world very little, and I would have escaped many cares, for God knows I have had enough of one kind or another. But I am getting gloomy, and looking either back or forward is not calculated to enliven me. One of the reasons why I quiz my friends in conversation is that it keeps me from thinking of myself. You laugh, but it is true."

To this conviction that he was journeying to his death he bowed his head with an unflinching resignation: from the first he accepted it as inevitable. " There was a helplessness about Byron, a sort of abandonment of himself to his destiny, as he called it, that commonplace people can as little pity as understand."

For we must remember that Byron, with all his earthiness, his excessive " empeiria and mondanité," as Goethe called it, was haunted by a morbid fear of the supernatural. Even now, in his thirty-sixth year, he would be frightened sometimes at night-time, and before entering the vast baronial bed which had so shocked the refined taste of Lady Blessington, he would ask Fletcher to make sure, to make quite sure, that there was no one, that there was *nothing*, lurking underneath ; and every night the pistols would be placed within his reach. Tita or Fletcher had contracted the habit of remaining within call should their master shriek with nightmare, and when he did so, they would hurry in with soda water and little brass Genoese oil-flares, and the shadows of the four coronets would sway and flicker thereat upon the vaulted ceiling. Byron would be reassured, and thank them warmly. They drew their own conclusions from these oft-repeated incidents. As for Tita, with his dog-like devotion, *he* had always known that milord, so generous and thoughtful on every occasion, was hopelessly, though very amiably, insane ; and Tita had ceased to wonder at such outbursts. But Fletcher, who remembered similar incidents in the old Newstead days, attributed their recent renewal to that Mr. Shelley, who had a habit, even when the company had just sat down to table, of hopping about screaming that he had seen a lady with eyes in her bosom, or a child calling to him from the sea, or even a phantom of himself passing, in a garden hat, in front of the window. This sort of thing had been very bad for his master, but it was not for Fletcher to criticise. " My lord," he would sigh, " may be very odd, but he has such a good heart." And he left it at that.

For Byron himself, this particular form of neurosis had confirmed his inherited tendency to believe absolutely in prophecies, coincidences, presentiments, and forebodings. "No consideration," he would say, "can induce me to undertake anything either on a Friday or a Sunday." At the back of his mind there remained the recollection of that destiny which Mrs. Williams, the fortune-teller of Cheltenham, had predicted to his mother in 1801. He was to marry twice, the second time to a foreign lady. This forecast had, in all but legal form, been oppressively fulfilled. And above all "he was to beware of his thirty-seventh year." The span of life vouchsafed to him by Mrs. Williams was approaching its conclusion ; it coincided with the term which had been allotted to his father. There could be no doubt that Mrs. Williams had prophesied correctly, and that it was this senseless journey to Greece which was to justify her warning.

Excessive always in the dramatisation of his own circumstances, Byron, from the moment that he realised the coincidence between this prophecy and his impending enterprise, assumed that sentence of death, irrevocable and ineluctable, had already been passed. It was as a doomed victim that he embarked at Genoa, picturing himself half-seriously and half-humorously as the Iphigenia of this second Iliad. And it was with the reckless fatalism thus engendered that he chose as the defiant date of his embarcation a Sunday and the 13th of the month.

II

The passengers who assembled under the hot evening sun upon the deck of the "Hercules" were, to say the least, heterogeneous. They were all, in their different ways, afraid of Byron. He stood there in his blue cap and his white trousers, silent, morose, and apparently disinterested, tugging and jerking his lace-fringed handkerchief between his small white hands. To some of them his insouciance, his melancholy, and his detachment were highly impressive; to Trelawny, however, they were merely exasperating. For Trelawny, it must be remembered, did not care for Byron.

This adventurous younger son of a Cornish family was then in his thirty-second year. He had in 1811 deserted from the Royal Navy, and launched upon those lurid personal experiences which he was in 1831 to weave into an autobiography of doubtful veracity, but of indubitable imaginative force. In 1813 he returned to England, married an extravagant and foolish wife, and disappeared from romance for seven years. He emerges again in the summer of 1820 in the company of his friend Captain Roberts, drinking his early morning coffee in the *salle à manger* of the Hôtel de l'Ancre at Ouchy. A party of hob-nailed and exuberant English tourists clattered into the room; there were two ladies, and a bony, angular gentleman with a strong Cumberland accent, his nose and lips blotched and blistered by exposure to the Alpine snows. Trelawny was impressed by the " dogmatic and self-confident " opinions expressed by this singular person, as well as by the " precision and quaintness " of his language. He was even more entranced when he heard from Captain Roberts that the strangers were Mr. William Wordsworth, with his wife and his sister Dorothy.

" Who," records Trelawny, " could have divined this ? I could see no trace, in the hard features and weather-stained brow of the outer man, of the divinity within him. In a few minutes the travellers reappeared; we cordially shook hands, and agreed to meet again at Geneva. Now that I knew that I was talking to one of the veterans of the gentle craft, as there was no time to waste in idle ceremony, I asked him abruptly what he thought of Shelley as a poet.

" ' Nothing,' " he replied, as abruptly.

" Seeing my surprise, he added, ' A poet who has not produced a good poem before he is twenty-five, we may conclude cannot, and never will do so.'

"'*The Cenci!*' I said eagerly.

"'Won't do,' he replied, shaking his head, as he got into the carriage; a rough-coated Scotch terrier followed him.

"'This hairy fellow is our flea-trap,' he shouted out as they started off.

"When I recovered from the shock of having heard the harsh sentence passed by an elder bard on a younger brother of the Muses, I exclaimed . . ."

It matters little perhaps what Trelawny exclaimed on that occasion, but his interest in Shelley, stimulated by Mr. Wordsworth's truculence on the subject, was within the next week fired by the enthusiasm of Thomas Medwin and the two Williamses, whom he met in Geneva. A few months later we find Trelawny in his one-horse cabriolet bumping through France and Switzerland, embarked in the company of Captain Roberts on a literary pilgrimage to Pisa. He arrived on January 14th, 1822. "Trelawny," records Mrs. Shelley in her diary five days subsequently, "is extravagant—'un giovane stravagante'—partly natural, and partly, perhaps, put on, but it suits him well; and if his abrupt but not unpolished manners be assumed, they are nevertheless in unison with his Moorish face (for he looks Oriental, yet not Asiatic), his dark hair, his Herculean form; and then there is an air of extreme good nature which pervades his whole countenance, especially when he smiles, which assures me that his heart is good."

In this Mrs. Shelley was mistaken: Trelawny had no heart at all; all that he possessed was a capacity, an excessive capacity, for egoistic enthusiasms. Besides, Trelawny was a liar and a cad.

His subsequent relations with the "lieta brigata" at Pisa; the story of how he arranged for Shelley's cremation; of how he snatched his heart out of the fire and gave it to Leigh Hunt, who refused at first to surrender it to Mrs. Shelley; of how he fell in love both with Claire Clairmont and with Mrs. Shelley, are recorded with an undoubted touch of genius in the letters edited in 1910 by Mr. Buxton Forman, and predominantly in the two astonishing volumes published in 1858 under the title " Recollections of the Last Days of Shelley and Byron," and republished in 1878 in an amended and watered form, and with the title altered to " Records of Shelley, Byron and the Author."

Trelawny, as I have already indicated, regarded Byron with a deep-rooted, if somewhat tortuous, dislike. The causes of this antipathy are not hard to discover. Whatever impression Trelawny may have desired to convey in the records which he published thirty-six years later, the essential purpose of his pilgrimage to Pisa was, we may well suppose, to visit Byron, whose *Lara* and *Conrad* he had taken as the models of his life and behaviour, and not, or at least not primarily, to see Shelley. But Byron, for his part, did not regard either Trelawny or his pilgrimage with any seriousness : he took a mischievous delight in adopting in his relations with Trelawny the very posture which, he well knew, would most effectively extinguish the ardour of that enthusiast—he adopted the posture of a regency beau. He would swim with Trelawny, and play billiards with him, and allow him to manage the yacht. But all the time he would make it clear how much his young friend had missed by not being a man of fashion, how very out of date and provincial it was of him to admire and to imitate the opinions and exploits of the Corsair. " How he hates Byron," the gullible Mr. William Graham remarked to Claire Clairmont fifty-five years later, when discussing Trelawny's book with that untruthful and, by then, senile wanton. " Well, Byron snubbed him, you know," replied Claire Clairmont : " he said, ' Tre was an excellent fellow until he took to imitating my *Childe Harold* and *Don Juan*.' This got to Trelawny's ears, and he never forgave Byron for it."

The injury which had thereby been inflicted upon Trelawny's rancorous vanity was still smarting when he embarked that evening upon the " Hercules." He was at pains, even, to explain to his particular cronies how it came that he, who had so defiantly, behind his back, derided the tin god of Europe, should now be found proceeding as a member of his staff to Greece. " Lord B. and I," he wrote to Captain Roberts, " are extraordinarily thick. We are inseparables ; but mind, this does not flatter me. He has known me long enough to see the sacrifices I make in devoting myself to serve him. This is new to him, who is surrounded by mercenaries."

And to Claire Clairmont he wrote as follows :—

> " I have long contemplated this, but I was deterred by the fear that an unknown stranger without money, etc., would be ill received. I now go under better auspices. L. B. is one of the Greek Committee ; he takes out arms, ammunition, money, and protection to them. *When once there I can shift for myself*—and shall see what is to be done."

The italics are mine.

The latent and watchful hostility of Trelawny stands in marked contrast to the affection and veneration with which their leader was regarded by the other members of the company. There was Pietro Gamba, conscientious, unfortunate, and evanescent ; there was M. Schilizzi, a Greek relative of Alexander Mavrocordato, who had been accorded a passage ; there was Fletcher, and Tita Falciere, and Lega Zambelli, the intendant of Byron's household ; there was Trelawny's negro groom, who was subsequently transferred to Byron's personal service ; there were the five horses ; there was the bull-dog " Moretto " and the Newfoundland " Lion," a present from Lieut Le Mesurier of the British Navy ; there were 10,000 Spanish dollars in ready money and bills of exchange for 40,000 more ; there were medical stores sufficient for the needs of a regiment ; and finally there was Dr. Francesco Bruno, " personal physician to Lord Byron," and the subsequent inheritor of much unpleasant notoriety.

THE BRIG 'HERCULES'

The selection of this intelligent but timid student of the art of medicine for the post of attendant surgeon and doctor was due partly to Byron's own instincts of economy, and partly to the inefficiency of Pietro Gamba. The former did not wish to engage an Englishman, who would doubtless demand a high salary, and the latter had no idea whatever how a suitable Italian could be secured. He wrote vaguely to Leghorn and Pisa, and asked Professor Vaccà whether he could recommend a young man from his own school of medicine. Gamba's letter, however, arrived too late to produce any very useful result. Vaccà replied that had he received the inquiry earlier, he would have been able to select one of his own more promising pupils; he would even have gone with them himself, were it not for the many ties and responsibilities which kept him at Pisa. The personal physician had therefore to be selected at the last moment, and almost at random, and it was upon the unfortunate head of the youthful Bruno, who was recommended by Dr. Alexander, the English doctor at Genoa, that the selection fell. Dr. Bruno, that "unfledged student," as Trelawny called him, was obviously ill at ease upon the "Hercules." He skulked about timidly, and started when he was spoken to. Many months later he confessed to Gamba that the first fortnight of his journey had been for him a period of "perpetual terror," since he had been informed that if he committed the slightest fault Lord Byron would have him torn to pieces by his dogs which he kept for that purpose, or would order his "Tartar" to dash his brains out. It was only when they reached the Adriatic that Dr. Bruno realised that the said "Tartar" was in fact but Tita Falciere, gentlest of all Venetian gondolieri, and that as for the dogs, "Lion" was in no way dangerous, and "Moretto" dangerous only if annoyed. But the "perpetual terror," as we shall see, remained with Dr. Francesco Bruno till the end.

99

III

The night of the 13th, the first of many nights upon the "Hercules," was spent in Genoa harbour. Their little brig, dark and ungainly amid the reflected spars and lanterns of larger vessels, rode gently at her moorings waiting for the breeze of dawn. The feeling of isolation, which descends on those who stoop together in the tallow-lit cabins of little ships, oppressed them with a sense of severance from all that was familiar in their usual identity. Schilizzi and Gamba, Trelawny and Bruno, all but strangers that morning, and now stooping together in a confined and airless prison, folding their so personal possessions into strange and sticky lockers—isolated and yet promiscuous, alien and yet under the sudden compulsion of the closest intimacy!

We have all, at moments, experienced this rapid wrench from the habitual, this immediate plunge into an impersonal and unknown microcosm. But for those five men who found themselves that night encased so suddenly, the sounds of a wider and more familiar world —the distant rattle of a coach upon the cobbles, the lilt of a Southern song across the water—came but as the echoes of an existence already sundered, as the faint reminiscence of a life which once, and long ago, had been their own. This physical isolation was but the symbol and the prelude of a more spiritual detachment: there was no similitude in their condition with the pleasurable ventures of other passengers on other ships; it was no fortuitous circumstance, but a compelling destiny, which had thus combined them; and as their leader was one who glittered as the cynosure of half the world.

The sun of the 14th of July rose upon an unruffled sea, and not a breath stirred the oily waters of the port of Genoa. Philosophically they accepted the anticlimax. They landed, unearthly visitants to the scenes of a past existence, and drove with Mr. Barry to the Lomellini

Gardens. For Byron, in his mood of depression, the choice was unfortunate. It was scarcely six weeks since he had been there with Lady Blessington; her voice— her gay, reproving voice—still echoed for him under the ilexes. He had, as usual, been telling her of all his weaknesses, hinting to her of the many enormities which he had not committed. She had laughed at him, and he had taken it in good part. He had said, "Don't shake your raven locks at me," and then they had all ridden back in the evening dust to Genoa. But Lady Blessington was by then at Naples, and here was he, Byron, a doomed and sombre victim, eating cheese and fruit under a tree with Barry, Gamba, and Trelawny. And to-morrow, that very evening perhaps, they would all sail again for the Morea.

They returned that night to the "Hercules," and at sunrise on the 15th they were towed out of the port by the boats of an American frigate. All day in the blazing sun they flapped and swayed outside the harbour, gazing at the distant villas and palaces of Genoa until the sun set and the lights quivered in the water. "The 'Pilgrim,'" records Trelawny, "sat apart, solemn and sad—he took no notice of anything, nor spoke a word."

Towards midnight the wind suddenly began to blow strongly from the west; the sails were shortened. The "Hercules," being constructed, as we know, "on the lines of a baby's cradle," reacted exuberantly to the motion of the waves. The less experienced passengers retired immediately to the cabin; the horses became frightened, and kicked at the flimsy partitions which had been erected; Trelawny and the negro groom went down to secure them; Byron remained morose and solitary upon the deck. The wind increased, and finally it was decided to return to Genoa. Gamba, for his part, was "half-dead with sea-sickness the whole night." Byron remained unaffected till towards the morning, when they were entering the harbour. "He appeared thoughtful," records Gamba, "and remarked that he considered a bad beginning a favourable omen."

The morning of the 16th found them therefore again at Genoa. Some English carpenters were procured to repair the damage which the horses had done to their partitions, and meanwhile Byron decided to revisit the Casa Saluzzo. "His conversation," says Gamba, "was somewhat melancholy on our way to Albaro : he spoke much of his past life and of the uncertainty of the future. ' Where,' said he, ' shall we be in a year ? ' It looked like a melancholy foreboding, for on the same day of the same month in the next year he was carried to the tomb of his ancestors."

This posthumous visit to the Casa Saluzzo was indeed a miserable experience. The Guiccioli had two days before been carried screaming to her travelling carriage, and had returned to Bologna. Charles Barry, who had decided to take on the Casa Saluzzo until the expiry of Byron's lease, had not yet established himself, and the vast rooms were almost empty, with wisps of straw blowing across the marble floors. The chapter was closed. It was but with morbid depression that he sat there in the empty house, toying with the completed pages. He lunched alone upon some cheese and figs, and then, tearing himself away from the perished associations of what had once been his home, he drove down to Genoa and embarked again upon the "Hercules."

In the afternoon of that day, the 16th of July, they again set sail with a favourable wind from Genoa harbour. Mr. Barry heard only when it was too late that Lord Byron had a second time landed at Genoa. There were several things he had wished to say to him. There was " a packet of some sort or other," which had arrived for him from Germany. There was the question of the journey money to be given to Leigh Hunt, and there was that bother about the geese. For on his first departure Byron had shouted to Barry at the last moment that he must not forget to look after the geese. Barry had never heard of the geese, but on going up to the Casa Saluzzo he found that there were, in fact, three geese which, the caretaker informed him, had been Lord Byron's special favourites. As a matter of fact he had bought them one day to test the theory of their longevity, but Barry was unaware of this, and of the reason for which his eccentric friend should attach such importance to their maintenance. Hurrying down to the harbour, he engaged a shore-boat and rowed out passionately, in the hope of catching the " Hercules " as it left the harbour. He was not successful. He went back to his office in a mood of depression. He despatched the geese and the " packet of some sort or other " by land to catch Byron at Leghorn, and he sat down and wrote to him by the same post a letter from which the following is an extract :—

> " You said that I should be glad when you got off, but I hope you don't think so. Believe me, My Lord, I am too proud of having known you not to regret most unfeignedly your absence. I cannot cry like the tailor's boy, but I feel the loss as acutely as if I did, and most sincerely do I hope that your return to Genoa will not be at a very remote period."

A few days later Charles Barry moved into the Casa Saluzzo. He wandered regretfully about the rooms, thinking of the miraculous friend and client who had passed out of his life, perhaps for ever. There were some pieces of furniture still remaining in the villa, and notably the writing bureau in Byron's own study. He opened one of the drawers, and was pained to find therein a long tress of golden hair, which could only have emanated from the Countess Guiccioli.

At which discovery Charles Barry became even more convinced that Lord Byron was a very singular and unaccountable person.

IV

It took the " Hercules " five days of favourable weather to reach Leghorn : she averaged no more than twenty miles a day. They spent the interval in completing their installation and acquiring their sea legs ; they abandoned the heated cabin for the deck, and there they slept and took their meals. Byron, as before, remained aloof, lying in the stern and reading such books as Scott's " Life of Swift," la Rochefoucauld, Grimm's " Correspondence," and Colonel Hippisley's " Expedition to South America." The conviction of voluntary immolation still hung heavily upon his spirits ; he did not mix with his companions.

On July 21st they entered Leghorn, and were gratified and somewhat startled to receive from another vessel in the harbour a salute of fifteen guns. She was a Greek frigate under the command of a certain Vitali. This gentleman, who had already been promised a passage to Greece in the " Hercules," immediately came on board, accompanied by " some Greek patriotic merchants " of Leghorn. The latter informed Byron confidentially that their friend Vitali was in fact in the pay of the Sultan, and that he would, on their arrival in Greek waters, deliver him over to the Turks ; as for Schilizzi, they confided that he also was a spy and an impostor, and that he was accompanying Byron in the capacity of an agent for the Russian Government. " This," comments Trelawny, " was our first sample of the morality of the modern Greeks." But upon Byron, who possessed more philosophy, as well as past experience in such matters, the incident made but a fleeting impression, and both M. Vitali and M. Schilizzi were accorded their few feet of space in the congested cabin of the " Hercules."

At Leghorn they remained two days. There was much business to be transacted : there were stores and gunpowder to be loaded from the emporium of Mr. Dunn, and the horse-boxes were again strengthened. Byron was rowed ashore, and proceeded to the office of Mr. Barry's partner, the aged Webb. The latter had made out bills of exchange for their correspondents in Cephallonia, the house of Corgialegno. He had also received some letters forwarded by Mr. Barry from Genoa. The geese had not yet arrived, nor did they reach the astonished Mr. Webb until after Byron's departure. There exists no record of their ultimate disposal.

There was another passenger besides M. Vitali who joined the "Hercules" at Leghorn. This was Mr. Hamilton Browne of Scotland, a young man who had been dismissed from the British service in the Ionian islands on the score of his Hellenic sympathies, and who possessed, apart from his knowledge of the Romaic language, considerable experience of the Levant and of the character of the Greek people. It was on Browne's advice that they decided to proceed at first not to Zante, as had been arranged with Blaquière, but to Argostoli in Cephallonia, the Resident of which island, Colonel Napier, was said by Browne to be the only British official who had any sympathy with the Greek insurgents or their supporters.

By the 23rd of July the stores and gunpowder had been safely stored in the capacious hold of the "Hercules." They prepared for their departure. At the last moment, however, Captain Grant, a friend of Trelawny's, came on board with the latest papers and reviews from England, and with the first volume of Las Cases' "Memoirs of Napoleon," which he presented to Byron. He also brought with him certain further letters which had just arrived from Genoa. Among them was that mysterious "packet of some sort or other" to which Barry had referred in his letter. On opening it, Byron discovered that it contained a note from a young Mr. Sterling, to whom in the early spring he had given a letter of introduction to Goethe at Weimar. The letter had been delivered, and in return Goethe had addressed to Byron three grave and complimentary stanzas. The verses, in Goethe's handwriting, were enclosed :—

" Ein freundlich Wort kommt eines nach dem andern
Von Süden her und bringt uns frohe Stunden ;
Es ruft uns auf zum Edelsten zu wandern,
Nie ist der Geist, doch ist der Fuss gebunden.

" Wie soll ich dem, den ich so lang begleitet,
Nun etwas Traulich's in die Ferne sagen ?
Ihm der sich selbst im Innersten bestreitet,
Stark angewohnt das tiefste Weh zu tragen.

" Wohl sey ihm doch, wenn er sich selbst empfindet !
Er wage selbst sich hoch beglückt zu nennen,
Wenn Musenkraft die Schmerzen uberwindet,
Und wie ich ihn erkannt mög' er sich kennen."

Byron descended to the little aft cabin which he had chosen for himself and replied as follows :—

" *Leghorn,*
" *July* 24 (sic), 1823.

" ILLUSTRIOUS SIR,
" I cannot thank you as you ought to be thanked for the lines which my young friend, Mr. Sterling, sent me of yours ; and it would but ill become me to pretend to exchange verses with him who, for fifty years, has been the undisputed sovereign of European literature. You must therefore accept my most sincere acknowledgments in prose—and in hasty prose too ; for I am at present on my voyage to Greece once more, and surrounded by hurry and bustle, which hardly allow a moment even to gratitude and admiration to express themselves.

" I sailed from Genoa some days ago, was driven back by a gale of wind, and have since sailed again and arrived here, ' Leghorn,' this morning, to receive on board some Greek passengers for their struggling country.

" Here also I found your lines and Mr. Sterling's letters ; and I could not have had a more favourable omen, a more agreeable surprise, than a word of Goethe, written by his own hand.

"I am returning to Greece, to see if I can be of any little use there. If ever I come back I will pay a visit to Weimar, to offer the sincere homage of one of the many millions of your admirers. I have the honour to be, ever and most respectfully, y(our)

"Obliged adm(irer) and se(rvant),
"NOEL BYRON."

The cover to this letter was addressed :—

"A Son Excellence
"Le Baron von Goethe,
"etc., etc., etc.,
"Weimar."

"Aux soins de
M. Sterling."

and was ever afterwards preserved among the most treasured of Goethe's papers.

V

A few minutes later the "Hercules" weighed anchor and, threading her ungainly course among the congested shipping of the harbour, drifted out gently into the Mediterranean. Slowly the quays and warehouses that fringed the dock blurred down into a confused unity, and from behind emerged the trees and terraces of the surrounding villas. Over there was Montenero; and to the right, already behind them, Pisa; and, still further behind, the white stucco rampart of the Carrara Mountains and the fringe of sand which runs to Viareggio.

This then was the ultimate farewell, the final severance! He crouched there, watching the narrow pathway of their wake, the little rippling eddies which slipped away below him, swirling and eager as they glided from the stern, swirling again less eagerly as they dropped behind, fusing finally into the wide texture of the sea. Whether for separation or deliverance, for loneliness or freedom, for exile or escape, for further failure or renewed renown, the dim horizons of his past were fading, failing, and in front was offered, inevitable and unknown, the final cause, the last occasion of his destiny.

The final cause! From this concluding and dramatic occasion there would be no honourable, or even feasible, escape. Persistent and inalienable, his fame enclosed him within its vast and cruel circle; wherever he might move he was encompassed by the far-flung horizon of his own renown. The eyes of the world, more searching and pitiless in their present approbation than ever in their reproof, were peering towards him. How could he hope to evade, to justify, or even to withstand such scrutiny? To other idle men it would be given to fulfil their reputation and their dignity through the facile and submissive qualities of endurance and self-sacrifice; from Byron the world expected energies both more excessive and more dominant. From the first they had confused his genius with his character; in the force of his imagination he had flamed for them as something virile and volcanic; with the unrealities of his own temperament he had been able to flick and flibbit in a most engaging manner, but to the glacial honesty of his judgment the realities of his nature were revealed in all their stark insufficiency. He knew that he was weak. His life-long struggle to attain to absolute objectivity had led him into many a pathetic affectation, had led him to aspire to the functions and manner of a man of action. These pretensions would now, and before the gaze of all the world, be drastically exposed: he knew, poor, tired sensationalist, that he would fail to stand the test. He knew that the only positive action of which he was still capable was death.

And was it positive? No wonder that he crouched there, sullen and despairing, in the stern.

As the days, the empty, detailed days of life upon a

little sailing-ship, succeeded each other in cloudless
monotony, the spirits and the confidence of Byron began
gradually to revive. He boxed with Trelawny; he
fenced with Gamba; he dined alone on cheese and
pickled cucumbers and cider; he fired at the gulls with
his pistols; he joined his companions in the hatchway
over a glass of grog; he bathed when they were becalmed;
he played with his dogs; and he chaffed and ridiculed the
experienced, but drunken, Captain of the "Hercules."
They passed along the coast of Italy, sighting the muddied
mouths of the Tiber, the line of the Alban Hills, and the
distant peak of Soracte; they sailed close to the islands
of Ponza, which then, as now, were used as a convict
settlement, and on the subject of which Byron endeavoured, but in vain, to compose a tirade against the
oppressive measures of the Neapolitan Government.
The whole of one night they lay off Stromboli, and he
remained on deck, absorbing local colour for a fifth canto
of *Childe Harold*. The next morning they passed
through the Straits of Messina, and clung to the coast of
Calabria, watching the cloud of smoke hanging upon the
summit of Etna.

"I never was on ship-board," records Trelawny,
"with a better companion than Byron. He was
generally cheerful, gave no trouble, assumed no authority,
uttered no complaints, and did not interfere with the
working of the ship; when appealed to he always
answered, ' Do as you like.' "

Meanwhile Byron had induced Trelawny to transfer
to him the negro groom which the latter had picked up
on his way to Genoa. Nor was this the only trans-
ference of property. One day Trelawny had told this
groom to bring on deck a parcel, which he had ordered
from a military tailor at Vienna. This parcel contained
a dark green cavalry jacket decorated with a considerable
quantity of braiding of a lighter shade. Trelawny was
unable to struggle into it, and threw it on the deck with
a gesture of annoyance. Byron, who was sitting near

him, picked it up. "Fletcher," he said, "what have I got to land with in Greece?" "Nothing, My Lord, but your ordinary clothes." "Haven't I got a jacket?" "Only your old plaid one, My Lord." Byron then tried on Trelawny's jacket. "It fits you exactly," remarked Fletcher. It was this little green and frogged jacket, therefore, which he wore at Missolonghi, and which, faded but still showing the original colours, is now preserved in his rooms at Newstead Abbey.

At times his reviving spirits became positively uproarious. The following story is retailed with considerable gusto by Trelawny:—

"No boy cornet enjoyed a practical joke more than Byron. On great occasions when our Captain wished to be grand he wore a bright scarlet waistcoat. As he was very corpulent, Byron wished to see if this vest would not button round us both. The Captain was taking his siesta one day, when Byron persuaded the boy to bring up the waistcoat. In the meantime, as it was nearly calm and very hot, I opened the coops of the geese and ducks, who instinctively took to the water. Neptune (*sic*), the Newfoundland dog, jumped after them, and Moretto, the bull-dog, followed.

"'Now,' said Byron, standing on the gangway, with one arm in the red waistcoat, 'put your arm in, Tre. We will jump overboard, and take the shine out of it.'

"So we did.

"The Captain, hearing the row on deck, came up, and when he saw the gorgeous garment he was so proud of defiled by sea-water, he roared out, 'My Lord, you should know better than to make a mutiny on board ship' (the crew were laughing at the fun). 'I won't heave to, or lower a boat; I hope you will both be drowned.'

"'Then you will lose your *frite*' (for so the

Captain always pronounced the world freight),
shouted Byron.

"As I saw the dogs worrying the ducks and geese,
I returned on board with the waistcoat, pacified the
skipper, lowered a boat, and with the aid of a boy
sculled after the birds and beasts; the Newfound-
lander brought them to us unharmed; but Moretto,
the bull-dog, did not mouth them so tenderly."

On another occasion, when Byron and Trelawny were
sitting in the stern, they overheard a conversation between
Fletcher and Captain Scott, in which the former expressed
in vivid language what Byron had always known to be his
opinions upon the cause of Greek independence. This
dialogue is also recorded by Trelawny :—

"'What,' inquired Captain Scott, who was
sipping his grog with Fletcher in the gangway, 'is
your master going to such a wild country of savages
for ? My mate was at Corfu, and he says an officer of
the garrison crossed over to Albania to shoot, and
was shot by the natives; they thought the brass
buttons on his jacket were gold.'

"'When I was there,' said Fletcher, 'the Turks
were masters, and kept them down.'

"*Captain.* 'What may the country be like?'

"*Fletcher.* 'Bless you! there is very little
country; it's all rocks and robbers. They live in
holes in the rocks, and come out like foxes; they
have long guns, pistols, and knives. We were
obliged to have a guard of soldiers to go from one
place to another.'

"*Captain.* 'How did you live?'

"*Fletcher.* 'Like dogs, on goat's flesh and rice,
sitting on the floor in a hovel, all eating out of one
dirty round dish, tearing the flesh to pieces with
their fingers; no knives, no forks, and only two or
three horn spoons. They drink a stuff they call

III

wine, but it tastes more of turps than grapes, and is carried about in stinking goat-skins, and every one drinks from the same bowl. Then they have coffee, which is pounded, and they drink it, dregs and all, without sugar. They are all smoking when not sleeping; they sleep on the floor in their clothes and shoes; they never undress or wash, except the ends of their fingers, and are covered with lice and fleas. The Turks were the only respectable people in the country. If they go, Greece will be like bedlam broke loose. It's a land of flies, and lice, and fleas, and thieves. What my lord is going there for the Lord only knows, I don't.' Then, seeing his master was looking, he said, 'And my master can't deny what I have said is true.'

" ' No,' said Byron, ' to those who look at things with hog's eyes, and can see nothing else. What Fletcher says may be true, but I didn't note it. The Greeks are returned to barbarism; Mitford says the people never were anything better. Nor do I know what I am going for. I was tired of Italy, and liked Greece, and the London Committee told me I should be of use, but of what use they did not say, nor do I see.'

" *Trelawny*. ' We shall have excitement; the greatest of all—fighting.' "

Such incidents and such conversations, recorded by Trelawny in his particularly vivid and untruthful manner, indicate that as the journey progressed Byron was able to conquer his early diffidence and self-absorption. It is not to be supposed, however, that the old impressions and presentiments did not recur to him. "His sadness," records Trelawny, "intermitted, and his cold fits alternated with hot ones." And one night, when Byron had been sitting silent on his usual seat by the taffrail, and when all was shrouded and asleep but for the figure of the helmsman and the mate keeping watch, he reverted

suddenly to the subject which was so consistently weighing
on his heart and brain :—

"If Death," he said, "comes in the shape of a cannon-
ball and takes off my head, he is welcome. I have no
wish to live, but I can't bear pain. Mind you, Trelawny,
don't repeat the ceremony you went through with Shelley
—no one wants my ashes."

"You will be claimed," replied Trelawny, "for Westminster Abbey."

"No," sighed Byron, "they don't want me, nor would
I have my bones mingled with that motley throng. There
is a rocky islet off Maina—it is the Pirates' Isle; it
suggested *The Corsair*. No one knows it; I'll show it
to you on the way to the Morea. There is the spot I
should like my bones to lie."

"They won't let me do so," replied Trelawny, "without you will it."

"I will do so," replied Byron, "if you are with me
when I die; remind me, and don't let the blundering,
blockhead doctors bleed me, or when I am dead maul my
carcase—I have an antipathy to letting blood."

Their journey was drawing to its conclusion. By
sunset on the 2nd of August they found themselves
between the islands of Cephallonia and Zante, and in
front of them stretched the calm outline of the Morea.

"I don't know why it is," said Byron, pointing to those
distant mountains, "but I feel as if the eleven long years
of bitterness I have passed through since I was here were
taken off my shoulders, and I was scudding through the
Greek Archipelago with old Bathurst, in his frigate."

That night they hove-to in the channel between the
two islands, and next morning, the 3rd of August, they
worked into Argostoli and anchored near the town.

CHAPTER VI

ARGOSTOLI, CEPHALLONIA

August 3—September 6, 1823

I

THE Heptanesos, the seven islands of Corfu, Paxos, Levkas, Ithaca, Cephallonia, Zante, and Cythera, had for nearly six hundred years—that is from 1205 to 1797—formed part of the possessions of Venice, the indolent domination of the Adriatic Republic being relieved at times by less stagnant interludes under the Despots of Epirus or the royal house of Naples. From 1797 to 1799, and again from 1807 to 1814, the larger islands had been occupied by the French, the interval between these two occupations being marked by the emergence of a Republic, at first under Turkish and then under Russian protection. In 1815 the seven islands were constituted into the "United States of the Ionian Islands," and placed under the protection of Great Britain, in which condition they prospered and protested until November 14th, 1863, when they were transferred, wisely and spontaneously, to the Kingdom of Greece.

By the summer of 1823, therefore, the islands had already enjoyed British protection for some eight years, and this protectorate had, since December 1815, been exercised in a very original and authoritative manner by Sir Thomas Maitland, known to his friends and enemies as "King Tom of Corfu." The passionate, but on the whole benevolent, despotism of this alcoholic autocrat had earned for him the dislike and veneration not only of the islanders themselves, but of the officials who served and trembled under his direction. The

114

policy pursued by Sir Thomas Maitland was not without its justification. The object which he aimed at was stability, and he realised from the first that this could only be secured by dramatic vigour and unflinching consistency. Over Corfu he ruled with iron despotism; he quite openly declared himself a dictator, and he encouraged his Residents in the other islands to become dictators in their turn.

With the outbreak of the Greek War of Independence, the wisdom of Sir Thomas Maitland's method was abundantly demonstrated. He conceived it his duty to interpret and to enforce the intentions of the Government at home, or, in other words, the intentions of Lord Castlereagh. He realised fully that the slightest sign of yielding or of sympathy on his part would render the Ionian Islands not only an asylum for the Greek insurgents, but an actual base for their operations. There was obviously no alternative between a rigid, and at moments a ruthless, enforcement of Ionian neutrality, and unstinted license for the Ionian islanders to assist their compatriots across the water. Sir Thomas Maitland was not a man to follow so negative a course, and in enforcing very positive regulations to prevent all communication between the islands and the Greek mainland, he incurred, as was inevitable, the fierce hostility not only of the Greeks, but of the foreign Philhellenes.

Violent and eccentric as King Tom indubitably became, yet he possessed certain definite and rough-hewn qualities of honour and acumen. Above all, he was quick to recognise a similar capacity in others, and it was thus that, when Colonel Charles Napier was sent out to Corfu, as inspecting field officer in the Ionian Islands, his chief recognised that the services of this active, though possibly troublesome, person were all too valuable to lose. He sent his unruly subordinate on a confidential mission to Ali Pasha of Janina, and it was during this mission that Napier resolved " to gain an exact knowledge of the Greeks as a people," having already formed the conviction "that England may now create a new kingdom, enthusiastic, vigorous, united in opinion (*sic*), and in a form suited for the aiding of our maritime power." On his return from Albania, Napier requested leave to travel in Greece proper. The request was refused by the Deputy High Commissioner, Sir F. Adam, who, throughout the course of their subsequent relations, was to pursue Napier with affable and tortuous malevolence. At last, in the year 1821, Napier obtained his wish, and for the first three months of that year he travelled across Continental Greece examining the social conditions and strategical possibilities of the country. He returned a convinced Philhellene, and proceeded to England, where he published anonymously his pamphlet, "War in Greece." On resuming his duties at Corfu, where he was looked upon with suspicion by his immediate superiors and colleagues, he was appointed by the unconventional Sir Thomas Maitland as Resident of Cephallonia, the second largest of the seven islands. With the assistance of John Pitt Kennedy, his Secretary of Public Works, Napier flung himself passionately into the task of improving the sanitary conditions of the island and its capital, in building quays, warehouses, market halls, and lighthouses, and in constructing throughout the island a network of admirable roads. "I would rather," he wrote twenty-two years afterwards, when he had become a national hero and the conqueror of Scind, "have finished the roads of Cephallonia than have fought Austerlitz or Waterloo." His sympathy and his affection for the Greek people never left him. On returning to Cephallonia in March 1825, he wrote as follows :—

"Now I am once more among the merry Greeks, who are worth all other nations put together. I like to see, to hear them ; I like their fun, their good humour, their Paddy ways, for they are very like Irishmen. As to cleanliness, they cannot brag. Yet they are cleaner than Italians and don't love dirt like the Venetians; they only suffered it out of politeness when the last were their masters, and are now leaving it off in compliment to us. All their bad habits are Venetian; their wit, their eloquence, their good nature are their own. . . . I am enjoying their good company, their fine climate, their magnificent mountains, their pretty scenery, liking them and all belonging to them, and wishing all belonging to me were here. No, not here in Corfu, but in Cephallonia, which is so dear to me that every hour not employed to do her good seems wasted."

In January 1824, Colonel Napier, fired by Byron's example, determined to throw up his appointment under the British Government and to place his services at the disposal of Greece. Byron furnished him with a letter of introduction to the Greek Committee in London. "Colonel Napier," he wrote, "will present you this letter. Of his military character it were superfluous to speak; of his personal, I can say from my own knowledge, as well as from all rumour and private report, that it is excellent as his military—in short, a better or a braver man is not easily to be found. He is our man to lead a regular force or to organise a national one for the Greeks. Ask the army; ask anybody! He is, besides, the personal friend of Mavrocordato, Colonel Stanhope, and myself; and in such concord with all three that we should pull together, an indispensable as well as a rare point, especially in Greece at present." The London Committee, however, were too busy to accept Napier's services; they were engaged at the time on a very acrid discussion regarding the menu for their next public dinner; moreover they were already involved in their endless negotiation with Lord Cochrane. Colonel Napier, for his part, did not appreciate the London Committee. "I promised," he wrote, "Byron and Mavrocordato to be of what service I could in explaining the real state of Greece to the Committee in London. I saw and heard the famous

Committee—from any further connexion with which the Lord deliver me."

"Perhaps," comments Finlay in one of his rare moments of sly illumination, "the man who was subsequently selected by the Duke of Wellington to command the Indian Army at a critical moment might have succeeded in organising an efficient army in Greece."

There can, indeed, be little doubt that had Napier's services been accepted by the Greek Committee the protracted misery of the Greek War of Independence would have been curtailed by several years. Even in the opinion of Trelawny, who was not lavish in his appreciation of others, Colonel Napier and Commodore Rowan Hamilton were the only British officers who ever understood the Greek situation. Such, however, was not the view of the Greek Committee; they chose, instead, Colonel Stanhope, of whom more hereafter; they chose Lord Cochrane, who malingered, and General Church, who had no force of character at all.

For my present purpose, however, it is sufficient in this way to indicate that when Byron arrived, diffident and irresolute, at Cephallonia, he found in Napier a person of remarkable originality and decision; a soldier who, while discounting, even as Byron did himself, the faults of the Greeks, never wavered for an instant in his affection for them or in his conviction of their ultimate triumph; a man of action who, while expert in the science of warfare, was also skilled in the arts of civil administration; and finally, a man of infinite humour (" peccavi," he assured an anxious Governor-General when he had exceeded his instructions by annexing Scinde, " peccavi—I have sinned "), of infinite energy, and, above all, of infinite resolution.

For it was Napier who inspired the despondent Byron with that self-confidence which vitalised him during those last months at Cephallonia, and which carried him, finally, gay but determined, across to Missolonghi.

II

The Bay of Cephallonia runs some eight miles into the mountains. On the left, as one enters, lies the little town of Lixuri, and on the east, around the Cape of St. Theodore, the inlet takes a hair-pin bend, and the whitewashed houses of Argostoli, garish with their green and vermilion shutters, stand splashed against the brown and arid hillside.

The " Hercules " anchored opposite the lazaretto, and awaited the visit of the Captain of the Port. He arrived, romaic and voluble, and gave them their first news of the affairs of Greece. The country, he said, was now united : all parties were preparing for an offensive against the Turks. It was true that for the moment the Turkish fleet had regained the command of the sea, and that the Greek squadrons were hiding behind the island of Hydra. Such inaction, however, was merely temporary : they would shortly emerge and sweep the crescent from the seas. " A little truth," records Gamba of their visitor, " and a great deal of boasting and conceit."

Shortly afterwards another boat put off to the " Hercules." It contained Captain Pitt Kennedy, the Resident's Secretary. Colonel Napier, he explained, was temporarily absent ; he had accompanied Sir F. Adam and Admiral Moore to a conference regarding some recent Turkish infractions of Ionian neutrality. He assured them, however, that they could depend on Colonel Napier's readiness to assist them in so far as " his orders to observe strict neutrality " would allow. Meanwhile the news from Greece was uncertain ; a sullen apathy appeared to have descended upon both the combatants, and the Greeks were profiting by this inaction to revive their internal discussions. Captain Kennedy regretted that he could not furnish any information either more encouraging or more precise.

There was one fact, however, which Captain Kennedy

disclosed which caused Byron considerable annoyance. Edward Blaquière, whom they had expected to find waiting for them at Zante, had passed through Cephallonia only a fortnight before on his way home to England. He had left a note for Byron. " Circumstances," he wrote, " having arisen which render it necessary, for the interests of Greece, that I should absent myself for a short time before your arrival. . . ." On reading this " paltry note " Byron exploded into one of his fits of passion. It was all very well for Blaquière to talk of " circumstances having arisen "; Byron knew very well that he had hurried home merely to get his book through the press while the interest in Greek affairs was still effervescent. The Committee, it was evident, were merely using the name of Byron as a decoy. They had no consideration for his feelings, nor did they attribute any real importance to his future co-operation. " Now that they have got me thus far," he expostulated to Trelawny, " they think I must go on, and they care nothing as to the result. They are deceived: I won't budge a foot farther until I see my way; we will stay here. If that is objected to I will buy an island from the Greeks or Turks; there must be plenty of them in the market." With this explosion, he retired to his cabin and remained there sulking till the evening sun had dropped behind Lixuri.

In that airless, land-locked creek, shut in by the bare flanks of the surrounding mountains, the little noises from the town, the smell of the thyme and the gumcystus upon the hills, furnished a not unwelcome sedative. The lights of Argostoli sparkled in the water, and from time to time the bugles of the English garrison would echo to each other from the bastions. It was all very like being at Malta again; and Malta had been the prelude to his first Grecian journey. It was not a very satisfactory prelude. The garrison officers, indifferent to his title, had been arrogant and supercilious. It would be worse this time: he was by now a moral outcast; the officers of the garrison would visit upon him the moral indignation which had caused his exile. Byron was exceedingly uneasy as to the reception which he would receive at Argostoli.

On the next morning they were awakened by the rattle of the Greek language and of little boats bumping along against the side. These were the Souliot refugees, who had lost no time in putting themselves under Byron's protection. The crew and staff were disconcerted by the fierce aspect and heroic cries with which these ruffians clambered over the gunwale. Lega Zambelli rushed to the money chest and coiled himself upon it " like a viper." Captain Scott, incensed by this invasion, was about to drive away the Souliots with hand-spikes. In the midst of this confusion Byron appeared from his cabin, toying serenely with his scented handkerchief. He was overjoyed to see again the clean fustanellas and the dirty stockings of his friends the Souliots, to feel again the pungent incongruity of the East. " As was his wont," remarks Trelawny, " he promised a great deal more than he should have done ; day and night they clung to his heels like a pack of jackals, till he stood at bay like a hunted lion, and was glad to buy them off by shipping them to the Morea."

On the following day Colonel Napier returned to Cephallonia, and came on board the " Hercules." He discoursed at length upon the condition of Greece ; he spoke of the incurable optimism of the Greek leaders, of the manner in which their early successes had led them to believe that their independence was actually assured ; of the embarrassment of their finances and of the refusal of the ship-owners to allow the fleet to put to sea without immediate payment ; of the appalling dissensions which had again broken out between the military and the civilian leaders. He spoke also of the apparent apathy of the Turks, of the facility with which, if they made a real effort, they could even now crush the revolution and reoccupy the Morea ; of the general stagnation which had descended upon the whole conduct of operations. He approved of Lord Byron's decision to remain for the time being at Cephallonia, and he assured him that, provided, as he felt certain would be the case, Lord Byron behaved with adequate discretion, it would be possible for him, Colonel Napier, to soothe the anxieties of Sir Thomas Maitland at Corfu, and to shut a benignant eye to the real purpose which had brought the " Hercules " and her strange company to Argostoli. He urged Byron to land, and offered him the hospitality of the Residency, an offer which, in his desire to avoid causing any unnecessary complications, Byron had the wisdom to refuse.

" I hope," Napier wrote to him from shore, " if you are in want of anything I can assist you in that you will make use of me. I have not called on you because I am afraid of boring you. Pray remember that there are two rooms and two beds always at your service and the service of Count Gamba, when you choose to visit ' the Capital ' and enjoy its round of pleasures."

III

For two days Byron remained on board the " Hercules " without landing. The civility with which he had been received by Pitt Kennedy, and the friendship which had been offered to him by Colonel Napier, should have convinced a man less diffident or self-conscious than Byron that his countrymen in this outpost of the Empire did not look upon him with the hostility which he persistently imagined to be his lot. He was convinced, in his morbid, self-centred way, that he had become an object of loathing and ridicule to every Englishman, and he shrank with feminine timidity from exposing himself to any converse with them. And in all this he was mistaken. The subalterns of the 8th (the King's) Regiment of Foot, quartered at Argostoli, regarded Byron with anything but aversion ; on the contrary, they had from their boyhood learnt by heart the stock passages of his romantic poems, and on joining their regiment they had found that *Don Juan* was of all forms of reading that which was least ill regarded in the mess. They were very anxious indeed to make his acquaintance, and they accordingly invited him to dinner.

Byron was astonished and deeply touched by this attention. "Nothing," he wrote to Charles Barry, "can be kinder than the officers . . . have been individually to us, as far as their duty will permit. I say this the more readily as I neither expected it nor had cause to expect it." He accepted the invitation, and with some diffidence and anxiety attended the dinner. At the conclusion of the banquet, which, as Gamba points out, was somewhat of a strain upon his "Pythagorean habits," the officers rose to drink Lord Byron's health. His reply was characteristic. His soft voice trembled a little with what in truth was a sincere emotion and an unaffected nervousness, as he expressed his great satisfaction at finding himself again in the society of his countrymen, and of seeing so many of them together. He added that he was so conscious of the honour they had done him that he regretted he could not adequately express his sense of obligation, since he had been so long in the practice of speaking a foreign language that he could not easily convey his sentiments in English. We may doubt whether the officers of the garrison were wholly pleased by this little gesture of affectation, but Byron for his part was delighted when he again resumed his seat. He leant towards the Colonel flushed and excited. "Had it been a success?" he asked. "Had he said what was required?" He sat on there beside Colonel Duffie, puzzled and delighted by their kindness, blinking a little at all those young boyish faces, and feeling very shy and happy and perturbed.

And then they all rowed back to the "Hercules."

IV

Meanwhile Byron had sent a messenger to Missolonghi to ascertain the whereabouts of Marco Botzaris, the Souliot chief, to whom he had been recommended by the Greeks in Italy. Pending a reply to this communication he decided to visit the neighbouring island of Ithaca.

The expedition to Ithaca, which lasted eight days, constitutes a curious interlude before his final establishment in Cephallonia, and as such bridges the transition between the diffident and irresolute mood which had clung to him since he left Genoa and the gay and confident assurance which he temporarily absorbed from Napier in the weeks which followed.

On the first day they rode across the island of Cephallonia on mule-back, over the arid stretch of hills which separate Argostoli from the roadstead of Santa Eufemia. On reaching this little quarantine station, the local English magistrate advised them to spend the night in his house before crossing to the island opposite. Byron was as usual impatient, and having procured an open four-oared boat they rowed shouting and singing across the little strait, and reached the coast of Ithaca at sunset. They landed upon the rocks below the Eagles' Crag, the narrow isthmus of only half a mile in width which joins the northern and the southern mountain masses of the island. There was no sign of human life, only the rough crags covered with arbutus and agnus castus, falling to the sea. They were tired by their six hours' ride across Cephallonia, and by their sun-scorched journey across the strait. They rested there, the eight of them, Byron, Trelawny, Gamba, Hamilton Browne, and Dr. Bruno, with three servants and luggage, hesitating as to what should be their next movement, and picking the grapes which grew upon the hill. Byron proposed to pass the night in one of the caves on the coast, but Gamba, thinking that this might prove injurious, decided to push on, in the hope of discovering some more suitable resting-place. With Hamilton Browne he clambered up the hill, and after an hour discovered a cottage among the trees. The cottage belonged to a merchant of Trieste, who had lost all his money, and who was living there upon his little patch of land with his wife and son. He could only provide one mule, and on hearing of the numbers of the party he advised them to spend the night in his own cottage. They all climbed up in single file to the little house among the trees. Their host provided them with grapes and figs and wine, and discoursed to them at length upon the cause of the Greeks, upon his own misfortunes, and upon the Homeric ruins which existed in the island. Above them, he explained, was the Castle of Ulysses, and over there the grotto of the Nymphs, and beyond, the Fountain of Arethusa. Byron was irritated by this encyclopædic discourse : " Do I look," he muttered to Trelawny, " like one of those emasculated fogies ? I detest antiquarian twaddle. Do people think I have no lucid intervals, that I came to Greece to scribble more nonsense ? I will show them I can do something better ; I wish I had never written a line, to have it cast in my teeth at every turn." Irritably, he interrupted the lecture to which they were being treated. The night was cool, and he went out under the stars. The sea and the islands were around them. Byron was soothed ; he limped about under the dome of night, " talking much of his former travels in Greece, and of the real happiness he felt amid such magnificent scenery."

They all slept together in a small room, wrapped in their cloaks, and in the morning Hamilton Browne started early for the town of Vathy, bearing a letter of recommendation from Colonel Napier to Captain Knox, the Resident. The latter at once despatched mules and guides, together with one of his own officers. In the afternoon they arrived at Vathy, where Captain and Mrs. Knox received them with lavish hospitality. " The

Pilgrim," Trelawny records, " was received as if he had been a prince."

Mr. Charles Mackay, in his book, " Medora Leigh," has published an interesting narrative written by an English solicitor, a Mr. S——, who was travelling in Ithaca at that time, and who on that first evening at Vathy came into Captain Knox's dining-room to find Byron and his companions seated around the table.

" I had been informed," writes this gentleman, " of Lord Byron's presence, but had no means of finding him out, except by recollection of his portraits ; and I am not ashamed to confess that I was puzzled, in my examination of the various countenances before me, where to fix upon ' the man.' I at one time almost settled upon Trelawny, from the interest which he seemed to take in the schooner in which I had just arrived ; but on ascending to the drawing-room I was most agreeably undeceived by finding myself close to the side of the great object of my curiosity, and engaged in easy conversation with him, without presentation or introduction of any kind.

" He was handling and remarking upon the books in some small open shelves, and fairly spoke to me in such a manner that not to have replied would have been boorish. ' " Pope's Homer's Odyssey "— hum !—that is well placed here, undoubtedly. "Hume's Essays "—" Tales of my Landlord " ; there you are, Watty ! Are you recently from England, sir ? ' I answered that I had not been there for two years. ' Then you can bring us no news of the Greek Committee ? Here we are all waiting orders, and no orders seem likely to come. Ha ! ha ! I have not changed my opinion of the Greeks,' he said. ' I know them as well as most people ' (a favourite phrase), ' but we must not look always too closely at the men who are to benefit by our exer-

tions in a good cause, or, God knows, we shall seldom
do much good in this world. There is Trelawny
thinks he has fallen in with an angel in Prince
Mavrocordato, and little Bruno would willingly sacrifice his life for the *cause*, as he calls it. I must say
he has shown some sincerity in his devotion, in con-
senting to join it for the little matter he makes of
me.' I ventured to say that, in all probability, the
being joined with him in any cause was inducement
enough for any man of moderate pretensions. He
noticed the compliment only by an indifferent
smile. ' I find but one opinion,' he continued,
' among all people whom I have met since I came
here—that no good is to be done for these rascally
Greeks, that I am sure to be deceived, disgusted,
and all the rest of it. It may be so ; but it is chiefly
to satisfy myself upon these very points that I am
going. I go prepared for anything, expecting a
deal of roguery and imposition, but hoping to do
some good.'

" ' Have you read any of the late publications on
Greece ? ' I asked.

" ' I never read any accounts of a country to which
I can myself go,' said he. ' The Committee have
sent me some of their " Crown and Anchor "
reports, but I can make nothing of them.' "

From these topics, after a slight digression on the
subject of Lady Byron and Ada, with which, as was his
wont, Byron acutely embarrassed the company, they proceeded to discuss their plans for the following morning.

" The next morning," continues Mr. S—'s account,
" about nine o'clock, the party for the Fountain of
Arethusa assembled in the parlour of Captain Knox ;
but Lord Byron was missing. Trelawny, who had
slept in the room adjoining his lordship's, told us
that he feared he had been ill during the night,
but that he had gone out in a boat very early in the

morning. At this moment I happened to be standing at the window, and saw the object of our anxiety in the act of landing on the beach, about ten or a dozen yards from the house, to which he walked slowly up. I never saw, and could not conceive the possibility of such a change in the appearance of a human being as had taken place since the previous night. He looked like a man under sentence of death, or returning from the funeral of all that he held dear on earth. His person seemed shrunk, his face was pale, and his eyes languid and fixed on the ground. He was leaning upon a stick, and had changed his dark camlet-caped surtout of the preceding evening for a nankeen jacket embroidered like a hussar's—an attempt at dandyism, or dash, to which the look and demeanour of the wearer formed a sad contrast. On entering the room, his lordship made the usual salutations, and, after some preliminary arrangements, the party moved off, on horses and mules, to the place of destination for the day.

" I was so struck with the difference of appearance in Lord Byron that the determination to which I had come, to try to monopolise him, if possible, to myself, without regard to appearances or 'bienséance,' almost entirely gave way under the terror of a freezing repulse. I advanced to him under the influence of this feeling, but I had scarcely received his answer when all uneasiness about my reception vanished, and I stuck as close to him as the road permitted our animals to go. His voice sounded timidly and quiveringly at first; but as the conversation proceeded, it became steady and firm. The beautiful country in which we were travelling naturally formed a prominent topic, as well as the character of the people and of the Government. Of the latter I found him (to my amazement) an admirer. 'There is a great deal of fine stuff about that old Maitland,' he said; 'he knows the Greeks well. Do you know if it be true that he ordered one of their brigs to be blown out of the water if she stayed ten minutes longer in Corfu Roads?' I happened to know, and told him that it was true. 'Well, of all follies, that of daring to say what one cannot dare to do is the least to be pitied. Do you think Sir Tom would have really executed his threat?' I told his lordship that I believed he certainly would, and that this knowledge of his being in earnest in everything he said was the cause, not only of the quiet termination of that affair, but of the order and subordination in the whole of the countries under his government."

On the third day of their visit they went by boat to what is known as the " School of Homer," drinking gin and water on the way from two stone jars provided by Tita. They were entertained by the native governor of Ithaca.

After a large meal they again embarked for their return to Vathy, Byron at first moody and sullen, but regaining his spirits as the wind filled the sails, and taking obvious pleasure in the anxiety shown by the civilian passengers at Trelawny's romantic steering. Thus they sailed on, drinking more gin and water, and listening to Byron's opinions on *The Bride of Lammermoor*, and on the charm of Sir Walter Scott's personality, and on Campbell's *Ode on the Death of Sir John Moore*. " The next morning," records the authority quoted by Mr. Mackay, " the accounts we heard of Lord Byron were contradictory: Trelawny, who slept in the next room to him, stating that he had been writing the greater part of the night, and he alleged it was the sixteenth canto of *Don Juan*; and Dr. Bruno, who visited him at intervals, and was many hours in personal attendance at his bedside, asserting that he had been seriously ill, and had been saved only by those ' benedette pillule,' which so often had had that effect. His lordship again appeared rowing in from his bath at the Lazzaretto, a course of proceeding (bathing and boating) which caused Dr. Bruno to wring his hands and tear his hair with alarm and vexation."

Before leaving Ithaca Lord Byron deposited with Mr. Knox the sum of 250 dollars for the relief of Greek refugees in the island, and he at the same time caused a whole family of these refugees of the name of Chalandritsanos, who had once been well-to-do people in Patras, to be transported to Cephallonia, where they were to be maintained at his expense under the direction of his banker, Mr. Corgialegno. The return journey was made by the same route which they had followed in coming to Ithaca. They rode across the island till they reached the Eagles' Crag, where a boat had been sent to fetch them by the collector of Santa Eufemia, Mr. Toole. On landing again in Cephallonia they were met by Mr. Toole in a formal manner, his whole establishment uncovered and bowing. He had prepared a large meal for their reception, of which, as was inevitable when he actually saw food in front of him, Byron partook without moderation. After dinner they were informed that sleeping accommodation had been reserved for them at a monastery on the hill of Samos across the bay. The Abbot of the monastery had been warned of their arrival, and, as they approached, files of monks stood on each side of the pathway bearing flaming torches of pine. The following account of their visit is given by Trelawny, who, with his usual inaccuracy, describes it as having taken place at Ithaca, and not, as was undoubtedly the case, on the first night of their return to Cephallonia :—

"On coming up to the walls we saw the monks in their grey gowns, ranged along the terrace; they chanted a hymn of glorification and welcome to the great lord, saying, 'Christ has risen to elevate the cross and trample on the crescent in our beloved Greece.' The Abbot, clad in his sacerdotal robes, received Byron in the porch, and conducted him into the great hall, illuminated for the occasion; the monks and others clustered round the honoured guest; boys swung censers with frankincense under the Poet's nose. The Abbot, after performing a variety of ceremonies in a very dignified manner, took from the folds of his ample garments a roll of paper, and commenced intoning through his nasal organ a turgid and interminable eulogium on my 'Lordo Inglese,' in a polyglot of divers tongues, while the eyes of the silent monks, anxious to observe the effect of the holy father's eloquence, glanced from the Abbot to the Lord.

"Byron had not spoken a word from the time we entered the monkery; I thought he was resolved to set us an example of proper behaviour. No one was more surprised than I was, when suddenly he burst into a paroxysm of rage, and vented his ire in a torrent of Italian execrations on the holy Abbot and all his brotherhood. Then, turning to us with flashing eyes, he vehemently exclaimed:

"'Will no one release me from the presence of these pestilential idiots? They drive me mad!' Seizing a lamp, he left the room.

"The consternation of the monks at this explosion of wrath may be imagined. The amazed Abbot remained for some time motionless, his eyes and mouth wide open. Holding the paper he had been reading in the same position, he looked at the vacant place left by Byron, and then at the door through which he had disappeared. At last he thought he had solved the mystery, and in a low, tremulous voice said, significantly putting his finger to his forehead :—

"'Eccolo, è matto poveretto!'"

The circumstances of the night that followed are important, since they indicate that Byron was then assailed by one of those sudden convulsive fits which had previously attacked him, and which were to be renewed in force on his arrival at Missolonghi. The account is given in the narrative quoted by Mr. Mackie, and there can be little doubt of its authenticity :—

"Lord Byron retired almost immediately from the ' sala ' ! Shortly afterwards we were astonished and alarmed by the entry of Dr. Bruno, wringing his hands and tearing his hair—a practice much too frequent with him—and ejaculating : ' O Maria, santissima Maria, se non è gia morte—cielo, perche non son morto io ! ' It appeared that Lord Byron was seized with violent spasms in the stomach and liver, and his brain was excited to dangerous excess, so that he would not tolerate the presence of any person in his room. He refused all medicine, and stamped and tore all his clothes and bedding like a maniac. We could hear him rattling and ejaculating. Poor Dr. Bruno stood lamenting in agony of mind, in anticipation of the most dire results if immediate relief were not obtained by powerful cathartics, but Lord Byron had expelled him from the room by main force. He now implored one or more of the company to go to his lordship and induce him, if possible, to save his life by taking the necessary medicine. Trelawny at once proceeded to the room, but soon returned, saying that it would require ten such as he to hold his lordship for a minute, adding that Lord Byron would not leave an unbroken article in the room. The doctor again essayed an entrance, but without success. The monks were becoming alarmed, and so, in truth, were all present. The doctor asked me to try to bring his lordship to reason : ' He will thank you when he is well,' he said, ' but get him to take this one pill, and he will be safe.' It seemed a very easy undertaking, and I went. There being no lock on the door, entry was obtained in spite of a barricade of chairs and a table within. His lordship was half undressed, standing in a far corner like a hunted animal at bay. As I looked determined to advance in spite of his imprecations of 'Back! Out of my sight! Fiends, can I have no peace, no relief from this hell? Leave me, I say!' he lifted the chair nearest to him, and hurled it direct at my head. I escaped as I best could, and returned to the 'sala.' The matter was obviously serious, and we all counselled force and such coercive measures as might be necessary to make him swallow the curative medicine. Mr. Hamilton Browne, one of our party, now volunteered an attempt, and the silence that succeeded his entrance augured well for his success. He returned much sooner than expected, telling the doctor that he might go to sleep; Lord Byron had taken both the pills, and had lain down on my mattress and bedding, prepared for him by my servant—the only regular bed in the company, the others being trunks and portable tressels, with such softening as might be procured for the occasion. Lord Byron's beautiful and most commodious patent portmanteau bed, with every appliance that profusion of money could provide, was mine for the night."

On the following morning Byron was all dejection and penitence. They started back to Argostoli about noon, riding over the Black Mountains and across the moors and marshes of the island. As always when in motion, Byron's spirits revived, and as the dusk closed in upon them he rode ahead singing, " at the pitch of his voice," the little ditties which Tom Moore had taught him, and snatches from the popular songs of 1812.

By night-time they reached Argostoli, and proceeded at once on board the " Hercules."

V

On his return from his eight days' visit to Ithaca, Byron found certain letters awaiting him. The messenger whom he had sent to Corfu had arrived with confirmation of the report that Edward Blaquière had left for England. As some compensation for this irritating intelligence, letters were at the same time received from England appointing Byron the principal agent in Greece of the London Committee. " We cannot doubt," wrote John Bowring, " the importance of Your Lordship's presence in Greece—for the sake of the Greeks, for the sake of our Committee, and on every account. The knowledge of your presence there will increase our funds and our influence at home and abroad. People will have a confidence in the cause itself, and in the appropriation of whatever they shall give to the cause." This letter concluded, however, on a note of pessimism : " We have not made," wrote Bowring, " the progress we expected. The Spanish cause has absorbed attention, and we begin to fear unworthily." The news which reached them from Greece itself was anything but encouraging. A report was abroad that Mavrocordato had been assassinated, and that Colokotronis had established his authority in the Morea. This rumour was shortly afterwards corrected by more accurate information. The second National Assembly, which had met at Astros in February 1823, had dissolved in May, after having reaffirmed the supremacy of the civil party, as represented by Mavrocordato, over the military party led by Colokotronis and Odysseus. The seat of the Government had been moved from Nauplia to Tripolitza, where it was expected that the legislative and executive bodies, representing the administration of the whole of Greece, would be able to consolidate their authority. Neither Colokotronis nor Odysseus, however, was willing to accept this arrangement. The former coerced the executive body into

electing him their Vice-President and delegating to him
the whole control of the Morea; the executive body
thereupon escaped from their Vice-President to Salamis.
The legislative body, or the Senate, as it was called,
were more courageous; while remaining at Tripolitza,
they elected Mavrocordato as their President, in the
hope that he would be able to establish his influence
in opposition to Colokotronis. Mavrocordato, however,
showed some hesitation in accepting the honour thus
thrust upon him, and the Senate were obliged formally
to summon him on July 3rd, 1823, and to threaten him
with prosecution unless he accepted their presidency.
Scarcely, however, had Mavrocordato reached Tripolitza
and assumed his office when the dictates of prudence
recurred to him, and after handing in his resignation he
fled secretly to Hydra. The Senate, thus deserted, in
their turn abandoned the Morea, and hurriedly joined
the executive at Salamis.

By the middle of August 1823, therefore, it was
uncertain which was either the *de jure* or the *de facto*
Government of Greece, or indeed whether any such
Government existed. In Eastern Greece the control
rested with the military chieftain Odysseus, who for the
moment had some working understanding with Colokotronis, the actual despot of the Morea. Western
Greece still acknowledged Mavrocordato as its leader,
although the latter was for the moment a refugee in
the island of Hydra. The legislative and executive
bodies, who were supposed to derive their authority
from the successive national assemblies of Epidaurus and
Argos, had ceased to oppose the military chieftains, and
were by now conducting futile and quite inconclusive
discussions in the island of Salamis. Meanwhile the
Turks under Omer Pasha were in force in Western
Greece, and their fleet was blockading the whole coast
from Missolonghi to Navarino. The Greek vessels,
owing to lack of funds, still sheltered idly in the islands
of Hydra, Psara, and Spetsai.

The news of Byron's arrival had by now spread throughout Greece, and the emissaries of each of these contending parties flocked to Cephallonia in the hope of securing his adherence. "To nobody," says Finlay, "did the Greeks ever unmask their selfishness and self-deceit so candidly. . . . Kolokotrones invited him to a national assembly at Salamis. Mavrocordatos informed him that he would be of no use anywhere but at Hydra, for Mavrocordatos was then in that island. Constantine Metaxa, who was Governor of Mesolonghi, wrote saying that Greece would be ruined unless Lord Byron visited that fortress. Petrobey used plainer words. He informed Lord Byron that the true way to save Greece was to lend him, the bey, a thousand pounds."

In face of these clamorous solicitations Byron adopted a non-committal, if somewhat languid, attitude. "As I did not come here," he records in his journal at Cephallonia, "to join a faction, but a nation, and to deal with honest men, and not with speculators or peculators (charges bandied about daily by the Greeks of each other), it will require much circumspection to avoid the character of a partisan, and I perceive it to be the more difficult as I have already received invitations from more than one of the contending parties, always under the pretext that *they* are the 'real Simon Pure.' After all, one should not despair, though all the foreigners that I have hitherto met with from amongst the Greeks are going or gone back disgusted.

"Whoever goes into Greece at present should do it as Mrs. Fry went into Newgate—not in the expectation of meeting with any especial indication of existing probity, but in the hope that time and better treatment will reclaim the present burglarious and larcenous tendencies which have followed this General Gaol delivery.

"When the limbs of the Greeks are a little less stiff from the shackles of four centuries, they will not march so much 'as if they had gyves on their legs.' At present the Chains are broken indeed; but the links are still clanking, and the Saturnalia is still too recent to have converted the Slave into a sober Citizen. The worst of them is that (to use a coarse but the only expression that will not fall short of the truth) they are such damned liars; there never was such an incapacity for veracity shown since Eve lived in Paradise."

At one moment, during the third week in August, he appears to have decided to proceed himself to the Morea in order to examine conditions on the spot. The captain of the "Hercules," however, showed little inclination to risk his vessel in an attempt to rush the Turkish blockade. Their first intention was to start on the Sunday. "No, My Lord," Captain Scott expostulated, "you must not play these tricks with me; there shall be no heathenish and outlandish doings on board my ship on a Sunday." When it was suggested that the expedition might start on the Monday or the Tuesday following, Captain Scott shifted his ground. He would only consent, he said, if Byron would undertake to guarantee him the full value of his vessel in the event of capture. Lord Byron did not insist. It would, after all, be supremely ridiculous if he were captured by the Turkish forces without landing in Greece, and even if he did manage to reach the mainland, it was questionable whether his presence would not do more harm than good. He decided, therefore, to remain for the present at Cephallonia, to release the "Hercules," and to allow Captain Scott to return to England.

On the 22nd of August he had received a reply to the letter which he had addressed to Marco Botzaris. The answer was dated the 18th of August, and was worded as follows :—

"Your letter, and that of the venerable Ignazio, have filled me with joy. Your Excellency is exactly the person of whom we stand in need. Let nothing prevent you from coming into this part of Greece.

The enemy threatens us in great number; but, by the help of God and Your Excellency, they shall meet a suitable resistance. I shall have something to do to-night against a corps of six or seven thousand Albanians, encamped close to this place. The day after to-morrow I will set out, with a few chosen companions, to meet Your Excellency. Do not delay. I thank you for the good opinion you have of my fellow-citizens, which God grant you will not find ill-founded; and I thank you still more for the care you have so kindly taken of them. Believe me," etc.

That very night Botzaris had attacked the camp of Omer Pasha at Carpenisi, and had been shot in the head by a musket ball. His body was recovered and conveyed to Missolonghi. Thus of the two leaders to whom Byron had been specially recommended, one was a refugee in the island of Hydra, and the other had already lost his life. " This melancholy state of affairs," records Gamba, " neither deceived nor disheartened Lord Byron. Not a fanatic, not a blind enthusiast, he was prepared for the worst. But there was little good to be reaped from proceeding at present. To learn the real state of affairs, to become acquainted with the men concerned, and to be known to them, was the best method of acquiring an influence which he might afterwards employ in settling their internal discords."

In these circumstances Byron decided to disembark at Cephallonia, and to await further developments. He felt that it would be indiscreet to accept the hospitality offered him by Colonel Napier and the other officials of the Government. He considered, even, that it would be preferable to establish himself at some distance from Argostoli, and he therefore decided upon the little village of Metaxata, at a distance of four miles from the capital.

His last days upon the " Hercules " were spent in

securing as a personal bodyguard the services of some forty of the Souliots. After some bargaining with their chiefs, Djavella, Draco, and Fotomara, he agreed that he would pay them four dollars a head. It was not a successful experiment. It was soon discovered that a large proportion of the forty were neither Souliots nor Greeks, that their three chiefs claimed the emoluments and the position which they held at home, and that the rank and file accused them of keeping back their pay. So soon as he had decided to remain indefinitely in Cephallonia, Byron realised that the presence of this turbulent bodyguard was not only unnecessary, but constituted an undue strain upon his purse and temper. With some difficulty, and with Colonel Napier's assistance, he induced the British authorities to restore to them the arms which had been confiscated when they took refuge on the island, presented them with the equivalent of two months' pay, and shipped them, at considerable expense, to Missolonghi.

In the intervals of this troublesome negotiation he would row in the afternoon across the harbour and bathe with Trelawny on the opposite rocks, sitting afterwards in an olive grove and eating his supper under the trees. On one of these occasions he held out his right leg to Trelawny saying, " I hope this accursed limb will be knocked off in the war."

" It won't improve your swimming," Trelawny answered. " I will exchange legs if you will give me a portion of your brains."

" You would repent your bargain ; at times I feel my brains boiling, as Shelley's did whilst you were grilling him."

Trelawny, meanwhile, was becoming impatient. One day, when Byron was having his siesta, Trelawny came and called him, at first in a low voice, and then louder and louder. Byron started up in terror. With a convulsive sigh he said, " I have had such a dream ! I am trembling with fear. I am not fit to go to Greece."

Trelawny could not tolerate such neurosis. He suggested that he should himself at once proceed to the Morea to ascertain the real state of things. Byron begged him to defer until the whole company could go together. For a few days Trelawny consented, but when it was clear that Byron had decided to pay off the "Hercules," and to establish himself on shore, Trelawny determined to leave him. "I well knew," he wrote, "that, once on shore, Byron would fall back on his old routine of dawdling habits—plotting, planning, shilly-shallying, and doing nothing."

And thus on the 6th of September Byron, Gamba, and Dr. Bruno moved to Metaxata, and parted from Trelawny for ever. For two days the latter remained on the "Hercules," and then with Hamilton Browne he left for the Morea. On the day following Byron's departure Trelawny sent up a farewell note to Metaxata. "We missed you sadly," he wrote, "last night at grog time." But, in spite of this, we may assume Trelawny was not really sorry to have separated from Byron.

CHAPTER VII

September 6—December 27, 1823

I

THE house which Byron rented at Metaxata is still extant, and bears above its gateway an inscription in modern Greek recording that it was here that the celebrated English poet and Philhellene resided immediately before his departure for the Greek mainland. The little cottage, which to-day shines white and trim against the dun background of the mountain and over the jumbled roofs of the surrounding hovels, has of late been restored: the ivy, which in Byron's day draped the outside walls in so incongruous a manner, has been stripped, and the walls themselves have been replastered and white-washed, the old balcony on which Byron would sit in his tartan jacket has been renewed and redecorated; the chimney and the gutters have been modernised; and finally, the ground floor, originally a vague, arcaded store-house for olives, grapes, and lemons, has been accorded windows and partitioned into four extra rooms.

In 1823 this villa of the Metaxas family was less commodious: it consisted of the top floor only, containing but four rooms—a bedroom and a sitting-room for Byron, a common room for Gamba and Bruno, and a kitchen for the servants. Apart, however, from the congestion of their actual quarters, it can scarcely be said that Byron and his staff were roughing it at Metaxata. For this village nestles in one of the richest and most pleasant of all Ionian valleys. Behind, protecting it from the north, rise the colourless but aromatic slopes of the Black Mountain; around the village itself, and running down to the shore, is a luxuriant sweep of vine and cypress, of olive groves and oranges; while in front, framed by the twin southern capes of Cephallonia, stretches a purple segment of the Ionian Sea. Nor was this the sole amenity; for from the eastern slopes of Cephallonia the neighbouring coast of Greece might have appeared a little too contiguous, a little imminent perhaps, and, as it were, insistent. The view from Metaxata was marred, however, by no such incessant reminder: only on rare occasions, in the early dawn, would the dark and distant outline of Southern Greece appear for a moment above the water. And as the sun rose, this vision would fade again into the sea, leaving only the contours of Zante to break the hard blue line of horizon.

The manner of their life was organised with extreme simplicity. At 9 a.m. Byron would appear from his bedroom and would work with Gamba till eleven. Then would come breakfast, consisting only of a cup of tea without sugar, followed by a ride upon the mountain. At 3 p.m. there would be the main meal of the day, Byron eating only cheese, olives, salad, and a little fruit. Then would follow pistol practice at a paper target set in a split reed against the hillside. Till seven Byron would retire, with one of Scott's novels, to his bedroom, and from then on there would be conversation till midnight.

The visitors who rode out to Metaxata in the cool of evening were at least variegated. There were the young officers of the garrison, who would come in twos and threes, and drink gin and water and listen, aghast and admiring, to the more lurid portions of Lord Byron's biography; there were Dr. Scott and Dr. Muir and Colonel Duffie; on occasions, busy, limping, and short-sighted, Napier himself would appear, bringing them the news from Greece and England. Count Delladecima, an Ionian noble deeply interested in Greek party politics, would ride out upon his mule and sit there on the balcony,

talking about the past history and future regeneration of
Hellas. " As a final analysis," he would say, in his
Venetian dialect; but Byron was not deeply impressed
by the analyses of Count Delladecima. At frequent
intervals there came Dr. Stravolemo, who had been
physician to Ali Pasha of Janina, and who had many
stories to tell of that obese adventurer, and of M. Pouqueville, the French Consul, and of the curiously impulsive
methods of the Turks. It would amuse Byron to egg
Dr. Stravolemo on to medical discussions with Francesco
Bruno, at which the latter would become very flushed
and excitable, and quiver up to a high falsetto, and
quote what the great Vaccà used to say at Pisa, and end
by bursting into tears. And there was Mr. Hancock, of
the firm of Barff and Hancock, bankers, of Cephallonia
and Zante.

For the firm of Cariddi and Corgialegno, to whom
Webb & Co. had given Byron letters of credit, had
proved highly unsatisfactory :—

" Of your two Correspondents," wrote Byron to
Charles Barry, " to whom you gave me letters of Credit,
Mr. Cariddi is unwilling and Mr. Corgialegno (is that
the name?) willing, but hardly competent, to advance
money on even the best bills of Exchange. Mr. Cariddi
not only declined, but declared that he had no connexion
with the house of Webb at Genoa; and when referred
to the letters for the proof that it was of the *same firm*
with that of Leghorn, he replied that it was all the
same—he had no connexion with either."

Gamba, in his narrative, is almost vehement upon this
subject : " I must not omit," he records, " the conduct
of the Ionian bankers towards Lord Byron, which grieved
him much. He had sent his letters of credit from one
of the first houses of the Mediterranean, directed to
Messrs. Cariddi and Corgialegno, two of the richest
proprietors and merchants in the island. The former,
either from fear of political consequences, or from
incapability, replied, and perhaps truly, that he could

not answer his bills. But the uncourteous manner was what offended Lord Byron. He neither came in person, nor sent an answer in writing, but a clerk with the refusal. M. Cariddi suffered afterwards, not only by the public contempt, but by the loss of much business with Messrs. Webb, which affected him, I should think, much more. M. Corgialegno was more courteous, but still betrayed a little of the Jew."

Barry from Genoa replied to Byron's protests in the sense that it was not his fault if the arrangements had miscarried: it was the fault of "old Webb," who had insisted, in his omniscient way, that Cariddi and Corgialegno were well known to him; and in fact so indignant had Barry been, that this incident had almost led to the disruption of his own partnership with the house of Webb of Leghorn. Byron was appeased; but his financial arrangements were thereafter entrusted to Mr. Hancock, whom he treated with that touch of gay familiarity which, on all occasions, so endeared him to persons of Hancock's quality and which has led the admirable Miss Mayne into the fallacy of contending that Byron was essentially "a man's man"; although, if we come to think of it, he was nothing of the sort.

A further, and particularly welcome visitor to Metaxata was Lord Sidney Osborne, with whom Byron was intimately, if somewhat intricately, connected. For Lord Sidney was the son, by a second marriage, of that Duke of Leeds whose first wife, the unhappy Lady Carmarthen, had eloped with Byron's father to become the mother of Augusta Leigh. In order to escape his London creditors, Lord Sidney had entered the Government service, and had been appointed State Secretary at Corfu. His varied duties brought him frequently to Cephallonia, where he would be greeted uproariously at the little ivy-covered house at Metaxata, and there would be much conversation about their mutual and rather flamboyant relations, by which conversation both Bruno and Gamba would be very considerably impressed.

Finally there were the emissaries of the various Greek parties, who flocked to Metaxata, attracted like vultures by the savour of Byron's fabled wealth. There were emissaries from Colokotronis, who would represent how their enlightened patron had by now firmly established his humane government throughout the Morea, and how Mavrocordato, that dishonest and incompetent phanariot, had been forced by popular clamour to fly the country. There were emissaries from Mavrocordato, who would explain how the Klepht leader Colokotronis, with his big nose and brigand mercenaries, had destroyed the legal government of Greece, had prevented the fleet from sailing, or the elected deputies from proceeding to England to secure their loan. There were emissaries from Odysseus, who would point out that Athens, and Athens alone, constituted the spiritual capital of Hellas, and that it was only by proceeding to the Acropolis and allying himself with the Captain of Eastern Greece that Byron could secure the unity and liberation of the country. There were emissaries from Petro Bey of Maina, who would contend that Maina alone had for centuries resisted Turkish authority, and that the final emancipation of Greece could only be secured by supporting the feudal movement in the south. There were emissaries from Missolonghi, from Anatolikon, from Salamis, from Gastouni, and from the islands. There were emissaries from Crete and Southern Albania. There were emissaries, even, from Mount Athos. Byron would receive these conflicting missions impartially; he would amble towards them across his sitting-room, smiling at them and offering them his rough, rush-plaited chairs; καθήσετε κύριε, he would say to them: it was about all the Greek he remembered. And at times, when they arrived together, he would confront them the one with the other; and Count Delladecima would act as interpreter, summarising, in his prolific way, the voluble insults which they would hurtle at each other across the little room; forgetting at moments to interpret, and launching out, upon his own, into a torrent of argument and invective.

And in this manner the month of September slid unnoticed to its conclusion—words and the confusion of tongues, and the gestures of angry disputants; the barking of dogs at night-time, and beyond, framed by the little valley and the stern slopes of the Black Mountain, the indigo horizon of the Ionian Sea.

II

As a relaxation from all these politics, external and internal, Byron engaged in an extended controversy on the subject of religion.

Attached to the garrison at Argostoli was a Scotch doctor, a Mr. James Kennedy. This excellent gentleman had been much distressed by the "free and deistical sentiments" which prevailed among the officers of the British garrison. He had also been much stimulated by the arrival of Lord Byron, and by the "vague and unrestrained wonder" which this arrival had occasioned. He had already decided that it was his duty to expound to the officers of the garrison the true nature of Christian doctrine and the evidences on which that doctrine was based. He was able, somewhat to his surprise, to indulge his other curiosities owing to a sudden decision on the part of Lord Byron that he, also, would attend these gospel-meetings.

"His Lordship," records Mr. Kennedy, "sat on the sofa, Colonel N. in a chair beside him; the others formed a circle round the table. I began by apologising for my boldness in undertaking such a task."

And then the exposition began. It was a very long exposition, but they sat there patiently while Dr. Kennedy was speaking. For an hour he continued, and then, to their relief, he paused. "I now said," Dr. Kennedy records, "that to relieve their attention by variety, and myself from the fatigue of speaking—to which I was little accustomed—I would read to them a brief and distinct summary of the fundamental doctrines of Christianity, supported by appropriate quotations from the Scriptures. . . . I had, on a different occasion, found them productive of much utility to two persons of excellent understanding and of great candour; but on the present occasion I was disappointed. Whilst speaking, I was listened to with attention; but I had not proceeded far in reading before I observed signs of impatience in some of them, especially in N. and his lordship. I endeavoured to obviate this, by saying that I should soon finish; but I had proceeded a short way further when I was interrupted by his lordship. . . ."

With this interruption the conversation became more general, and, as a result, more desultory. Byron displayed considerable knowledge of the Scriptures, and recalled many of the passages which he had learnt in the old Aberdeen days from Mary Gay; he mentioned, also, several well-known works on theological subjects with which even Dr. Kennedy was unacquainted. The audience was impressed as much by his erudition as by his patience. At last he rose to leave, having listened courteously to Dr. Kennedy for four hours.

"After this," records Dr. Kennedy, "there were seven or eight meetings held on the Sunday forenoons. His Lordship . . . was not present on these occasions. . . . I read the testimonies of Manetho, Eupetinos, Artapanes, Tacitus, Diodorus Siculus, Strabo, Justin, Juvenal, Porphyry, Julian, and Mahommed, to show that Moses was a real character, and not a mythological person, as some have impudently asserted, and that he lived long before Sanconiathon, who, according to them, lived before the Trojan war.

"The history of the destruction of Sodom and Gomorrah is attested by Diodorus Siculus, Strabo, Solinus, Tacitus, Pliny, and Josephus. Barnes, Alexander Polytresh, Nicolaus Damascenus, Artapanes, and other historians cited by Josephus and Eusebius, make honourable mention of Abraham, Isaac, Jacob, and Joseph."

All this did not, however, put an end to the conversations between Dr. Kennedy and Lord Byron. The former was a few weeks later invited up to Metaxata. He was well received, and embarked at once upon a discussion regarding Warburton, Gibbon, the Methodists, the Socinians, and the morals of Percy Bysshe Shelley. Dr. Kennedy contended that the untimely death of the latter constituted " a striking warning to others as to the opinions they should form, the mode in which they should live, and the necessity for preparing for death and judgment." Byron did not share this view. " I should have been pleased," he said, " that you had known Shelley. I should have liked to have seen you argue together. You very much remind me of him, not only in countenance, but in your manner of speaking . . . but I see that it is impossible to excite in your mind sympathy for an unfortunate man of fine genius and imagination." Besides, it was getting dark, and it was time for Dr. Kennedy to ride back to Argostoli.

Immediately after this second conversation the doctor developed a severe sore throat, attended by the loss of his voice, and the conversion of Lord Byron was thereby temporarily suspended. Meanwhile the news of their meetings and of Dr. Kennedy's self-appointed mission had spread through the island :—

" The wits of the garrison made themselves merry with what was going on, and passed many jokes on the subject. Some of them affected to believe, I know not on what ground, that Lord B.'s wish to hear me proceeded from his desire to have an accurate idea of the opinions and manners of the Methodists, in order that he might make Don Juan become one for a time, and thus paint their conduct with the greater accuracy and fidelity. Some of them did not hesitate to tell me that this was the case, and that, if I were wise, I should let his lordship alone.

"My answer was short and decided. 'I could not affirm that Lord B. had not the intentions they ascribed to him, but if he had, he did not act like a gentleman in wishing, of his own accord and at his own request, to be introduced to me, to hear me on these subjects; but if such were his design, it would have no effect upon me, as I neither feared his ridicule nor his poetry, and would therefore converse with him on the subject till such time as it was more certain what his secret intentions were."

On recovering the use of his voice, Dr. Kennedy, therefore, again rode out to Metaxata :—

"'Has your lordship,' I said, 'read any of the books I took the liberty of sending?' 'I have looked into Boston, but have not had time to read far. I am afraid it is too deep for me!' 'Be not afraid,' I said, 'but continue, and you will find it easier than you imagine; for how can that be deep which the most illiterate people understand? The scroll that I sent you about Warburton perhaps you will not be able to make out; if you will give it to me now, I will read it to you, as you may find my hand-writing difficult.' 'Not at all,' said his lordship, 'I mean to give all you have sent me a serious perusal. . . . I have begun very fairly: I have given some of your tracts to Fletcher, who is a good sort of man, but still wants, like myself, some reformation, and I hope he will spread them among the other servants, who require it still more. Bruno and Gamba are busy reading some of the Italian tracts, and I hope it will have a good effect upon them! . . . You have sent me an account of the death of Lord Rochester, as a tract, *par excellence*, having a particular reference to me.' 'Something of this sort was in my mind when I put up this tract with the others; but my principal wish was to give you a copy of each of the tracts in my possession, in hope that, as they are all good and short, something in one or other of them might arrest your attention.' 'But,' added he, 'I am not quite satisfied with Lord

Rochester's conversion; there will always remain this uncertainty about it, that perhaps had he recovered, and been placed among his former companions, he would have relapsed; and while this uncertainty prevails, we can never be assured of his real conversion.' I admitted that this was true; yet I added, 'We shall be perfectly satisfied if we find that your lordship, who follows him in some points, should also preserve a resemblance of him at his departure.' "

The discussion upon the repentance of Lord Rochester was still proceeding when there came the noise of horses in the lane below; Lord Sidney Osborne had arrived on one of his visits. Dr. Kennedy thereupon took his departure. "Sidney," exclaimed Byron, "you have saved my life. Saint Kennedy was boring me to distraction and, but for your arrival, I could never have got rid of him."

This remark was not, however, overheard by Dr. Kennedy, who was already riding slowly along the dusty road to Argostoli, thinking, as he rode, of all the forceful and brilliant arguments with which he might have convinced Lord Byron of the sincerity and potential permanence of Lord Rochester's death-bed reformation.

On his third visit Kennedy inquired of Byron whether "he had looked into my paper on the doctrine of eternal punishments." "No," replied Byron, "I must confess I have not—something or other always comes in the way; but that and the other books I intend to peruse diligently, though I fear I shall not have time to do so before I go to Greece; but I shall take care to send them all to you before I go, whether I read them or not."

Dr. Kennedy did not, as will have been gathered, succeed in his conversion of Lord Byron. But Byron, for his part, had succeeded admirably in the conversion of Dr. Kennedy. "From what has occurred," the latter assured him at their last meeting, "I shall ever feel a warm interest and anxiety in whatever concerns you, especially till such time as I hear that you have arrived at that point of religious knowledge and improvement towards which I have, in our conversations, been desirous of leading you. You have complained that many, who professed themselves strict Christians, have inveighed against you. Be assured that there is one at least who will not do so, but who will, on the contrary, always pray for your welfare, particularly for that of your soul.

" ' I shall always feel myself indebted to you,' said Lord B."

And in general Dr. Kennedy's impression was as follows :—

" His appearance and manner gave the idea of a kind-hearted, benevolent, and feeling man, with an amiable and pleasing countenance, but a man who was led by passions, by prejudice, and not by coolness of judgment, nor the steady self-denial and heroical feelings of Christian principles. . . . I often looked at Lord Byron with admiration, sympathy, and compassion : admiration for his great abilities, sympathy with his unfortunate life, and compassion for one who, with all the wealth, rank, and fame which fell to the lot of few, and which, when founded on a proper basis, are calculated so much to promote happiness, appeared unhappy ; not merely because he was not virtuous, but because he was not religious. Many talents he possessed, calculated to excite wonder and envy ; yet the highest of all blessings, piety, he possessed not. . . . Yet Lord B. excited intense sympathy in my mind. . . . His patience in listening to me, his candour in never putting captious objections, his acknowledgment of his own sinfulness, gave hope that the blessing of religious truth might be opened to his understanding ; and though these were damped by an occasional levity, at least by the want of that seriousness which the subject required, yet, on the whole, the general result was favourable."

Dr. Kennedy did not live to complete the notes from which the engaging volume of his " Conversations on

Religion with Lord Byron " was subsequently compiled. In the following year he was removed to Jamaica, where in September of 1827 he died of yellow fever. But sufficient material exists in the published volume to furnish a curious and not wholly incidental comment upon the diversions and preoccupations of Lord Byron in Cephallonia.

And I, for one, am of opinion that in his conversations with Dr. Kennedy Lord Byron was in no way guilty of insincerity. For had the doctor been a Catholic, and not a Methodist, the result might well have been a dramatic and emotional conversion. Which, I suppose, would have proved of considerable subsequent assistance.

III

Trelawny, as we have seen, having already found Byron " not romantic enough," had left for the Morea. From Pyrgos he and Hamilton Browne had travelled through the devastated country as far as Tripolitza, and then on to Argos and Nauplia. At Corinth they had an interview with Colokotronis " and other predatory chiefs," and had then crossed to Salamis to visit the legislative and executive bodies, who were then engaged in mutual indictments of each other for the embezzlement of public funds. " Here, too," writes Trelawny, " we saw the most potent leaders of the chief Greek military factions — Primates, Hydriotes, Mainotes, Moreotes, Ipsareotes, Candiotes, and many others—each and all intent on their own immediate interests. There, too, I saw the first specimens of the super-subtle Phanariotes, pre-eminent in all evil, reared at Constantinople, and trained in the arts of deception by the most adroit professors in the world. These pliant and dexterous intriguers glided stealthily from tent to tent and from chief to chief, impregnating their brains with wily suggestions, thus envenoming their feuds and causing universal anarchy. Confounded at this exhibition of rank selfishness, we backed out of these civil broils, and sailed for Hydra, one of our commissions being to send deputies from that island to England to negotiate a loan."

Meanwhile Byron himself, with Gamba and Bruno, was prolonging his inactive if expectant sojourn at Metaxata. He was perfectly happy. It was a period of pleasurable, and quite justifiable, transition between the worries and humiliations of Italy and the period of action which would, sooner or later, have to follow. He had his books; he had his horses; he fenced with Gamba; he could defeat them all, in spite of his trembling hand, at pistol practice; he could beat Dr. Kennedy in his citations of the Scriptures; he could compete with Colonel Napier in his realistic and prudent judgment of the Greek character; he could even share with him in appreciating the essential and vivid charm of that maligned nation; he could cope with the emissaries who visited him, voluble and solicitous, from the mainland; he could write long and splendidly sensible letters to the Greek Committee in London, and to Hobhouse; his health was now better than ever; he had disengaged himself, and not too discreditably, from the past; the future began to glimmer, under the stimulus of Napier, with the reviving shimmer of hope and of romance.

" I like this place," he said to Dr. Kennedy—" I do not know why—and dislike to move. There are not, to be sure, many allurements here, neither from the commodiousness of the house nor the bleak view of the black mountain; there is no learned society, nor the presence of beautiful women; and yet, for all that, I would wish to remain, as I have found myself more comfortable, and my time passes more cheerfully than it has for a long time done."

It was not only pleasant to remain there at Metaxata; it was also wise. Again and again we find Byron pointing out to his correspondents how very wise, how almost masterly, was his inaction. He knew that Europe had echoed to the announcement of his coming; that they

would expect something quick, dramatic, and excessive.
He decided to show them that his main characteristic
was deliberation and prudence. He knew also that the
leader of every Greek party was endeavouring to secure
the auspices and the dollars of Lord Byron for his own
faction; he determined to show them that Lord Byron
could not so easily be gulled, that they had to cope with
an impartiality as impervious as granite. He knew that
his friends at home, Hobhouse and Kinnaird, disbelieved
as much in his patience as in his resolution; he would
show them that they were mistaken. " The fact is," he
wrote to Hobhouse in September, " that matters are in
great disorder—no less than three parties and one con-
spiracy going on amongst them at this moment; a few
steps further, and a civil war may ensue. On all sides
they are (as you perceive) trying to enlist me as a partisan; but I have hitherto declared that I can recognise
only the Greek Government, without reference to the
persons who may compose it; and that, as a foreigner,
I have nothing to do with factions, or private preferences
of individuals.

" I have not yet gone to the Main because, to say the
truth, it does not appear that I could avoid being considered as a favourer of one party or another; but the
moment I can be of any real service I am willing to go
amongst them."

And again : " I mean (unless something out of the
way occurs to recall me) to stay up in the country itself,
or the neighbourhood of Greece, till things are either
better or hopeless, and in every case will take advantage
of circumstances to serve the *Cause* if the patriots will
permit me; but it must be *the Cause*, and not individuals
or *parties*, that I endeavour to benefit."

We may doubt whether either Hobhouse or Kinnaird
was wholly convinced by all these excellent explanations.
To them, doubtless, it appeared that Byron was once
again malingering; that once again the old indolent
stagnation had descended as a cloud upon him. They

did not realise that he was clutching at these potent justifications for delay mainly because he flinched from the responsibilities which he visualised so clearly ; mainly because he was acutely, torturingly diffident. The temptation to remain in Cephallonia was indeed all but invincible : he had proclaimed himself a man of action ; from the moment he landed in Greece this pretension would, he knew too well, be pitifully exposed. At Metaxata he could be generous, be acute, be prudent ; at Missolonghi he would have to *control*. And so he lingered there, hoping that something would emerge to strengthen him ; hoping that something would emerge to keep him there for ever ; hoping, predominantly, that the Committee would send out someone else. If only it could be Napier ! The hope alone sufficed to give him courage :—

" I shall continue here," he wrote to Hobhouse, " till I see when, and where, I can be of use, if such a thing at least be practicable. I have hitherto only contradictory accounts. If you send out a military man, he will have every co-operation from me ; or if you send out any other person, I have no objection to act as either his coadjutor, or subordinately, for I have none of those punctilios."

And in the meantime he could at least place his fortune at their disposal. No strength of character, no dominance, was required for that. " Get together," he wrote to Kinnaird, " all the means and credit of mine we can, to face the war establishment, for it is ' in for a penny, in for a pound,' and I must do all that I can for the ancients. I have advanced them four thousand pounds, which got the squadron to sea ; and I made them forward the Deputies for the loan, who ought to be soon in England, having sailed some weeks ago. . . . In the meantime I stand paymaster, and what not ; and lucky it is that, from the nature of the warfare, and of the country, the resources even of an individual can be of a partial and temporary service. . . . If I can but succeed in reconciling the two parties (and I have left no stone unturned there*for*) it will be something; and if not, why, we must go over to the Morea with the Western Greeks, who are the bravest, and at present the strongest, now that they have beaten back the Turks—and try the effects of a little *physical* advice, should they persist in rejecting *moral* persuasion. . . . Once more (as usual) recommending to you my affairs, and more especially the reinforcement of my strong-box, and credits from all lawful sources and *re*sources of mine, to their practicable extent (and, after all, it is better playing at Nations, than gaming at Almack's, or Newmarket, or piecing, or dinnering), and also requesting your Honour to write now and then one of those pithy epistles ' touching the needful,' so agreeable to the distant traveller."

Meanwhile there came the gratifying and at the same time disturbing intelligence that his journey to Greece had already produced in Europe some practical impression. "An immense number of half-pay officers," Barry wrote to him from Genoa in August, " only want the word to start for Greece. Your going there has given a sort of encouragement, and if you write home anything favourable, you will have a Host out looking to you for instructions."

And in another letter Barry wrote : " The papers do not speak ill of you now, nor ever would had your character been better known."

All this, perhaps, was satisfactory. He was not—of course he was not—wasting time : he was wisely waiting there at Metaxata to hear from Trelawny and Hamilton Browne ; to hear that the fleet had sailed from Hydra ; that the deputies were proceeding to England ; that the stores which the Committee were sending had arrived.

"Much credit," remarks Dr. Millingen, " is certainly due to Lord Byron for the prudence which, under these circumstances, characterised his conduct."

There were moments when even Byron felt that Dr. Millingen was right.

IV

At the beginning of October news of their mission was received from Browne and Trelawny. Although they confirmed the report that Colokotronis was the master of the Morea, and that the civil party were for the moment powerless, yet they spoke highly of the general condition of public opinion and of the determination of the peasants to continue the struggle. They were of opinion, apparently, that the immediate necessities were, first to induce the Greek fleet to leave Hydra and to break the blockade, and secondly to despatch the two Greek deputies to London for the purpose of concluding the loan which the Committee stated could now easily be floated. They foresaw that, if such a loan could be given to the constitutional Government, the usurped authority of the military chieftains would from that moment diminish. And the event proved that they were correct in this assumption.

Byron was gratified by this intelligence : it gave him something definite to do ; it gave him an added excuse for remaining at Metaxata. Throughout October he concentrated his efforts on securing the departure of the fleet and the despatch of the two deputies to London. On receiving a letter from Mavrocordato inviting him to proceed to Hydra, he instructed Hamilton Browne and Trelawny to journey there in his place, and he himself sent a letter to Mavrocordato informing him that he was determined to remain " as a looker-on until he could see the favourable moment of co-operating with advantage in the national cause."

Meanwhile he maintained his ostensible attitude of confidence tempered by realism. He discouraged undue pessimism, which he regarded as a pathological reaction to the enthusiasm with which the glamour and early successes of the Greek cause had filled the superficial. " All this comes," he wrote to Colonel Napier, " of what

157

Mr. Braham pronounces 'Entusymusy,' expecting too much and starting at speed. It is lucky for me so far that, fail or not fail, I can hardly be disappointed, for I believed myself on a fool's errand from the outset, and must, therefore, like Dogberry, 'spare no wisdom.' I will at least linger on here or there till I see whether I *can* be of *any* service in *any* way; and if I doubt it, it is because I do not feel confidence in my individual capacity for this kind of bear-taming, and not from a disbelief in the powers of a more active or less indifferent character to be of use to them, though I feel persuaded that that person must be a military man.

"But I like the Cause at least, and will stick by it while it is not degraded nor dishonoured."

And again in the same month he wrote as follows :—

"It is very expedient that the Committee should support me with their authority; and if they were to frame a memorial to the Greek Government on the subject of their existing differences and the expulsion or secession of Mavrocordato, it would probably have more effect than any *individual* attempt of mine to reconcile the parties; and until they *are* reconciled, it seems to be allowed very generally that their internal affairs will be in an unpleasant state of weakness. I would, of course, present such a memorial and enforce it by all lawful means in my power.

"All the stories of the Greek victories by sea and land are exaggerated or untrue : they *have* had the advantage in some skirmishes, but the Turks have also had the same in others, and are now before Missolonghi in force. And as for the fleet, it has never been to sea at all until very lately, and, as far as can be ascertained, has done little or nothing to the purpose. . . .

"I offered to advance a thousand dollars per month for the succour of Missolonghi and the Suliotes under Bozzari (who was since killed), but the Govt. have answered me (through Count Delladecima of this island) that they wish to confer with me previously—which is, in fact, saying that they wish me to expend my money in some other direction.

"Now, I will take especial care that it *is* for the public cause; otherwise, I will not advance a para. The Opposition say they want to cajole me, and the party in power say the others wish to seduce me; so between the two I have a difficult part to play. However, I will have nothing to do with their factions, unless to reconcile them if possible.

"I know not whether it be true that 'Honesty is the best policy,' but it is the only kind that I am disposed to practise or to sanction."

At the end of October an agent of the executive body, or, as they called themselves, the Government of Greece, arrived at Metaxata with a definite invitation to Byron to proceed to Tripolitza. After some hesitation, he decided to respond to this appeal. They were to start in the second week of November, and preparations were immediately made. The luggage was packed, the boats were ordered, and a guard of fifty Souliotes, under the command of Djavella, with mules, were sent across from Missolonghi to Pyrgos, on the coast of the Morea, to await his coming.

Two days, however, before the moment came for their dash across the intervening sea, Hamilton Browne returned from Hydra, bringing with him the two deputies who were to proceed to London to conclude the loan. The deputies begged Byron that, pending the definite conclusion of the loan in London, he would advance to them the sum of 300,000 piastres for the immediate payment of the fleet, and promised that with this payment a squadron of fourteen vessels would immediately put to sea. Byron agreed to advance them 200,000 piastres, or £4000, out of his private purse. Considerable difficulty was experienced in raising this money from the house of Cariddi and Corgialegno, who insisted upon usurious terms. Byron refused to submit to these impositions, and decided to obtain the money from Malta. At the last moment, however, Messrs. Barff and Hancock came forward and offered to discount his bills on the most advantageous conditions. Whereat the deputies departed with Hamilton Browne for London, well contented with their visit to Metaxata.

V

The information which Hamilton Browne was able to give Byron convinced him, somewhat to his relief, that it would after all be preferable to avoid the Morea, and to wait in his home at Metaxata until Mavrocordato and the fleet had arrived at Missolonghi. His conviction of the impossibility of achieving anything in the Morea, which was still under the influence and domination of Colokotronis, was confirmed by a letter which he received in November from M. Schilizzi, who had been his fellow-passenger on the " Hercules." M. Schilizzi wrote as follows :—

" Puisque la sagesse de Milord l'à empêché jusqu'à présent de faire des pas précipités, il est essentiel qu'il soit informé de tout ce qui se passe ici, et alors il pourra prendre le parti qu'il lui paraîtra le plus convenable. Les affaires sont tout à fait dans un autre état que ce que Browne avait écrit de Salamine, et ce qu'il m'a engagé aussi de passer içi après avoir beaucoup de difficultés et de désagréments sur notre route, manquant presque tous les soirs de villages pour nous arrêter la nuit et étant obligés de la passer quelques fois sur les montagnes et parmi les précipices ayant la pluie sur le dos. Nous sommes à la fin arrivés à Napoli de Romania le cinquième jour de notre départ de Prygos.

" Napoli est une petite ville dévastée. Toutes les maisons sont brulées ou dégradées, et il est impossible de trouver une seule qui soit un peu

convenable. Les deux meilleures maisons de toute
la ville (c'est à dire celle de Petrobei et de Coloco-
troni) n'ont ni porte ni fenêtre,—ainsi songez ce qui
doivent être les autres.

" Si vous me demandez du Gouvernement, c'est
un mot plutôt idéal que effectif : car les ordres du
corps exécutif ne vont pas plus loin que les murs
de Napoli ; comme ceux du corps législatif ne sur-
passent Argos ; mais cela ne ferait rien s'il n'était
séparé que par le local ; mais ils le sont d'intérêt,
d'opinions et aussi ennemis l'un de l'autre que les
turcs le sont avec les grecs.

" Les trois membres composant aujourd'hui le
corps exécutif qui se trouve à Napoli sont : (1) Petrobei, président, homme ignorant au suprême
degrès et très fier des grands exploits de sa famille,
qui ne sont autrement connus que de lui seul, mais
il est du moins honnête homme et il parait défendre
les intérêts du peuple. Le comte Mataxa est un
homme rusé, un peu plus instruit que les autres,
mais il sacrifie tous les intérêts de sa patrie pour
conserver sa place ; il est très mal vu du peuple.
Quant à Sotiris il est presque nul si ce n'est qu'il
trouve toujours de nouveau plan pour mettre le
peuple en contribution. Dehors de là c'est un vrai
paysan de Metaxata. Colocotronis et Zaimis les
deux autres membres sont retirés.

" Parmi le corps législatif on trouve quelques uns
des membres qui sont plus instruits que les premiers,
et ce qu'on trouve de mieux parmi eux ce qu'ils
sont unis entre eux et qu'ils cherchent à défendre
les intérêts du peuple.

" Pour vous faire une idée de la mésintélligence
qui règne entre les deux corps, vous saurez que le
corps exécutif se prépare à envoyer un nommé
Perouka comme député à Londres et contredire
Orlando dans ses entreprises. Je leur ai exposé que
s'ils font une telle chose elle fera peut-être cause

M

que l'emprunt n'aura pas lieu, mais le plus mauvais
de tout ce que je vous annonce est qu'il y a une
guerre civile. . . ."

And on this M. Schilizzi describes at length, and in a
manner both involved and unconvincing, the state of
actual civil war which had arisen in the Peloponnese.

Meanwhile, under the advice of the London Committee, and heartened by the auspices of Byron, further
British Philhellenes were drifting out to the scene of
action. In October Finlay, fresh from the University
of Göttingen, arrived, and was received by Byron at
Metaxata. The reception he met with was " more
poetical than agreeable." Byron sat upon the sofa and
stared and stared at Finlay with startled and anxious
eyes. " I thought," he explained afterwards, " that you
were Shelley's ghost." The resemblance also struck Tita,
who would refer subsequently to Finlay as " the gentleman who is so much like Mr. Shelley." But after they
had spoken nervously for some time about German
literature and Goethe, the shock of Finlay's personal
appearance was mitigated, and more normal intercourse
was established.

In November Julius Millingen, a young medical
student of Edinburgh, arrived at Cephallonia in the
company of Baron von Quass, Lieutenant Kindermann,
and Lieutenant Fels, three German officers who had come
to Greece to avenge the disaster of Peta. Mr. Millingen
was then but twenty-three years of age, and had been
sent out by the London Committee to dispense the
medical stores furnished by the Society of Friends, and
to place his inexperience at the disposal of the Greek
Government. They were interviewed by Byron in the
lazaretto at Argostoli. He informed them of the present
condition in Greece, and warned them of the disappointments and the " thousand crosses " which they would
have to bear, explaining that the task before them was
not one to be undertaken in a mood of idle Philhellenic

enthusiasm, but in a spirit of firm and bitter determination. The romantic feelings which had inspired them in their journey were somewhat damped by this prosaic realism. The three Germans proceeded with chilled emotions to Missolonghi; Dr. Millingen remained at Cephallonia, and shortly afterwards rode out to Metaxata to visit Lord Byron.

"On my arrival," he records, "I found him on the balcony of the house, wrapt in his Stewart tartan cloak, with a cap on his head, which he affected to wear as the Scotch bonnet, attentively contemplating the extensive and variegated view before him, terminated by the blue mountains of Ætolia, Acarnania, and Achaia.[1] The valley below the village is highly luxuriant, and even at this advanced epoch of the year was covered with verdure, and embellished by the evergreen olive, orange and lemon trees, and cypresses towering above the never-fading laurel and myrtle. Like an oasis in the sandy desert, its aspect produced the most pleasing impression on the eye, weary of the barren and cheerless rocks of Cephallonia."

It is necessary at this stage to explain that Dr. Julius Millingen, that "tall, delicately-complexioned, rosy-cheeked, dandy boy of simpering and affected manners," was not, in any way, a desirable person. He must figure with a certain unsavoury prominence in any record of the last adventure of Lord Byron, since he attended him in his illness, and in 1831 published a record of his doings and conversations, in which he bears much false, or at least exaggerated, witness. In this record Byron is represented as having heaped the most unmitigated abuse upon the Greek nation, and the whole volume is flavoured by exaggerated Turcophile sentiments. For in 1824 Julius Millingen deserted to, or, as he himself contended, was "captured by," the Turks. "Out of three thousand adventurers," writes Trelawny, "of all sorts and conditions, all serving for pay and plunder, one

[1] Dr. Millingen is, as usual, inaccurate. There is no such view from Metaxata.

163

man alone was mercenary and base enough to abandon the cause in which he was engaged, and for which he received pay, even to be a deserter to the enemy, and that . . . was Millingen, a self-styled Englishman." [1] Trelawny's judgments are not generally very authoritative, and we may perhaps dismiss as unfair his supplementary imputation that Dr. Millingen, while at Missolonghi, sold for his own account the medical stores entrusted to him by the Quakers. Nor need much credence be given to the bitter attack upon him published subsequently by his renegade son, Frederick Millingen, under the attractive title of " Sin and its Victims." The fact remains, however, that Dr. Millingen entered the Turkish service, resided for over fifty years at Constantinople as physician to five successive Sultans, and married four wives, the first of whom he treated abominably. He lingered on till the later 'seventies, a gaunt and sallow figure in his fez and stambouline, cut by the English colony, execrated by the Greeks, and pointed out to tourists as the man who had tended Lord Byron on his death-bed. And then in 1878 he died, and was buried in the British cemetery at Haidar Pasha, leaving it to his other sons, and particularly to his son Alexander, that gentle and accomplished scholar, to render the name of Millingen again respectable and respected.

At the stage of his career, however, when Millingen landed at Cephallonia, these later propensities had not developed : he confined himself, during those few days at Metaxata, to being very agreeable, to listening politely to Byron, and trying for his part also to look like Mr. Shelley, and writing to Bowring in London for more money. And early in December 1823 he crossed to Missolonghi.[2]

---

[1] Another such deserter, at least by implication, was incidentally E. J. Trelawny.

[2] I should add, perhaps, that all the above observations are strenuously contradicted by the surviving sons of Doctor Millingen.

CHAPTER VIII

December 28, 1823—*January* 5, 1824

I

ON the afternoon of November 22nd, Pietro Gamba, who had ridden down to Argostoli, sent up the following urgent note to Byron at Metaxata :—

" *Urgente.*

" MIO CARO BYRON,

"Questa notte è arrivato da Ancona in sette giorni un bastimento papale con a bordo 20 passageri e due colonelli, uno inglese e l'altro prussiano. Il primo si chiama *Canop*, il secondo *Dylon*."

Colonel the Hon. Leicester Stanhope, C.B., to whom Gamba thus impulsively alluded, was the third son of the Earl of Harrington, and a gentleman of the most diverse attainments and convictions. Born in 1784, he joined the Army in 1799, and was present at the attack on Buenos Aires ; in 1817 he had been appointed Deputy Quarter-Master-General in India, and had seen service in the Mahratta wars. His real interests were, however, far other than martial : he became deeply involved in such questions as Chancery reform, the Maine Liquor Laws, the Lancastrian system of education, and a free press for India. In the course of his researches into these subjects he had fallen deeply and hopelessly in love with the political theories of Mr. Jeremy Bentham. In September 1823 he offered his services as a substitute for Captain Blaquière to the Greek Committee in London, and on these services being accepted, he proceeded

165

with enthusiasm to Darmstadt. After interviewing the German Philhellenes at that unconvincing capital, he journeyed to Zürich, and from there to Lausanne, where he met Count Capo d'Istrias, the ex-Minister of the Tsar Alexander, to whom he expounded his opinions on the needs of republican Greece. "His Excellency," Stanhope wrote home to the Committee, " spoke as well as could be expected. . . . He highly approved of my wish to introduce the military system of Switzerland into Greece." But there was little time to lose : hurrying to Geneva, Colonel Stanhope purchased all the available works upon the Swiss constitution and the cultivation of the silk-worm. From there he dashed on to Milan, where he had just time to persuade the learned M. Mutoxidi to write a pamphlet bitterly attacking the administration of Sir Thomas Maitland. From Milan he hurried via Florence to Pisa, where he had a most unpleasant interview with the Metropolitan Ignatius. "The Metropolitan," he wrote home, " is of opinion that a king should be placed on the throne of Greece. (No king—no bishops.) He would prefer a foreigner. The Prince of Cobourg, or the son of the deposed King of Sweden. I have observed that this monarchical spirit is prevalent among the Greeks. With many eminent writers, they think that democracies are not suited to large states, because they possess less vigour and promptness. They talk of the prosperity of the small republics and the decline and fall of the large ones. They forget to cite the corruption and effeminacy, the disorders and convulsions, to which large monarchies are subject, and the stability and grandeur of America."

Colonel Stanhope's dismay at discovering that the poison of the Holy Alliance had infected even the Greek community at Pisa was mitigated by the reception of two inspiring although cryptic letters from Mr. Bentham. "Would," the Colonel wrote home, " that I had time to answer Mr. B.'s letters : they are the proud credentials which, however undeserved, I must respect. They are enough to turn the head of a soldier, whose virtues grow out of his vanities. But to the point: I will do my utmost to comprehend these papers, and to place them in the channels of usefulness."

Still puzzling over Mr. Bentham's apocalyptic letters, Colonel Stanhope embarked at Ancona with a representative of the German Committee, Colonel Delaunay, and on November 22nd he arrived, as we have seen, at Argostoli.

The news which Byron was able to impart to Colonel Stanhope was by now more reassuring. The Turkish army which had been threatening Missolonghi had suddenly, and for no very apparent reason, been withdrawn; the deputies, Luriottis and Orlando, had reached Cephallonia, and were about to leave with Hamilton Browne for London; and—most welcome news of all— the Greek fleet, on the strength of the advances promised them by Byron, had actually left Hydra, and were at any moment expected to raise the blockade of Western Greece. This " special interposition of the gods on behalf of the Greeks " was, however, negatived by the spread of internal dissensions. " They seem," wrote Byron to John Bowring, " to have no enemies in heaven or on earth to be dreaded but their own tendency to discord among themselves." It must be admitted, indeed, that by this December of 1823 the internal condition of Greece had degenerated into civil war. The executive Government had by then fallen completely under the influence of Colokotronis, and the Senate of Argos had endeavoured to break this domination by deposing one of the members of the executive and nominating another in his place. The executive retaliated by sending troops under the younger Colokotronis to capture the Senate and to seize their archives. The latter thereupon escaped to Kranidi, from where they proceeded to appoint a new executive under Conduriottis and Londos. The old executive refused, however, to be thus dissolved, and Petro Bey with

Colokotronis flung themselves into Tripolitza, where they were besieged by the constitutional party. It was only on the receipt by Mavrocordato of the first instalment of the English loan that the military party were eventually induced to surrender; but meanwhile, and throughout Byron's residence in Greece, the Morea was given up to civil war.

On the advice of Colonel Stanhope, Byron decided to address an open letter to the Greek Government, in which he drew attention to the fact that no loan would be forthcoming so long as these disturbances continued. To Mavrocordato, who was on his way with the fleet to Missolonghi, he wrote more explicitly :—

" I am very uneasy at hearing that the dissensions of Greece still continue, and at a moment when she might triumph over everything in general, as she has already triumphed in part. Greece is, at present, placed between three measures : either to re-conquer her liberty, to become a dependence of the sovereigns of Europe, or to return to a Turkish province. She has the choice only of these three alternatives. Civil war is but a road which leads to the two latter. If she is desirous of the fate of Wallachia and the Crimea, she may obtain it to-morrow; if of that of Italy, the day after; but if she wishes to become truly Greece, free and independent, she must resolve to-day, or she will never again have the opportunity."

Armed with this letter and his own republican enthusiasms Stanhope crossed in the first week of December to Missolonghi. Byron remained at Cephallonia, waiting to complete the formalities of his loan to the Greek fleet, waiting for the military stores which the Committee had despatched, and still determined not to leave for the mainland so long as civil war continued.

Meanwhile he and Napier between them had endeavoured to cool the effervescent ardour of Colonel Stanhope. "I am happy to say," Byron wrote to Bowring on December 26th, "that Colonel Leicester

Stanhope and myself are acting in perfect harmony together—he is likely to be of great service both to the cause and to the Committee, and is publicly as well as personally a very valuable acquisition to our party on every account. He came up (as they all do who have not been in the country before) with some high-flown notions of the sixth form at Harrow or Eton, etc.; but Colonel Napier and I set him to rights on those points, which is absolutely necessary to prevent disgust, or perhaps return; but now we can set our shoulders *soberly* to the *wheel*, without quarrelling with the mud which may clog it occasionally.

" I can assure you that Colonel Napier and myself are as decided for the cause as any German student of them all; but like men who have seen the country and human life, there and elsewhere, we must be permitted to view it in its truth, with its defects as well as beauties —more especially as success will remove the former *gradually*."

II

Encouraged by the cash advance guaranteed to them by Byron, the Greek fleet left the island of Hydra in the first days of December, and, with Mavrocordato in their wake, sailed for the Gulf of Corinth. On reaching Ionian waters they intercepted two Turkish corvettes, freighted with money for the Turkish garrison at Patras, as also with certain distinguished passengers, among whom was the nephew of Youssuf Pasha. The Turkish ships defended themselves virulently, and before surrendering ran ashore upon the coast of Ithaca. The Greeks thereupon pursued them on to the rocks, thereby violating the neutrality of the Ionian islands, and giving cause for many acrid complications in the future. The Hydriot squadron then proceeded to Missolonghi, where Mavrocordato was received with universal acclaim. The main Turkish fleet, which had been operating in the Gulf of Patras, retired thereupon to the inner Gulf of Corinth.

On December 12th, Colonel Stanhope arrived at Missolonghi. He lost no time in impressing the Government of Western Greece with his own unremitting energy and his own unremitting republicanism. He read aloud to them a letter from Lord Erskine (who by then was dead), replete with the most elevated expressions of goodwill. He convened a Committee, which he entitled " The General Committee in Greece," and which consisted of Colonel Delaunay as President, and of himself and a German lieutenant as subsidiary members. This Committee does not appear to have survived more than two inaugural meetings, or the arrival of Lord Byron. Within eight days from his descent upon Missolonghi Colonel Stanhope was in the position to write to the London Committee buoyantly, and as follows :—

" Your agent has now been at Missolonghi one week. During that period a free press has been established, a corps of artillery has been decided on, the funds furnished for its maintenance during nine months, and a person despatched to assemble it; means have been furnished to prevent the Greek fleet from dispersing, and a proper house and grounds have been procured for the establishment of a laboratory. This is a very encouraging commencement of our labours."

Nor had the more spiritual needs of Hellas been overlooked by Colonel Stanhope : " Money is what I want here : a little from the Committee ; a little from the Quakers. Schools, presses, posts, hospitals, all will then flourish. Elementary books on education, war, agriculture, etc., newspapers, useful pamphlets, Greek Bibles, the Monthly Repository, medical stores, blankets, bandages, matter for the press, and *two schoolmasters*, to teach the Lancastrian system, are all much required."

It appears from a subsequent letter that Colonel Stanhope was somewhat premature in stating in this way that the free press of Greece had already been established. It seems that the printer raised some objection to the prospectus which had been prepared for him. This prospectus contained a translation of passages from the works of Mr. Bentham, and Mavrocordato sent his secretary to Colonel Stanhope to explain that this translation was not in the good purged Greek which was necessary, and could not therefore appear ; " but sophistry," expostulated and proclaimed Colonel Stanhope, " would not do from one who was slily acting as censor over the press, and attempting to suppress the thoughts of the finest genius of the most enlightened age —the thoughts of the immortal Bentham."

On the second occasion it was the printer himself who objected to the insertion of the Benthamite translation. " I gave him another sound rating," Colonel Stanhope wrote home to the Committee, " and he yielded. . . . The high and sturdy tone assumed in these two conversations produced the desired result—the prospectus is printed ; and I feel proud that in Greece, as in Hindustan, I have contributed to the first establishment of a free press."

But there was one important point which Colonel Stanhope had forgotten : he had forgotten that the Hellenic public were unable to read.

III

The arrival of Mavrocordato at Missolonghi, and the activity which Colonel Stanhope had displayed in the few bustling days since his arrival, somewhat undermined the determination of Lord Byron to remain prudently at Cephallonia until the various Greek parties had coalesced. Of the three main sections into which Greece was now divided, the Morea, owing to the violence of Colokotronis and Petro Bey, had relapsed into the cheerful anarchy of civil war ; in Eastern Greece, the other prominent military leader, Odysseus, had established an independent authority, and had up to then committed himself neither to the civil government nor to the military leaders in the Peloponnese. The position of Western Greece was, however, different. In the first place, the military chiefs in that region, who were in fact the Souliot chieftains, were not unprepared to accept the civil authority of Mavrocordato. In the second place, Western Greece was for geographical reasons exempt from any menace on the part of Coloko-tronis. In the third place, Missolonghi furnished the obvious base for any attack upon the fortresses of Lepanto and Patras, the only two remaining Turkish assets in continental Greece ; and finally, Mavrocordato, in that he was the representative of the legislative assembly, or Senate, could claim with some justice to be the only constitutional ruler, and to have a right to the loan, which the English people, in their optimism, had collected for the provisional government of Greece.

In November, Byron had received from the Senate, which was then at Salamis, the following letter, in which they urged him deferentially to join forces with Mavro-cordato :—

"Now as it has been considered necessary that there should be sent to Missolonghi, for the direction of affairs in that locality and of whole Western Greece, that good patriot and president of the Legislative Party, Alexander Mavrocordato, Your Excellency is begged to help spontaneously, in any way you think best, at Missolonghi (which, with Patras, is suffering more than ever), in conjunction with M. Mavrocordato, who knows in detail the needs of that place, which he will represent to you. The gratitude to Your Excellency is common throughout the race. May you prosper."

Such an appeal could not be disregarded, nor could Byron now feel wholly justified in remaining at Cephallonia. His decision to leave the Ionian islands for the

mainland was also influenced by certain tentative inter-
rogations from home, as to whether it was true, as
reported, that he was living languidly in a villa in the
country and writing poetry. Of course it was not true :
he had put poetry behind him ; he was occupied only
with politics ; nor could the four-roomed cottage at
Metaxata be described by any twist of malignity as a
villa. It had been necessary, it had been right, it had,
above all, been prudent, that he should remain at
Metaxata. Dr. Millingen, and even Colonel Napier,
had been of the same opinion. There were, as he had
often explained, many admirable reasons why he should
not venture to run the Turkish blockade or commit
himself to any one of the Greek parties. By the end of
December, however, these very excellent excuses were
no longer very valid. There was now no prospect that
the parties would coalesce. The Government of Western
Greece was ostensibly and perhaps firmly established
under Mavrocordato, and could not be described as
anything but the legitimate Government of Greece ;
the fleet had come out, and the Turks had retired to the
Gulf of Corinth ; in a few weeks the Greek loan would
be floated on the London market ; Byron would be
expected to administer the proceeds ; and, after all, his
colleague, Colonel Stanhope, had, within a week of his
arrival, proceeded to Missolonghi, and was already
playing there a very prominent and destructive part.
The happy and facile justification for Metaxata was
wearing very thin, and Byron could no longer ignore
the appeals which Mavrocordato addressed to him from
the moment he arrived in Western Greece.

The first of these letters from Mavrocordato, which
are among the papers found in Byron's room after his
death, runs as follows :—

    " MY LORD,
        " After endless delays occasioned by unforeseen
circumstances and above all by contrary winds, I

have at last arrived at my destination. My delay
has done much harm, in that the enemy, appalled
by the news of the destruction of their fleet and the
rout of their armies in Eastern Greece, expecting
the arrival of a Greek fleet in these waters, and the
difficulty of beating a retreat should we disembark
in their rear, have precipitately withdrawn beyond
the frontiers of Western Greece. The Pasha of
Scutari, after waiting for two days in the neighbourhood of Prevesa, has continued his withdrawal
for the purpose of getting his troops home. Only
Omer Pasha, with a body of 1500 Albanians, remains
in Scutari. Arta has no troops; the garrisons of
Lepanto and Patras are disaffected and mutinous
since they have received no pay for fourteen months.
All these circumstances justify us in expecting a
successful issue to our enterprises if only we can
keep our flotilla together for some time longer;
and the co-operation of the ships is essential to the
execution of our plans. It is not in order to flatter
you, My Lord, that I assure you that I should have
hesitated to accept so vast a task had I not based
my hopes upon your co-operation. The Government also has counted on nothing else, as you will
see from the Senate's letter which I have the honour
herein to transmit to you. On reaching Missolonghi I found moreover that everyone was so
convinced of the truth of what I now tell you, that
you will be received here as a saviour. Be assured,
My Lord, that it depends only on yourself to secure
the destiny of Greece. Now that Lepanto and
Patras are encircled by land and sea, they must
soon capitulate; when once we are masters of those
two places we shall be able to elaborate our plans
for the occupation of Thessaly.

"I have ordered one of the best ships in our
squadron to sail for Cephallonia, although, for the
sake of precaution, I have told it not to enter the

port. M. Leli, who I am sending simultaneously
but in another boat, will bring you this letter. If
he has the honour of seeing you, he will be able to
inform you in greater detail of the condition of
affairs, as well as of the desirability, I would almost
say the necessity, of your presence. Should you
fall in with my views, which are those of the Senate
of the whole of Greece, the captain of the brig
will await your orders. I myself, rejoicing at being
able to co-operate with Your Lordship in securing
the independence of my country, will wait only for
the moment when we can join forces, and I beg you
to accept the reiterated assurance of my respect
and of the great consideration with which I have
the honour to be

" My Lord,
" Your Lordship's
" Most humble and obedient Servant
" A. MAVROCORDATO.

" P.S.—At the very moment when I was about to
send off my letter I have received, owing to the
arrival of Colonel Stanhope, your kind letter of the
2nd inst. Its contents and the assurance which
Colonel Stanhope has given me have kindled my
hopes to an even greater degree.

" Your observations on Greece are dictated by
that good sense which characterises your judgment.
Yes, My Lord, the present moment will decide the
fate of Greece. If ever I have done my duty, I
shall redouble my activity and my zeal when I find
you beside me. Opinion here is very well disposed,
and I hope that we shall have little to fear from the
contagion of the dissensions which rule the situation
in the Peloponnese : I feel assured even that these
dissensions will shortly terminate ; everything depends on the success of our plans. I am trying to
collect the Souliot corps, which will be very necessary

to us, and to put a stop to all misunderstandings between the chiefs here. A noble spirit of emulation will, under the eyes of a man like you, take the place of their former rivalries : they will wish to distinguish themselves; they will accomplish miracles. You will find enclosed a letter from Colonel Stanhope, who deserves in every respect the praise you have bestowed on him, and whose acquaintance I feel happy to have made. Again accept, My Lord, the assurance of my respect.

" A. M."

In order in this way to make certain of Lord Byron's inevitable arrival, Mavrocordato despatched to Argostoli a Spetsiot brig, which was not, however, allowed to anchor for more than twenty-four hours in the port, or to hold any communication with the shore. After cruising sadly in front of Argostoli for two days the ship returned to Missolonghi without Lord Byron. The disappointment was intense. Mavrocordato sent another ship with his own secretary, Mr. Praïdes, armed with even more urgent letters, but this gentleman again returned to Missolonghi, having been unable to establish contact with Lord Byron. Mr. Praïdes was a third time sent to Cephallonia with further letters from Mavrocordato and Colonel Stanhope. Mavrocordato's letter was as follows :—

" MY LORD,
 " Here is a third letter; but M. Praïdes, who arrived at the same moment exactly as Mr. Leli was to leave, is the reason for delay of the first expedition. I send him again to you with the letters which the first was instructed to bring you. All that I heard from M. Praïdes has only increased my desire that we should come together. As I have written already, I should never, in view of my retirement from public life, have accepted a task whose magnitude and difficulty I foresaw, had

I not counted upon the co-operation of Your Excellency. It is true that circumstances are such as to enable us to accomplish much; but it is absolutely necessary that we should act in this way without losing time; for all the money which you have recently given in response to our solicitations will shortly be expended, if we keep the ships here for long without employing them immediately and in conjunction with operations on land on the plan of getting possession of Lepanto (*sic*). M. Praïdes will place before you the details of this truth. We must play for time : every day gained, every hour, is a great advantage for us. Your presence will do the greatest good : our forces will be electrified; the enthusiasm of all will be kindled to follow the impulsion which you will give them. Do not let us lose this great opportunity, and you will have the pleasant satisfaction of having contributed to the work of our regeneration.

" I shall repeat myself no longer; My Lord, I only wait for the moment when we can join forces —the rest will soon be done.

" I am," etc.

Colonel Stanhope was even more excited and explicit :—

" The Greek ship," he wrote, " sent for your Lordship has returned : your arrival was anticipated, and the disappointment has been great indeed. The Prince is in a state of anxiety, the admiral looks gloomy, and the sailors grumble aloud. It is right and necessary to tell you that a great deal is expected from you, both in the way of counsel and money.

" In the first place, your loan is much wanted; and if the money arrive not speedily, I expect the remaining five ships (the others are off) will soon make sail for Spezia. I therefore think that a large portion of the loan should be immediately placed at the disposal of Mavrocordato.

N 177

" With respect to your coming here, all are eager to see you; they calculate moreover on your aiding them with resources for their expedition against Lepanto; they think you will take 1000 or 1500 Suliotes into your pay for two or three months.

" This town is swarming with soldiers, and the government has neither quarters nor provisions for them.

" I walked along the street this evening, and the people asked me after Lord Byron ! ! !

" L. S."

" Miss.
" Dec. 29th.

" Prince Mavrocordato and the admiral are in a state of extreme perplexity : they, it seems, relied on your loan for the payment of the fleet; that loan not having been received, the sailors will depart immediately. This will be a fatal event indeed, as it will place Missolonghi in a state of blockade, and will prevent the Greek troops from acting against the fortresses of Nepacto [*i. e. Lepanto*] and Patras.

" Under these circumstances, I hope your Lordship will proceed hither. You are expected with feverish anxiety. Your further delay in coming will be attended with serious consequences.

" L. S."

IV

On the receipt of these letters Byron at once left Metaxata for Argostoli. He decided not to embark upon any of the Greek brigs, but to hire local vessels at Cephallonia, and thereby to profit by the neutrality of the Ionian flag. This decision, as events proved, was a wise one. Two boats were hired : one, a large one, for the servants and luggage, called a bombard, the other, a light sailing vessel, called a mystico, for Lord Byron and his immediate attendants. In less than twelve hours everything was ready, and they embarked. The wind was against them, and they landed again at Argostoli and lodged for two days with Mr. Hancock. In the afternoon of December 28th the wind changed to a favourable quarter. Pietro Gamba was having tea with Dr. Kennedy when they came to tell him that the larger boat was ready. He rose at once, and taking in one hand the French Bible which Dr. Kennedy had just given him, and in the other a telescope, he walked down to the harbour and climbed on to the bombard. Dr. Kennedy then went round to Mr. Hancock's house to take farewell of Byron. He found him alone reading "Quentin Durward." Byron promised again that he would read the books which Kennedy had given him, and would continue the investigation of the subjects "about which we had conversed." At this stage Mr. Hancock came into the room with Dr. Bruno. The account of what followed is agreeably rendered by Dr. Kennedy :—

" ' Is Gamba gone ? ' asked Lord B. ' He is,' replied one of them. ' He has carried with him all my money. Where is Fletcher ? ' One of them answered he did not know. ' Send some one after him, we must embark immediately : send down to the Mess-house, you will probably find him there, taking a parting glass with some of his cronies.'

" ' If your lordship wants any money,' said the gentleman of the house, ' I can supply you with whatever sum you please.' ' I thank you,' said Lord B. ; ' I believe I shall have enough till I reach Zante.' He then went into the next room, and soon returned with fifteen dollars, which he presented to me. ' Take them,' said he, ' as a very small donation from me to the school for Greek females which Mrs. K. is establishing, as a mark of my approbation and sincere good wishes for the success of so useful an institution.'

" I thanked him, and said, ' that some of the ladies had requested me to ask his lordship's assistance, which I declined, knowing the many claims and applications which had been, and would yet be made upon his generosity.'

" ' The ladies did right, and you did wrong,' said Lord B.; ' for I should at any time be ready to lend my aid, however small, to such useful institutions.' I shook hands with him, and he said, ' I shall write to you, and give you an account of my proceedings in assisting Stanhope in establishing schools, and in forwarding the moral and religious improvement of the Greeks.' "

Mr. Hancock and Dr. Muir then walked down to the quay with Byron, who was " gay and animated at finding himself embarked once more on the element he loved." They rowed out to the mystico, which was lying in the little creek under the Convent of St. Constantino. As they rowed, Byron was assailed with one of his sudden outbursts of boyish spirits. He chaffed Hancock on his bad steering; he chaffed Muir on his thoughtful and serious expression; he laughed at Dr. Bruno; he laughed at Fletcher, who was getting drenched by the spray which broke over the boat. He then climbed on board the mystico, and as the sails streamed and bellied to the breeze, Hancock and Muir, rocking knee to knee in their little shore-boat, watched Lord Byron disappear gaily and enthusiastically behind the point.

By the morning of the next day, the 29th, they were at Zante, transacting business with Mr. Barff, and obtaining considerable specie. The local British authorities called on Byron, and the Commandant, Mr. Thomas, invited him to his house. The invitation was not accepted, and at six in the evening they all set sail again for Missolonghi, Lord Byron in the smaller boat and Gamba with money and papers in the bombard.

" We sailed together," records Gamba, " till after ten at night; the wind favourable, a clear sky, the air fresh but not sharp. Our sailors sang alternately patriotic songs, monotonous indeed, but to persons in our situation extremely touching, and we took part in them. We were all, but Lord Byron particularly, in excellent spirits. The mystico sailed the fastest. When the waves divided us, and our voices could no longer reach each other, we made signals by firing pistols and carbines—' To-morrow we meet at Missolonghi—to-morrow.' Thus, full of confidence and spirits, we sailed along. At twelve, we were out of sight."

V

When daylight dawned on Tuesday, December 30th, Gamba discovered that they were close to the rocks which terminate, on their western edge, the long lagoons of Missolonghi. There was no sign of Byron or the mystico, but in front of them and to the right loomed a large vessel bearing slowly in their direction. They thought at first that she must be a unit of the Greek fleet sent out to convoy Lord Byron. As the vessel approached nearer, however, the captain was unable to identify her as any of the Spetsiot vessels : she was too large, she was of a different build ; she was a frigate and not a brig. She was more than menacing : she was Turkish. Quickly they hoisted the Ionian colours. They were answered by the crescent fluttering threateningly in the dawn. Panic, intense and voluble, seized upon the crew of the bombard. The Turks were shouting hoarsely at them to send their captain on board with the ship's papers. Gamba kept his head. He told Captain Valsamaki to say that they were an Ionian vessel proceeding to the island of Kalamos, near Santa Maura, and in the service of an English Lord. The papers which they had obtained at Zante would bear out this story. The captain climbed timorously into the dinghy and rowed to the Turkish vessel. They watched him disappear up the gangway. Gamba meanwhile bundled

Byron's compromising correspondence into a packet weighted with shot : he gave it to one of his own servants, telling him to stand in readiness behind the sail and to drop the packet overboard should a boat put off from the Turkish vessel. They waited, silent and apprehensive, watching for any movement on the frigate. A Turkish sailor climbed slowly down the rope ladder which dangled into the gig at the stern. There was a sudden splash as Byron's correspondence disappeared into the Gulf of Patras ; and then the Turkish sailor climbed back again and they remained there waiting silently in the early morning sun. Three sails appeared to the east in the direction of Zante. The Turkish frigate awoke to sudden energy and veered round in the direction of Patras, shouting back at the bombard to follow in her wake. "Weeping bitterly," the crew strained to the sheet, and the bombard hove diagonally across the gulf, away from Missolonghi and into the jaws of Youssuf Pasha. They scanned the waters and the coast behind them : there was a small vessel taking refuge among the rocks. Gamba hoped fervently that this might be the mystico. Meanwhile, one thing alone was certain, and that was that Pietro Gamba, with 8000 dollars in specie, all the Committee stores, the negro groom, Tita, Lega Zambelli and the horses, had been captured outrageously but incontestably by the Turks, and were being brought in triumph to Patras. That in itself was a sufficient disaster. The crew whimpered as they pulled obediently at the ropes.

Suddenly the head and shoulders of their captain, Spiro Valsamaki, appeared upon the quarter-deck of the Turkish frigate. He waved at them and shouted. He said that " it was all right," that " he had arranged everything," that they were to be of good courage. It was not until they reached Patras that they retrieved their captain and learnt the meaning of these excited exhortations. For it appears that the commander of the Turkish frigate, Zacharia Bey, a native of Candia, had some years before been saved from shipwreck by this same Spiro Valsamaki, and had recognised him as he stepped on board the frigate—had, indeed, fallen in gratitude upon the neck of his present captive, and his former rescuer. So that when they all reached Patras that evening the examination was anything but severe. Gamba, who had the foresight to bring with him as presents a telescope and a bottle of rum, repeated the story about Kalamos, the effect of which was somewhat diminished by the fact that Valsamaki had, in the first moments of terror, told the truth. But Zacharia Bey was too deeply under the enervating influence of poetic justice to insist on blatant accuracy. He accepted Gamba's story; he asked him to dinner; he gave him a pipe; and he sent him along to the Castle of the Morea to interview the Pasha and with his story miraculously and unscrupulously confirmed. Meanwhile Gamba had been able to secure the assistance of the British Vice-Consul. For three days he waited on the Pasha's decision : he amused himself by shooting woodcock; he presented the woodcock to the Pasha and was very amiably received. On Sunday the 4th of January he was released, together with his servants and the contents of the bombard. He reached Missolonghi at noon of the same day. Lord Byron had not arrived.

The mystico which Byron had chosen for his own conveyance was a long open boat, of shallow draft, carrying two large latine sails and a little mizzen mast astern. He had with him some 16,000 dollars in specie, together with such of his papers and correspondence as had not been given to Gamba. He was accompanied by Dr. Bruno, Fletcher, the two dogs, Lion and Moretto, and his Greek page, Loukas Chalandritsanos. The latter, who was but fifteen years of age, was a younger member of that Patras family which Byron had transported from Ithaca to Cephallonia, and had maintained at his own expense under the supervision of M. Corgialegno. The boy Loukas had at the time been serving with Colokotronis in the Morea, but on hearing of the good fortune of his mother and sisters, he had come at once to Cephallonia and attached himself to Byron's service, in which he remained until the final tragedy.

After losing touch with the bombard on the night of Monday the 29th, the mystico pushed on quietly into the Gulf of Patras, which they entered while it was still dark. Between them and Missolonghi they could see the lights of a ship, signalling spasmodically with oil-flares. They approached close to her, thinking that she was a Spetsiot brig, and passed within pistol shot of the stern. A voice hailed them, and from her decks there arose the sudden clamour of a Turkish crew, who, in their turn, had mistaken the mystico for a Greek fireship. The captain of the mystico, hissing to them to lie quiet, put down the helm, and the little ship darted out under the dark stern of the frigate and was lost in the night. Not a shot was fired: even the dogs were silent; they had escaped by a "miracle of all the Saints."

When daylight dawned on the 30th the mystico was safe for the moment, hiding behind the rocks and in the shallow waters of the coast. Between them and Missolonghi the Turkish frigate still loomed, with the wind in her favour, and in the distance they observed another frigate in chase of Gamba's bombard. It was hopeless to make a dash for Missolonghi; on the advice of a little Zantiote boat, which signalled to them from the beach, they crept along in shallow water to the Scrofa rocks, between which it was hoped the Turkish frigate would be unable to penetrate. But Byron was still uneasy: the Turks might send armed boats into the shallows to attack them, and what resistance could they make with only two carbines, a fowling-piece, and no pistols? For the moment he contemplated abandoning the boat and the money, and swimming ashore. It was Loukas who was his chief anxiety. He told the boy if things came to the worst to climb upon his back and to cling there with his arms around his neck. The captain suggested

184

that they should row in to the shore and send a message to Missolonghi. Byron agreed, and scribbled a gay note to Stanhope, in which he told him of his danger, and asked that Draco should be sent with his Souliots to escort them round by land. This letter was given to Loukas, who, with another sailor, scrambled safely on to the rocks. Byron's main anxiety was thus relieved: " I would sooner," he had written in his letter to Stanhope, " cut him in pieces and myself too, than have him taken out by those barbarians . . . for you know what his fate would be."

Meanwhile the Turkish frigate had sighted them and was approaching. There was no alternative between that of abandoning the ship and money and of making a further dash along the coast. Byron decided on the latter. Keeping close to the shallows, they worked their way along to Petala, but, finding that roadstead too exposed both to the weather and the Turks, they crept on to Dragomestri, where they arrived by nightfall.

From Dragomestri Byron sent further messages to Missolonghi. It was his intention to proceed there by land, and he asked for transport and a detachment of troops. Meanwhile he waited for three days at Dragomestri. Since leaving Cephallonia he had not taken off his clothes, and had purposely exposed himself to every privation in order to harden his constitution. Fletcher meanwhile had caught a severe cold in the head, and the only mattress in the mystico was surrendered to him. In spite of these dangers and inconveniences, Byron was in the best of health and spirits. He wrote to Muir and Hancock, giving a delighted account of his adventures ; he bathed in the lagoon ; he composed a war-song called *The Song of Souli*, which is, perhaps, the most deplorable of all his many poetic failures ; and he watched the dawn of January 1st, 1824, spread green and gold behind the mountain of Akarnania.

On Saturday, the 3rd of January, messengers arrived

from Missolonghi with the following letter from Mavrocordato :—

"MY LORD,

"I have already replied to your kind letter of
yesterday by the hands of Liverius, my secretary,
whom I sent to you by sea, telling you that I had
also sent you, immediately after the arrival of your
letter to Colonel Stanhope dated from Scrophes,
M. Praïdes with three ships, of which one was flat-
bottomed, and for the purpose of looking for you at
Petala. I have every reason to suppose that M.
Praïdes will have gone as far as Dragomestri if he
has learnt of your departure for that place. I hope
also that M. Liverius, with my answer and the
orders to the military authorities of Xeromeros, will
arrive on one of our ships before this present letter.
I repeat again, my Lord, that you will have much to
suffer if you decide to come by land, whereas your
voyage by sea on the small boats offers no danger.
I am pleased to hope that you will be here before
this letter reaches you. As regards Count Gamba,
I have every hope that he will shortly be released,
with the boat and all his belongings, in view of the
fact that such a capture can never be good or be
admitted by the British authorities.

"I have the honour, etc.,

"A. MAVROCORDATO."

Shortly afterwards the Greek escorting vessels appeared
off Dragomestri ; the sudden sortie of the Turkish fleet,
ill-timed as it had been, was not of long duration.
Escorted by the Spetsiot brig, the "Leonidas," Byron
again started in the mystico on Sunday the 4th of
January for Missolonghi. On their way they were
overtaken by a violent squall, which threw the little
mystico upon the rocks. She was pushed off without
serious damage, but with a second gust of wind was
again, and with greater violence, flung back upon the

coast. The crew thereupon decided, with tears, to abandon the vessel. Byron insisted on their making another effort. The mystico was again launched, and by night-time had anchored safely and serenely at the entrance to the lagoon of Missolonghi.

Early the next morning Byron donned the scarlet regimentals which he had borrowed at the last moment from Colonel Duffie, and entered the little canoe, the local *monoxylon* which had been sent to convey him across the three miles of marshy waters which surround the village of Missolonghi. At 11 a.m. on Monday the 5th of January, 1824, he landed, amid salvos of artillery, the discharge of muskets, and the wild yells of the populace. At the door of the house which had been allotted to him he was received by Mavrocordato, Colonel Stanhope, and a crowd of Greek and European officers. The occasion was stupendous.

" Hope and content," records Gamba, " were pictured in his countenance. He was in excellent health, and appeared moved by the scene." Gamba, for his part, was equally stimulated by this reunion. " I cannot," he wrote in his journal, " easily describe the emotions which such a scene excited : I could scarcely refrain from tears : whether moved by the noise and signs of joy and delight, I know not ; or whether from gladness that we now met each other safe on the Grecian soil, after encountering, in the space of a few days, so many dangers."

CHAPTER IX

January 6—February 15, 1824

I

THE village of Missolonghi wallows untidily in the fœtid lagoon that runs parallel to the Gulf of Patras, from which it is separated, to an average depth of three miles, by a low bar of mud and sand. For eighteen other miles or so the lagoon straddles its shallow, tideless waters to right and left among the sedge of the surrounding marshes, taking a sudden loop to the north where it encircles the inland village of Anatolikon, sweeping sideways to the east again to be sweetened by the waters of the Phaidari, stopping abruptly where it meets the bastion cliff of Mount Varassavo. Behind, runs the indented circle of the Ætolian and Akarnanian mountains, shining grey with limestone or mottled brown with scrub, and in front, above the low barrier of the mud dune, stretch the waters of the Gulf, closed to the south by Cape Araxos, and to the north by the jagged point of Scropha. Between these two capes is hung the horizon of the Ionian Sea, with Zante as a blue cloud fifty miles away, and with Cephallonia, twelve miles nearer, outlined black against the sunset or glimmering opalescent in the dawn.

The beauty of this far-flung prospect, so delicate and yet so majestic, so crude and yet so diaphanous, serves only to emphasise the festering melancholy which exudes from Missolonghi. For that putrescent village can claim no share in the radiance of its surrounding mountains, or in the circean lure of sea, of promontory, and of island. No share, even, in that more meretricious

beauty which is the guerdon of other towns built glitter-
ingly into other waters; for the puddles which stagnate
among the piles and mud-banks of Missolonghi are too
sullen even to mirror the walls which totter above them,
too garbaged even to reflect the sparse and viscous
vegetation of their banks.

It has been asserted by those few travellers who have
visited Missolonghi that the present village bears but
little resemblance to the place where Byron suffered so
and died. My own conviction is that Missolonghi of the
to-day is in general impression exactly and very squalidly
what it was in 1824. It is true, of course, that the
original town or village was extensively destroyed by
the Turks when they captured the place in April 1826.
But, when eventually reconstructed, it was reconstructed
from the same materials, on exactly the same design, and
almost exactly on the same individual foundations.
And thus it remains. The four or five lanes which
intersect it from south to north and east to west are
still impassable to any but pedestrian traffic; the dingy
awnings of the one-storeyed booths which fringe these
thoroughfares still overlap from one side to the other,
attached to the gutter opposite by fly-clustered strings;
and down the centre, as of old, trickles an open, irides-
cent drain. Beyond these central and converging alleys
lie vague open spaces, littered asymmetrically with
cottages of one or two storeys constructed of jumbled
stones and plaster chipped and stained, surmounted by
the same primitive chimneys as in Byron's time, and by
the same moraine of mud-cemented tiles. In the centre
of these open spaces oozes, even in summer, a puddle
of stagnant water edged with green mud and intersected
at intervals by the very stepping-stones which figure in
the narratives of Gamba, Parry, Millingen, and Trelawny.
The claw-marks of the flea-ridden hens still star the
mud with their four-pronged pattern; the edges of the
puddles are still strewn with the ordures of the street.

The legend of Byron lingers somewhat fitfully, I fear,

at Missolonghi : the children have heard that the flippant white china statue down there by the old bastion is the memorial of a great general, of General Veeron ; the fishermen and the old women will assert that the heart of the said general is buried, with the bones of other heroes, in the mound of the Heroon ; and the officers of the local regiment, as they sip their ouzo under the pepper trees, will, in their friendly, garrulous way, inform the foreign visitor that Veeron was indeed a great English soldier, and that, like Mr. Lloyd George, he was a friend of Greece.

Fortunately, however, there lives to-day at Missolonghi a Mr. Aramandios Soustas, head master of the municipal school, and the repository of much authentic tradition. For Mr. Soustas was a friend of Costa Ghazis, the nonagenarian boatman, who, when a lad, had almost daily ferried Byron across the lagoon to where the horses waited by the olive grove ; and Ghazis, before his death, had carefully and repeatedly recounted to Mr. Soustas exactly where Byron's house was situated, and what it looked like, and, indeed, how Byron would always sing strange Western songs as they punted back together in the evening, and how, on the last day that he had thus conveyed the general, the latter had sat silent and shivering in the stern. Mr. Soustas had been acquainted also with Dr. Nieder, who had learnt from Dr. Treiber the exact spot in the Heroon where they had buried the jar containing the lungs of Byron ; and he had known also the daughter of the woman who had been employed to lay out the body. She had come back that wet April night to tell them all of the white skin of the general : " White," she had said, " like the wing of a young chicken." For those, says Mr. Soustas, were the very words she used.

It was thus with the assistance of Mr. Soustas, and of the bamboo canes that he had bundled under his arm, that I was enabled to identify, and in fact to mark out, the site and the dimensions of the house of Capsali, primate of Argostoli—of the house, that is, where Byron died. There can be no doubt, I think, as to the accuracy of this identification. The evidence of Mr. Soustas is detailed and at first hand; the surroundings correspond exactly to the picture of the house as given in Parry's volume. On the left there is the short strand of green-edged mud running into the lagoon; in front is the bare outline of the hillside; and behind is the open space where Byron's brigade paraded with the artillery.

The house, as it stood in 1823, consisted of three storeys, and was surrounded on the east by a courtyard and several outbuildings. The latter, as well as the large room on the ground floor, built originally for the storage of boats and sails, was chosen as quarters for the Souliot guard. On the first floor were the rooms selected for himself by Colonel Stanhope, and those retained by the proprietor of the house; and on the top floor were situated the apartments of Lord Byron— a bedroom and a sitting-room facing to the south and the lagoon, and two or three further rooms, looking on to the courtyard, for the staff and servants. The site of the courtyard and the back of the house is now occupied by a building which must have been erected before 1840. The ground from which rose the front portion of the house—the actual site, that is, of the rooms which Byron inhabited and where he died—is now a mere vague open space, muddied at the edge where it is washed by the lagoon, and in its landward portion employed by the citizens of Missolonghi as a public and very promiscuous latrine. This circumstance was, as he protested, a source of deep regret to Mr. Soustas; but to the English visitor it can only be a source of shame.[1]

On his arrival in that January of 1824 Byron discovered that the house possessed but few conveniences. There was little furniture, beyond a few bug-infected divans, and no drains at all : one simply slopped things into the lagoon below. It is just possible that the trim

[1] *Note to Second Edition.*—This fault, on the repeated instigation of Mr. Soustas, and in celebration of the centenary, has now been abundantly rectified.

Empire sofa, which is preserved with due veneration at the Garrick Club, did actually form part of the equipment of Lord Byron's bedroom; if so, we find no mention of it in contemporary records, and hear only of Byron sitting propped up on a mattress against the wall. I am inclined myself to identify the Garrick Club relic as the "settee" which is known to have stood in Colonel Stanhope's apartments, and on which Byron had been sitting just before his attack of epilepsy on the night of February 15th. For Colonel Stanhope had arrived three weeks before him, and was thus in a position to acquire for himself the only piece of European furniture of which the house of Capsali could boast.

The more essential fittings of Byron's bedroom are equally difficult to determine. The legend has it that the little portmanteau camp-bed which is now in the National Museum at Athens is the bed on which Byron died. I feel obliged to question the accuracy of this assumption. For although there can be no doubt that this camp-bed was the property of Byron, and that he brought it with him from Genoa to Greece for the needs of some possible campaign, yet I feel convinced myself that he made no use of it at Missolonghi, and that it was merely relegated with his other luggage to the box-room. For, in the first place, this little iron-trestled pallet stands but ten inches from the ground, is little more than two feet in width, and would be far less comfortable or commodious than the Turkish divans with which the house abounded. In the second place, the many accounts of Byron's final illness, although they omit no detail of the general squalor of his surroundings, make no mention of what would have been a very telling dramatic feature—namely, how he lay there almost on a level with the floor, upon so narrow a mattress that he could scarcely turn or move in his delirium, and that the doctors in order to reach him had to fall upon their knees. And, in the third place, the death-bed scene which figures among the illustrations to Parry's book shows a high and almost double bed, with a wide mattress and with heavy surrounding curtains. I cannot believe that Parry would have allowed his illustrator to mislead posterity in so essential a detail, and I conclude therefore that the camp-bed of the Athens Museum was not the bed upon which Lord Byron died.

Squalid and inadequate as were the rooms given to Byron in the house of Capsali, he endeavoured on his arrival to make the best of them. Upon the damp plaster of the sitting-room he arranged his collection of arms; he grouped them symmetrically so as to form various panoplies; swords and rifles, pistols and carbines, blunderbusses and daggers, helmets and trumpets, were suspended round the room in the form of a frieze; and above them, skied to the ceiling, he placed his books.

The conduct of his household was entrusted to Lega Zambelli, who had followed him from Italy. Zambelli did the accounts, and he did them very badly. Byron would spend hours putting them right again : the bills and the receipts which he left behind at Missolonghi are covered with little inconclusive additions and sub-tractions in his own handwriting and in that of Gamba. Nor was the household a very easy one to manage. There was Fletcher, grumbling but faithful, disapproving but persistent, claiming the privileges of an old servant and sulking about with an "I told you so" expression on his bearded face. There was Tita Falciere, dog-like, incompetent, and emotional, with his fierce black whiskers and his baby cheeks. There was the page, Loukas Chalandritsanos, for whom Byron had provided a garish livery, who flitted about with coffee and some olives on a plate, and a sly but ingratiating manner. And on the ground floor, redolent and murmuring, were the Souliot guard : undisciplined and squalid, they would stride about the house in their fustanellas, getting in every-body's way, banging their muskets against the banisters, smelling the house out with their rancid concoctions, keeping everyone awake at night-time with their high-

o   193

pitched, droning songs. There was no definite function, and no common tongue. The confusion which distracted Hellas had its counterpart, both in intrigue, in altercation, and in misunderstanding, in the very bedroom, damp and stinking, which became his ultimate refuge.

At the time of Byron's arrival at Missolonghi the chiefs and primates of Western Greece were assembled in the town to attend a conference convened by Mavrocordato. They had held meetings from December 23rd to December 30th, had formally accepted Mavrocordato as Governor-General of Western Greece, had divided the province into several administrative districts, and had discussed the future basis of their operations whether of offence or defence. On the conclusion of this conference they remained on at Missolonghi, in the expectation of Lord Byron's arrival, and within a few minutes of his entering his house they descended upon him in a tumultuous rabble, accompanied by their retainers, all shouting at the same time, and all expecting to be received immediately. " It was difficult," records Gamba, " to make them understand that he would fix certain hours to receive them, and that the rest of the day was allotted to business or domestic affairs." The unfailing accessibility which the Greeks even to-day expect their public characters and statesmen to practise, was equally looked for from the foreigners who came to Greece to assist in the War of Independence. Much time and patience were expended in such interviews, and to Byron, with his ingrained dislike of argument, they constituted a provoking but quite unavoidable experience. The yells and shouting which had pleased him that first morning at Argostoli when the Souliots had boarded the " Hercules," the disputes and vociferations which he had tolerated later at Metaxata, were as nothing to the incessant irruptions which were to deafen and exhaust him at Missolonghi. There would at any hour be a clatter on the wooden staircase, a muffled " Now

you get out of this " from Fletcher, and then a flood
of yelling voices, of fierce eyes, of hurtling invective,
and in a language which, when faced with it, he had to
admit that he was unable, in any possible way, to understand. Noise, noise, noise; and Byron sitting there
upon the divan, wishing that he were back even at the
Casa Saluzzo; wishing predominantly that Napier were
there to quell all this disturbance; wishing, rather
petulantly, that Hobhouse were there to see how devilish
difficult it all was; wishing, finally, that they would
leave him in peace.

But at no stage of the tragedy which then opened
was there to be peace, or any peace, for Byron at Missolonghi.

II

The immediate task which confronted him on his
arrival was of a military rather than of a political nature.
Although the Turkish armies had by then been withdrawn from Western Greece, and although it was im-
probable that the Sultan would resume offensive operations during the winter months, yet it was confidently
expected that with the spring a determined effort would
be made by the Turks to capture Missolonghi, and even
to re-establish their authority in the Morea. It will be
remembered that the enemy still retained at this date
the fortresses of Patras and Lepanto, together with the
two castles which commanded the entrance to the Gulf
of Corinth. If the Greeks could capture Lepanto before
the spring, they would not only diminish the immediate
menace to Missolonghi, but might even force the Turks
to evacuate Patras and the two castles. The prestige of
Mavrocordato would thereby be immeasurably enhanced;
the loan would arrive from England; the capitani would
submit; and Greece, liberated, independent, united,
solvent perhaps, possibly even recognised by the Great
Powers, could face the coming revenge of Turkey without
undue apprehension.

The optimism with which Byron during those first weeks of January flung himself into this project was not, however, inspired solely by these wide and radiant expectations. The scheme attracted him for reasons which were, perhaps, a little topical. For, in the first place, Lepanto, as a name in history, possessed considerable resonance; it would be highly effective to initiate his military career by such an assault and by such a capture; there were many very stimulating and curious analogies which could, and would, be drawn. And, in the second place, of all the Turkish fortresses, Lepanto was the easiest to take. The garrison, which consisted largely of Albanian mercenaries, had allowed it to be known that they would, for a slight monetary consideration, be not at all unwilling to surrender : they would find, indeed, a particular pleasure in surrendering to Lord Byron; all that they asked was that some apparent assault should be made upon the fortress, in order that they might safeguard their own honour by putting up some show of resistance. They indicated, however, that this resistance would not be either very determined or very protracted; nor would the price be very large. Byron fully agreed with Mavrocordato that this operation should take precedence of all other undertakings. What was required, however, was some organised and recognisable force which could be marched in some sort of order, and with adequately convincing menace, upon the crumbling Venetian walls of Lepanto. It would look better also if the fleet, or what remained of it, were to join in this operation. Of the fourteen units of the Greek fleet, which had with such difficulty been induced to leave Hydra, nine had already returned to that island under the impression that they would receive no pay. Five Spetsiot brigs, however, remained, and Byron was able to prevent them from absconding, by advancing out of his own pocket the money for their maintenance.

He then turned his attention to the organisation of a

regular land force. The Committee in London had some time previously informed him that they had despatched a director of artillery with a staff of artificers, and, in anticipation of these experts, Byron, with the aid of Stanhope and Mavrocordato, at once began to form the nucleus of an artillery brigade. He collected the foreign volunteers who had drifted expectantly to Missolonghi, and induced Colonel Stanhope to share in the expenses of their upkeep. Neither the numbers nor the enthusiasm of these Philhellenes was, however, as great as had been expected ; many of them, on their arrival, were in ill health, and asked only to be repatriated to Europe. In the end Byron was able to secure only two foreign artillery officers and some young volunteer pupils. He decided therefore to enrol a certain proportion of Greeks, and was immediately involved thereby in serious difficulties regarding rank and status. " The Germans," Gamba remarks, " were not altogether willing to forget their Prussian etiquette even in Greece." In spite of these difficulties, the nucleus of the brigade was in being by January 20th, and the Government handed over to them the large and rotting building called the Seraglio for their future requirements.

Byron next decided to organise a regular corps of infantry, the nucleus of which was to be formed by the Souliots. The disadvantage of the Souliots, however, was that they were not only brave, but also rapacious ; moreover, the heads of the several clans refused consistently to accept any one member of the tribe as their commander. Mavrocordato addressed to Byron a memorandum in which he explained in detail the internal jealousies by which the Souliots were sundered. Undeterred by this pessimistic document, and by the difficulties which he had himself experienced with the Souliots in Cephallonia, Byron determined to take five hundred of their number into his pay. They were loud in their protestations that although they would not serve under each other, they were prepared to serve under Lord Byron. In fact Draco, one of their leaders, explained that although he was willing to act as a common soldier under his lordship's orders, yet the honour of his house, which had been unsullied for three hundred years, forbade him to obey the commands of his equals, Botzaris or Djavella. These family quarrels among their officers would have affected the discipline of any force. Unfortunately, however, the men themselves took sides with one chief against the other, and the chiefs in their turn intrigued with the men in order to detach them from their rivals.

Had Byron subjected the Souliots to a more objective vision he would at once have realised, as others realised, that, far from being a suitable nucleus for an organised military force, they were the nucleus only of disruption, blackmail, and intrigue. His admiration for these rugged charlatans constitutes the first if not the greatest mistake that he committed at Missolonghi; his subsequent troubles and disappointments were in a large measure due to his obstinate predilection for his Souliot rabble, and throughout the last weeks of his existence we find him, although wary and courageous in other things, manifesting in regard to the Souliots a mixture of defiant imprudence and feminine timidity. And in this way came humiliation, failure, and despair.

III

The month of January therefore was occupied in preparing for the attack upon Lepanto. The artillery brigade would practise every morning in the muddied space in front of the Seraglio, and in the courtyard of Byron's own house a picked detachment of the Souliots were drilled daily as his personal bodyguard. The situation was, in semblance at least, encouraging. They were not losing time; the ships, or at least some of them, had been retained ; the artillery and infantry brigades were being organised ; the technicians from England, whom they were hourly expecting, would arrive to find everything in readiness ; and in a few weeks they could all proceed to a triumphant and quite convincing attack upon Lepanto.

Meanwhile Byron endeavoured to mitigate the brutality with which the operations had hitherto been conducted. On January 16th he heard that a Turk had been taken prisoner by a Greek privateer. He instructed Gamba to write officially to Mavrocordato asking that as a personal favour this prisoner might be handed over to his charge. The man was immediately delivered and lodged in Byron's house. The next evening, at a moment when Mavrocordato was himself on a visit to Byron, there was a scuffle in the doorway and two Greek sailors from the privateer burst into the room, demanding insolently that their prisoner might be returned to them. Byron refused, and as the sailors became threatening, he pulled out his pistols and threatened to shoot them if they did not immediately retire. They retreated from the room, and Byron turned upon Mavrocordato, who had sat there throughout the scene blinking sagaciously through his gold spectacles, and abused him violently for his lack of authority. On the next day the captain of the privateer came in person to apologise for the outrage, but Byron refused to see him unless he brought with him the two sailors who, on the previous evening, had behaved with such insubordination. The apology was humbly given, and the incident was for the moment closed. In order to convince Mavrocordato that this was no sudden whim, Byron thereupon demanded from him three further Turkish prisoners, and despatched the four of them to Youssuf Pasha at Patras with a courteous letter, in which he took occasion to thank him for his treatment of Pietro Gamba and the crew of the bombard.

The only reply which he received to this communication was in the form of a formal receipt for the four prisoners.

On the following day, the 18th of January, it poured with rain, and Byron was unable to take his usual ride. He chartered one of the canoes which ply among the lagoons, and he rowed about with Gamba, talking to him optimistically about the forthcoming expedition to Lepanto. He had, the evening before, been asked by Mavrocordato to head the expedition in the capacity of Archistrategos. He owned to Gamba that this post and title struck him as somewhat ridiculous, and that he had not much confidence in his troops. "After all," continued Gamba, " he discovered, unawares perhaps to me, that the romance and the peril of the undertaking were great allurements to him. He talked so much on this head, that I and others were always apprehensive that he would expose himself unnecessarily."

That evening, at about nine o'clock, they heard discharges of musketry in the town, "which continued longer, and were more frequent than usual." News was brought to them that the Souliots and the citizens had come to blows. They sat there waiting with their muskets across their knees, expecting that one party or the other would fly to Byron's house for succour. Gradually the noise abated, but an hour later M. Praïdes, Mavrocordato's secretary, came in to bring further ill news. The Turkish fleet had sailed out from Patras, and the Spetsiot brigs had weighed anchor and fled before them. Two days later they woke to find themselves blockaded. They discussed by what means the blockade could be broken. They decided that the only method was to attack the fleet from boats, and it was with difficulty that they dissuaded Byron from carrying this project into immediate and personal execution.

The 22nd of January was Byron's birthday. He was thirty-six. He came out of his bedroom in the morning to the next room, where Colonel Stanhope and his friends

were assembled. " You were complaining," he smiled,
" that I never write any poetry now; this is my birthday, and I have just finished something which I think
is better than what I usually write." And then he
showed them the famous verses, which are almost the
last which he composed :—

> " The Sword, the Banner, and the Field,
> 　　Glory and Greece, around me see !
> The Spartan, borne upon his shield,
> 　　Was not more free.
>
> " Awake ! (not Greece—she *is* awake !)
> 　　Awake, my spirit !　Think through *whom*
> Thy life-blood tracks its parent lake,
> 　　And then strike home !　. . .
>
> " If thou regret'st thy youth, *why live ?*
> 　　The land of honourable death
> Is here :—up to the Field, and give
> 　　Away thy breath !
>
> " Seek out—less often sought than found—
> 　　A soldier's grave, for thee the best;
> Then look around, and choose thy ground,
> 　　And take thy Rest."

" We perceived from these lines," writes Gamba, " as
well as from his daily conversations, that his ambition
and his hope were irrevocably fixed upon the glorious
objects of his expedition to Greece, and that he had
made up his mind to ' return victorious or return no
more.'　Indeed, he often said to me, ' Others may do
as they please—they may go—but I stay here, *that is
certain.*'　The same determination was expressed in his
letters to his friends; and this resolution was not unaccompanied with the very natural presentiment that
he should never leave Greece alive.　He one day asked
his faithful servant, Tita, whether he thought of returning to Italy ?　' Yes,' said Tita; ' if your Lordship goes,
I go.'　Lord Byron smiled, and said, ' No, Tita, I shall
never go back from Greece—either the Turks, or the
Greeks, or the climate, will prevent that.' "

IV

During the whole of that last week of January the rain descended black, persistent, almost tropical, upon the tideless lagoons of Missolonghi. He would stand there drumming with his manicured but bitten nails upon the window. In front was a wide whirl of smoking waters; and below him, as a coagulated fringe to the lagoon, swayed and festered the garbage of the town. And such was Greece! From time to time in the yard below a group of Souliot guards, their fustanellas splashed and dirty, would hop, with a sack covering their shoulders, from stepping-stone to stepping-stone across the mud. He could make out the outline of the Seraglio opposite; some German officers were drilling in the rain; out there in the gulf, behind the curtain of water, was the Turkish fleet blockading Missolonghi; and from the floor below came the nasal drone of Colonel Stanhope dictating another tonic article for the *Greek Chronicle*. Byron ground his teeth in fury. For his relations with Colonel Leicester Stanhope were already becoming strained.

It must be admitted that the divergence between the two representatives of the London Committee was more profound and temperamental than any passing disagreement on the methods to be pursued, or the immediate steps to be taken. For Colonel Stanhope possessed certain rigid convictions which were not dreamt of in Byron's more undulating philosophy. Colonel Stanhope believed in the immortal Bentham, and the Lancastrian system of education, and the American Commonwealth, and the perfectability of human nature; he believed also, fervently and with an elevated passion, in Colonel Stanhope. He pictured himself as something urgent and decisive, as something regenerative and Promethean; he had dashed out to Missolonghi as a bright herald of the new liberalism of the Crown and Anchor, bearing with eager but reverential hand the sacred fire from Queen Square to the Parthenon; and as he hopped and bustled through the mud, that hurried and inefficient apostle allowed no doubt to arise as to the meaning and the need of his enlightened mission.

Byron for his part shared none of these illusions. To him the future loomed more nebulous and less convincing. Subjective and sceptical, he was solaced by none of the confident convictions of his assistant. He did not believe very much in the Crown and Anchor : he had known them all too intimately. He did not believe unduly in the immediate perfectability of the Hellenic character : here again his experience militated against his credulity. He believed least of all in the efficiency of Lord Byron : his irradicable and realistic modesty precluded so seductive a fallacy. For him it was just a wet afternoon like any other; perhaps it would clear by four o'clock, and he could have his ride after all; meanwhile he might fence with Gamba; no, Gamba was in disgrace for the moment, because he had muddled the accounts at Cephallonia, and bought all those yards of red cloth that no one wanted. He drummed again upon the streaming windows. It was a bore being thirty-six. He was a fool to have come to Missolonghi; it was all the fault of Hobhouse and his vapid radicalism. What a curious trick Mavrocordato had of fluttering his eyelids behind his gold spectacles : he never looked one in the face. Was it duplicity or only astigmatism? Stanhope's voice continued intoning from the room below; he was summarising the "Fragment of Government" for the next number of the *Chronicle*. Tugging his handkerchief between his hands, Byron limped down the damp and smelling staircase to the basement. After all, he could always play with the two dogs, and to-morrow, perhaps, the artillery expert would arrive, and they could attack Lepanto. That, at least, was something definite; that, at least, would be more efficacious than the "Fragment of Govern-

ment." He paused for a moment by the door of
Stanhope's sitting-room. Yes, he was still dictating.

The origins of this divergence can be traced in the
endless but informative letters which every evening
Stanhope, in his small and florid writing, would address
to the Committee in London. "His Lordship," he
had written home on his arrival at Argostoli in November,
" has been here about three months ; the first six weeks
he spent on board a merchant vessel, and seldom went
on shore except on business. Since that period he has
lived in a little villa in the country, in absolute retirement." How different, by implication, was the unremitting energy and force of the Committee's second
representative ! Had he not crossed, within ten days,
to Missolonghi, and was not the *Greek Chronicle* already
in being, in spite of the tortuous opposition of Mavrocordato and the prevailing " feudalism " with which he
had had to compete ? " Your agent," he had written
on December 20th, " has now been at Missolonghi one
week," and with justifiable gratification he had been
able, as we have seen, to supplement that announcement with a formidable list of work accomplished. A
fortnight later Byron had joined him. " His Lordship,"
wrote Stanhope on January 6th, " has given £100 towards
the support of the artillery corps, and £50 in aid of the
press. His Lordship, however, thinks the press will
not succeed. I think it will." In the immediately
ensuing reports which Stanhope addressed to the Committee the references to Byron are merely incidental,
but by January 21st it is evident that as a result of the
flippancy of his colleague's intervening conversation
Colonel Stanhope had come to be visited with doubts
as to the purity, the absolute Queen Street purity, of
Byron's radicalism. He feels it his duty to sound a
note of warning :—

" Lord Byron," he reports on that date, " possesses
all the means of playing a great part in the glorious
revolution of Greece. He has talent ; he professes

liberal principles; he has money; and is inspired with fervent and chivalrous feelings. . . . Thus advantageously circumstanced, his Lordship will have an opportunity of realising all his professions. In his course he will be closely watched and scrutinised by his countrymen, and by the whole world. His fame, like that of other prominent men, must depend on his conduct."

The anxiety which this letter must have caused the Committee in London, their relief that so efficient and dependable a utilitarian as Colonel Stanhope should be there " closely to watch " the illiberal vagaries of Lord Byron, can only have been increased by the sinister report which they received three days later :—

"I am in the habit," wrote Stanhope on January 24th, " of putting written questions to Lord Byron for his decision. The following have received his Lordship's answers, and I am desirous of submitting them to the Committee.

" *1st.*—Will your Lordship allow me to make over a certain quantity of Greek and Roman types to the editor of the *Greek Chronicle* ?—Yes.

" *2nd.*—Will your Lordship subscribe £50 for the support of the Greek paper ?—Yes.

" *3rd.*—Will your Lordship allow me to take round the printing press, etc., to the seat of the Greek Government, *i. e.* of the legislative body ?— We will talk over this article.

" *4th.*—Will your Lordship subscribe £100 toward the support of the German artillery ?—Yes.

" *5th.*—Will your Lordship allow £100 of your loan to the Greek Government to be made over to the German Committee, they having advanced that sum to the said Government on my guaranteeing its repayment ?—Yes.

" *6th.*—Would your Lordship approve of Mr. Hesketh being appointed Sub-intendant of Stores ? —Yes.

" 7th.—Would your Lordship approve of my exchanging the Greek Committee's press for the one belonging to the editor there ?—This article I do not quite understand, but will talk it over with you.

" The following one has given rise to some discussion between his Lordship and myself, with the substance of which I think it necessary that the Committee should be acquainted. I have, therefore, subjoined the heads of a conversation which has passed between us on the subject.

" ' Your Lordship stated yesterday evening that you had said to Prince Mavrocordato that, " were you in his place, you would have placed the press under a censor ; " and that he replied, " No, the liberty of the press is guaranteed by the constitution." Now I wish to know whether your Lordship was serious when you made the observation, or whether you only said so to provoke me ? If your Lordship was serious, I shall consider it my duty to communicate this affair to the Committee in England, in order to show them how difficult a task I have to fulfil in promoting the liberties of Greece, if your Lordship is to throw the weight of your vast talents into the opposite scale on a question of such vital importance. To this question I solicit a written answer, lest I should misrepresent your Lordship's opinion and sentiments.'

" After Lord Byron had read this paper, he entered into conversation with me on the subject. He said that he was an ardent friend of publicity and the press ; but he feared that it was not applicable to this society in its present combustible state. I answered that I thought it applicable to all countries, and essential here, in order to put an end to the state of anarchy which at present prevailed. Lord B. feared libels and licentiousness. I said that the object of a free press was to check public licentiousness and to expose libellers to odium. Lord B. had mentioned his conversation with Mavrocordato to show that the Prince was not hostile to the press. I declared that I knew him to be an enemy to the press, although he dared not openly to avow it. His Lordship then said that he had not made up his mind about the liberty of the press in Greece, but that he thought the experiment worth trying."

It was four days after the date of this letter that Byron's patience and good temper for a single thundery moment deserted him. A discussion arose with Colonel Stanhope on the recent visit to Missolonghi of Captain Yorke of H.M.S. "Alacrity," charged with the enforcement of certain claims against Mavrocordato's Government for the violation of Ionian neutrality. The latter had, "with that promptness which distinguishes the negotiations of our seamen," demanded satisfaction from Mavrocordato in the form of an ultimatum. Byron advised compliance, but Colonel Stanhope was indignant.

"In the evening," he reported to the Committee on January 28th, "Lord Byron conversed with me on the subject. I said the affair was conducted in a bullying manner, and not according to the principles of equity and the law of nations. His Lordship started into a passion. He contended that law, justice, and equity had nothing to do with politics. That may be; but I will never lend myself to injustice. His Lordship then began, according to custom, to attack Mr. Bentham. I said that it was highly illiberal to make personal attacks on Mr. Bentham before a friend who held him in high estimation. He said that he only attacked his public principles, which were mere theories, but dangerous, injurious to Spain, and calculated to do great mischief in Greece. I did not object to His Lordship's attacking Mr. B.'s principles : what I objected to were his personalities. His Lordship never reasoned on any of Mr. B.'s writings, but merely made sport of them. I would, therefore, ask him what it was that he objected to ? Lord Byron mentioned his Panopticon as visionary. I said that experience in Pennsylvania, at Millbank, etc., had proved it otherwise. I said that Bentham had a truly British heart ; but that Lord Byron, after professing liberal principles from his boyhood, had, when called upon to act, proved himself a Turk.—Lord Byron asked, ' What proofs have you of this ? '—' Your conduct in endeavouring to crush the press, by declaiming against it to Mavrocordato, and your general abuse of liberal principles.'—Lord Byron said that if he had held up his finger he could have crushed the press.—I replied, ' With all this power—which, by the way, you never possessed—you went to the Prince and poisoned his ear.'—Lord Byron declaimed against the liberals whom he knew.—' But what liberals ? ' I asked : did he borrow his notions of free-men from the Italians ?—Lord Byron : ' No ; from the Hunts, Cartwrights, etc.'—' And still,' said I, ' you presented Cartwright's Reform Bill, and aided Hunt by praising his poetry and giving him the sale of your works.'—Lord Byron exclaimed, ' You are worse than Wilson, and should quit the army.'—I replied, ' I am a mere soldier, but never will I abandon my principles. Our principles are diametrically opposite, so let us avoid the subject.'

" If Lord Byron acts up to his professions, he will be the greatest, if not, the meanest, of mankind. —He said he hoped his character did not depend on my assertions.—' No,' said I, ' your genius has immortalised you. The worst could not deprive you of fame.'—Lord Byron : ' Well, you shall see : judge me by my acts.' When he wished me good-night, I took up the light to conduct him to the passage ; but he said, ' What ! hold up a light to a Turk ! ' "

And it was at this stage that the third emissary of the London Committee, Mr. William Parry, the expert in artillery, arrived at Missolonghi.

V

Mr. William Parry, or, as he subsequently styled himself, " Major Parry of Lord Byron's Brigade, Commanding Officer of Artillery and Engineer in the service of the Greeks," had first been mentioned to Byron in a letter from Mr. Bowring of August 18th, 1823. " The Committee," Mr. Bowring had written, " feel a great difficulty in expressing their wishes with respect to Greece in any other than general terms. After long consultations amongst the military gentlemen who belong to it, a plan of Colonel Gordon has been adopted to send to Greece, under the control of a very intelligent fire-master who was General Congreve's right-hand man, and understands the manufacture of every species of destructive arms and missiles, a small body of labouring artificers, with forges, laboratories, and every implement necessary for the fabrication of the *material* of war. His name is Parry, and he, with his men, will be immediately addressed to Your Lordship, from whom we hope (*sic*) that you will induce the Greek Government to put his services into immediate and active requisition. We understand that large quantities of spoiled powder were found at Nauplia. Now Parry can make it as serviceable as if it had been made yesterday. He will also make Congreve rockets—Greek fire—and a variety of other mischievous things which will inspire terror into the Turks. He is master of all the improvements in gunnery and of the maritime service of war."

A delay of nearly six months intervened before this

artillery expert, his artificers, and his staff arrived at Dragomestri. Their arrival, belated as it was, came at an opportune moment. It was hoped, with the artillery which Parry would at once be enabled to manufacture, to reduce to dust the Turkish fortresses in the Gulf of Corinth. And by the use of the Congreve rockets, which had caused such damage to the French fleet in 1809, and contributed to the panic of the French armies at the Battle of Leipzig, to destroy the Turkish frigates, and once and for all to establish Greek command of the sea.

From the first, however, it became apparent that General Congreve's right-hand man did not know how to manufacture the Congreve rocket. It transpired also that Mr. Parry had merely been a clerk in the civil department of the Woolwich arsenal, and that his only experience of the manufacture and management of artillery had been derived from a previous service as fire master in the Navy. The expedition sent out by the Greek Committee under Mr. Parry proved for these reasons a very bitter and unexpected disappointment to the Greeks. The Greek cause and the conditions at Missolonghi proved in their turn a very bitter disappointment to Mr. Parry. The immediate results of such mutual disillusionment did not contribute to the amity and good order of the artillery brigade which had been established in anticipation of Parry's arrival. It may be said, indeed, that from first to last the artillery expert and his staff were a cause of dissension, jealousy, and disruption, and that when in May 1824 Parry returned to England, he left his mission unaccomplished, and the stores which he had brought still rotting unused in the arsenal at Missolonghi.

In the eleven weeks, however, which he remained at Missolonghi, Parry figured prominently in the fortunes and the affairs of those with whom this narrative is concerned. He quarrelled with the artificers whom he had brought from England; he quarrelled with the

German officers who formed the nucleus of the artillery brigade; he quarrelled with the Greeks; he quarrelled with Stanhope, with Millingen, with Bruno, and even with Fletcher. Trelawny, when he met him, was not favourably impressed. "A rough, burly fellow," he dubbed him, "never quite sober. But he was no fool, and had a fund of pot-house stories, which he told in appropriately slang language. . . . All he did was to talk and to drink." To Millingen he appeared "as ignorant as he was presumptuous." Dr. Kennedy was told by Lieut. Hesketh that Parry was "officious, pompous, and jealous of any having access to or influence with Lord Byron." Descriptions of Parry as a "pot-house buffoon" even reached Leigh Hunt, in his retirement at Florence.

How came it, therefore, that this personage should have attained over Byron an ascendancy which, throughout the last weeks of his life, was exclusive and predominant? The explanation is furnished by the very remarkable book which Parry himself published in 1825. There are those, I know, who contend that Parry's book on the last days of Lord Byron must have been edited for him by some more expert hand. I am not convinced by this explanation. In the first place, the style of the book accords very fully with the style of Parry's letters; and, in the second place, the book is written with a vivid personal touch, and with that note of rancorous plausibility, coupled with naif hero worship, which can only have been given to it by Parry himself. For Parry was no fool. Uneducated but shrewd, besotted but vigorous, pretentious and yet devoted, plausible and yet in his own way sincere, crude and yet intensely emotional, Parry emerges as a very definite, and not wholly unsympathetic, personality. One can conjecture, not only from Parry's own book, but from the confirmatory evidence provided in Byron's letters, and in the accounts of other witnesses, exactly the appeal which Parry made to Byron. His simplicity came as a relief from the diffident subtlety of Mavrocordato; his crude materialism as a relief from the vapid idealism of Stanhope; his rough common sense as a relief from the romantic excesses of Trelawny; his shrewd efficiency in little things as a relief from the timid bungling of Gamba. Nor was this all. Parry both shared and stimulated Byron's increasing dislike of the London Committee. He could give a somewhat gross, but extremely entertaining, imitation of his own interview with Mr. Jeremy Bentham. He became the recipient of Byron's complaints against Stanhope, and the safety valve for all his suppressed invectives. And finally, Parry was always there; burly and sodden, he would keep people away and manage the accounts, and advise infinite schemes for doing nothing. Parry was a relief and a stand-by. His admiring devotion to Byron solaced the increasing diffidence with which that unhappy person was assailed. There were times when the husky outbursts of Parry served as the conductor for many an electric storm.

And, after all, there was no one else on whom Byron could rely. Mavrocordato, Stanhope, Trelawny, even Gamba, had failed him; Napier and Gordon showed no signs of coming to his assistance; Hobhouse was no good at all. There was, it is true, a certain Captain Hastings who would write him endless letters offering advice, co-operation, and service. But who was Captain Hastings? Obviously another of these enthusiasts, and one, moreover, with a whole hive of bees in his bonnet. For did not Captain Hastings fill his letters with strange tales of Egyptian preparations for a descent upon Crete? And did he not pester Byron with some plan for one of these new steam-driven vessels with which to assail the Turks? The thing was laughable; it would explode at once—of course it would explode. The letters from this Captain Hastings remained unanswered.

And the tragedy of it all is that Frank Abney Hastings, the most intelligent and unsullied of all English Philhellenes, was in the right; and that, had Byron met him personally, this whole foolish story would have undoubtedly been otherwise.

VI

Parry, with his artificers and his stores, arrived at Dragomestri on the last day of January. On Sunday, the 1st of February, Byron proceeded with Mavrocordato on a visit to Anatolikon, at the opposite end of the lagoons, where they were entertained by the Archbishop with plum-pudding and champagne. They returned by water, they were caught in drenching rain, and both Gamba and Loukas the page were attacked by fever. They arrived on February 3rd to find that Parry's stores had reached Missolonghi, and were being removed from the quay to the Seraglio. The 4th of February was a holiday, and the Greeks refused to handle the stores, which lay there under the pouring rain. Byron lost all patience, and running down to the shore, he began with his own hands to move the material. His example finally induced the Greeks to come to his assistance and to place the stores under cover.

The handling of these munitions of war rekindled Byron's military ambitions. "Tell Muir," he wrote to Charles Hancock on February 5th, "that, notwithstanding his remonstrances, which I receive thankfully, it is perhaps best that I should advance with the troops; for if we do not do something soon, we shall only have a third year of defensive operations and another siege, and all that. . . . As for me, I am willing to do what I am bidden, and to follow my instructions. I neither seek nor shun that nor anything else that they may wish me to attempt. As for personal safety, besides that it ought not to be a consideration, I take it that a man is on the whole as safe in one place as another; and, after all, he had better end with a bullet than bark in his body. If we are not taken off with the sword, we are like to march off with an ague in this mud basket; and, to conclude with a very bad pun, to the ear rather than to the eye, better *martially* than *marsh-ally*—the situation of Missolonghi is not unknown to you. The dykes of Holland when broken down are the Deserts of Arabia for dryness, in comparison."

Parry himself, who had remained behind at Drago-mestri to supervise the final disembarkation of the stores, did not arrive at Missolonghi until February 7th. He brought with him eight English mechanics and four volunteer officers, of whom two were English, one German, and one a Swede. His first act on arrival was to apply to Colonel Stanhope for an advance of money. Stanhope refused, and referred him to Byron :—

"I felt abashed and ashamed," Parry records in his narrative, "to come before Lord Byron for the first time in the character of a beggar. He was a nobleman, a stranger, and a man of exalted genius. I had understood I might be of service to him and to Greece, but, on the contrary, I found myself immediately obliged, that I might be enabled even to subsist my men, to have recourse to him for pecuniary aid.

"It was under these mingled feelings of regret and expectation that I had my first interview with Lord Byron. In five minutes after Colonel Stanhope had introduced me, every disagreeable thought had vanished; so kind, so cheering, so friendly was his Lordship's reception of me, that I soon forgot every unpleasant feeling. He gave me his hand, and cordially welcomed me to Greece. 'He would have been glad,' he said, 'to have seen me before; he had long expected me, and now that I was come, with a valuable class of men, and some useful stores, he had hopes that something might be done.' This was highly flattering to me, and I soon felt a part of that pleasure which beamed from his Lordship's countenance. . . .

"Lord Byron was sitting on a kind of mattress, but elevated by a cushion that occupied only a

part of it, and made his seat higher than the rest.
He was dressed in a blue surtout coat and loose
trowsers, and wore a foraging-cap. He was attended
by an Italian servant, Tita, and a young Greek of
the name of Luca, of a most prepossessing appearance. Count Gamba, too, came in and out of the
room, and Fletcher, his servant, was also occasionally
in attendance. His Lordship desired me to sit
down beside him; his conversation very soon
became animated, and then his countence appeared
even more prepossessing than at first.

"He began to rally me on the length of my
voyage, and told me he had supposed I meant to
vie with my namesake, and that I was gone to
explore the South Pole instead of coming to Greece.
My arrival at length, he added, had taken a load off
his mind, and he would not complain if he at last
saw Greece flourishing and successful. 'Why,' he
asked, observing that I did not share his satisfaction,
'was I not as well pleased as he was?' Then,
with a hint at my sailor habits, he said he knew I
wanted refreshment, and sent Tita to bring me
some brandy and water. This, however, had not
all the effect his Lordship wished, and he still
rallied me on my dissatisfied appearance, bade me
be at home, and explain to him why I was not
contented.

"I told his Lordship that I felt my situation very
irksome; that I had come to render assistance to the
Greeks, and found myself, on the instant of my
arrival, obliged to ask him for assistance; that his
Lordship's kindness, and what he had said to me,
had heightened my regret, and that if he had received
me haughtily and proudly, I should have had less
objection to trouble him; 'for,' I added, 'Colonel
Stanhope informs me that he has no funds to assist
me, and has recommended me to ask your Lordship for money.' On hearing this, he rose, twirled

himself round on his heel (which I afterwards found was a common, though not a graceful practice of his), and said, ' Is that all ?—I was afraid it was something else. Do not let that give you any uneasiness ; you have only to tell me all your wants, for I like candour, and, as far as I can, I will assist you.' When his Lordship rose, I observed that he was somewhat lame, but his bust appeared perfectly and beautifully formed. After a few moments' reflection, he again took his seat, and said he would take some brandy and water with me, on condition that I should tell him all the news in England, and give him all the information in my power. . . .

" My first interview with Lord Byron lasted nearly three hours, and his Lordship repaid my candour, and the information I had given him, by explaining to me how much he had been harassed and disappointed since his arrival in Greece. Of these subjects I shall hereafter have more to say, and shall enter more into details ; I shall therefore now only observe that his Lordship, when speaking on these topics, displayed a great degree of sensibility, not to say irritation, that his countenance changed rapidly, and expressed great anxiety. He seemed almost to despair of success, but said he would see the contest out. There was then a pallidness in his face and knitting of his brows that indicated both weakness and vexation. I have since thought that his fate was sealed before my arrival in Greece, and that even then he was, so to speak, on his death-bed."

Byron's own record of this conversation is as follows :—
" Parry seems a fine rough subject, but will hardly be ready for the field these three weeks ; he and I will (I think) be able to draw together—at least, *I* will not interfere with or contradict him in his own department. He complains grievously of the mercantile and *entusymusy*, as Braham pronounces enthusiasm, part of the

216

Committee, but greatly praises Gordon and Hume. Gordon *would* have given three or four thousand pounds and come out *himself*, but Kennedy or somebody else disgusted him, and thus they have spoiled part of their subscription and cramped their operations. Parry says Blaquière is a humbug, to which I say nothing. He sorely laments the printing and civilising expenses, and wishes that there was not a Sunday-school in the world, or *any* school *here* at present, save and except always an academy for artilleryship.

"He complained also of the cold, a little to my surprise; firstly, because, there being no chimneys, I have used myself to do without other warmth than the animal heat and one's cloak, in these parts; and, secondly, because I should as soon have expected to hear a volcano sneeze, as a firemaster (who is to burn a whole fleet) exclaim against the atmosphere. I fully expected that his very approach would have scorched up the town like the burning-glasses of Archimedes.

"Well, it seems that I am to be Commander-in-Chief, and the post is by no means a sinecure, for we are not what Major Sturgeon calls 'a set of the most amicable officers.' Whether we shall have 'a boxing bout between Captain Sheers and the Colonel,' I cannot tell; but, between Suliote chiefs, German barons, English volunteers, and adventurers of all nations, we are likely to form as goodly an allied army as ever quarrelled beneath the same banner."

And again four days later he writes as follows :—

"Parry and I get on well *hitherto*. How long this may last, Heaven knows, but I hope it will, for a good deal for the Greek service depends upon it; but he has already had some *miffs* with Col. S(tanhope), and I do all I can to keep the peace amongst them. However, Parry is a fine fellow, extremely active, and of strong, sound, practical talent, by all accounts."

Encouraged by this arrival, and by the assistance of this active and downright coadjutor, Byron again turned his thoughts eagerly to the expedition against Lepanto.

CHAPTER X

MISSOLONGHI : THE SECOND STAGE

February 15—April 9, 1824

I

THE first fortnight of February 1824 marks the turning-point in Byron's last journey. Until February 15th he managed to cope defiantly with the difficulties which beset him : after that date his health and his optimism failed him, and for the few weeks that remained he drifted despairingly and irritably towards the only conclusion.

For, in the first place, he was alone :—

> " I soon perceived," writes Parry, " not only that Lord Byron had no friend in Greece, but that he was surrounded by persons whom he neither loved nor trusted. Beyond the walls of his own apartment, where he seemed to derive amusement from his books, and from his dog, Lion, and pleasure from the attachment of his servants, particularly from the attentions of Tita, he had neither security nor repose. He had the ungovernable Souliotes both to appease and control. Against the intrigues of the very persons he came to help and benefit he was obliged to be constantly on his guard ; and while he necessarily opened his purse for their service, he was exposed to be made their prey. His confidence even in Prince Mavrocordato was not always unshaken. His youthful friend Count Gamba was destitute of experience, and was rather an additional burthen on him than a means of lightening his load. The foreign officers and English adventurers were all dissatisfied, and either appealed to him

to improve their condition or wearied him with their complaints. Whether he had actually received promises of greater succour from England than had ever been sent, or whether he had only formed an idea that supplies would be transmitted abundantly, I know not; but it was evident to me, from the very commencement of our acquaintance, that he felt himself deceived and abandoned, I had almost said betrayed. He might put a good face on the matter to others, because he would not be thought Quixotic or enthusiastic; he might even be, as in fact he sometimes was, the first to laugh at his own difficulties, to prevent others laughing at his folly; but in his heart he felt that he was forlorn and forsaken."

And, in the second place, he was distracted by discord and disunion among those who ought to have been either his subordinates or his assistants. It was all very well that Byron should, as Parry wrote to Bowring, have discovered " the inutility of theoretical fools and designing puppies." Such a discovery was useful only if it led to improvement : if it could be followed, that is, by action. But what action was possible? Napier long ago had told Trelawny that no one should assume any direction in Greek affairs " without two European regiments, money in hand to pay them, and a portable gallows." Byron possessed only one of these means of persuasion, and even his purse was not unfathomable.

So long as the projected expedition to Lepanto glimmered before him, Byron was able to lighten his discouragement with the stimulus of that impending adventure. It was his very own experiment; for this operation he had been rendered solely responsible. It was a chance of action : he would get away from the mud and the eternal swamps of Missolonghi; he would show the world that he could do more than write poetry : he would return with the fortress of Lepanto, which was a more resounding achievement than any of Stanhope's chronicles or societies. With his own Parry and his own Souliots he would win the second battle of Lepanto. And what would Hobhouse say then ?

II

The first blow to these aspirations was the discovery that Parry had brought no Congreve rockets and was unable in fact to manufacture them; moreover there was no coal with which the arsenal could function. The London Committee, as well as Byron himself, had forgotten about the coal. The mechanics who had come over from England were moreover becoming disaffected, and the German officers engaged for the artillery brigade objected to serving under Parry, whom Byron had appointed as their commander, and one of them, Major Kindermann, in spite of Byron's protest, promptly surrendered his commission.

In the face of these obstacles and objections, he still persisted in his preparations, encouraged by further reports which reached him of the dissatisfaction among the Turkish garrison of Lepanto. He sent for additional dollars from Zante ; he sent for some old artillery which was at Corinth ; nd above all he charged Gamba with the task of organising the Souliot brigade. By the 13th of February all was in readiness, and Gamba with the advance guard of the expedition was ready to start for Lepanto on the following evening.

Intelligence of the projected expedition had, however, reached Colokotronis, who was quick to realise that the capture of Lepanto would enable his rival, Mavrocordato, inconveniently to enhance the military prestige of the Government of Western Greece. Colokotronis at once collected all the Souliots he could find in the Peloponnese and sent them secretly to Missolonghi for the purpose of sowing dissatisfaction among the main body of their compatriots. His endeavours in this direction were crowned with immediate success. At 5 p.m. on February 14th, the moment timed for the departure of the advance guard, the Souliots at Missolonghi stated that they would not march unless the Government increased their pay and agreed to appoint from their ranks two generals, two colonels, and two captains, with inferior officers in the same proportion ; in other words, out of a total unit of three or four hundred they demanded that one hundred and fifty should receive the rank and pay of commissioned officers. Unless their demands were immediately accorded they would be unable, they said, to join the expedition : they had not been engaged, they contended, to fight against stone walls.

On learning of this ultimatum, Byron " burst into a violent passion, and protested that he would have no more to do with these people." His decision was conveyed to the Souliots by Gamba and Mavrocordato on the morning of Sunday, the 15th of February. Constantine Botzaris alone of the chieftains expressed some contrition, and stated that he was too sensible to all the benefits which Byron had conferred upon the men of Souli thus to abandon him at a crisis ; that he would for his part be prepared to serve under his Lordship as a private soldier if but five men remained. This offer made some impression upon the other chieftains, and a compromise was thereupon arranged whereby the original Souliot organisation was to be dissolved and a new corps, directly under Lord Byron's orders, was to be recruited from those, whether Souliots or others, who were willing to accept his orders and to submit to discipline. Nothing, however, could disguise the fact that the inspiriting prospects of the assault on Lepanto would now and for ever have to be abandoned.

Byron realised at once that there was no alternative but to accept this wretched compromise ; but the disappointment was overwhelming. He retired to his room, where Gamba found him lying upon the divan in the dark, crushed and humiliated. " I am not asleep," he called, "come in—I am not well." A few minutes later Parry entered, and for Parry there was only one remedy for such situations : he proposed a strong concoction of brandy punch, and induced Byron to drink it.

Parry, in his vivid, innocent way, has well recounted the scene that followed :—

"In the evening, about eight o'clock, he came downstairs into the Colonel's room, where I was. He seated himself on a cane settee, and began talking with me on various subjects. Colonel Stanhope, who was employed in a neighbouring apartment, fitting up printing-presses, and Count Gamba both came into the room for a short time, and some conversation ensued about the newspaper, which was never, to Lord Byron, a pleasant topic, as he disagreed with his friends concerning it. After a little time, they went their several ways, and more agreeable matter of conversation was introduced.

"His Lordship began joking with me about Colonel Stanhope's occupations, and said he thought the author would have his brigade of artillery ready before the soldier got his printing-press fixed. There was then nobody in the room but his Lordship, Mr. Hesketh, and myself. There was evidently a constrained manner about him, and he complained of thirst ; he ordered his servant to bring him some cider, which I entreated him not to drink in that state. There was a flush in his countenance, which seemed to indicate great nervous agitation ; and as I thought his Lordship had been much harassed for several days past, I recommended him, at least, to qualify his cider with some brandy. He said he had frequently drunk cider, and felt no bad consequences from it, and he accordingly drank it off.

"Lord Byron had scarcely drunk the cider, when

he complained of a very strange sensation, and I noticed a great change in his countenance. He rose from his seat, but could not walk, staggered a step or two, and fell into my arms. I had no other stimulant than brandy at hand, and having before seen it administered in similar cases, with considerable benefit, I called for some of that liquor, which was brought by Mr. Hesketh, and we succeeded in making him swallow a small quantity. In another minute his teeth were closed, his speech and senses gone, and he was in strong convulsions. I laid him down on the settee, and with the assistance of his servant kept him quiet.

"When he fell into my arms, his countenance was very much distorted, his mouth being drawn on one side. After a short time, his medical attendants came, and he speedily recovered his senses and his speech. His first care was to call for Colonel Stanhope, as he had something particular to say to him, should there be a probability of his not recovering. Colonel Stanhope was accordingly sent for, and came from the adjoining room. On recovering his senses, Lord Byron's countenance assumed its ordinary appearance, except that it was pale and haggard; and no other effect remained from his illness than a great degree of weakness. His Lordship was then carried upstairs and put to bed; and we left him in charge of his servants and medical attendants."

The anxieties of that evening were not, however, thereby concluded. Within half an hour of Byron's attack of epilepsy, the alarm was given that the Souliots had risen and were marching on the Seraglio with the intention of seizing the arms and ammunition stored in that building. Gamba, Parry, and Stanhope ran out into the night, leaving Byron alone; the artillery brigade was called to arms, the sentinels were doubled, and the

Seraglio was put in a state of defence. The panic which had arisen proved unfounded ; but while the others were absent, two drunken Germans, whose wild behaviour had caused the original alarm, forced their way into Byron's house and into the very room where he was lying, weak and bewildered, in his bed. They shouted to him in German that the Souliots had risen, that the arsenal had been stormed, that they themselves had come there to protect him. They waved their arms and shouted at the man lying there motionless upon the bed. He did not understand what they were saying. He was helpless and alone. The noise around him was pierced by the falsetto protests of Bruno. Bruno was already in tears. To Byron's fuddled consciousness the scene in the damp and ill-lit room adjusted itself gradually to a vague turmoil of confusion, helplessness, and terror.

And above and behind it all came the sound of rain pouring relentlessly upon the roof, and splashing from the gutters upon the mire of the yard below.

III

On the next day, Monday, February 16th, Byron rose at noon. He still felt weak and ill, and he had " a sensation of weight in his head." Drs. Bruno and Millingen decided that he should be bled : eight leeches were applied to his forehead, but owing to an oversight they were placed too near the temporal artery, and the flow of blood could not be arrested. Lunar caustic was applied to the veins, but by then their patient had already fainted. Parry, who was standing there officiously, intervened in indignation ; he snorted in speechless contempt at Bruno ; he rated Millingen more directly and in the English language. " When I saw them," he writes, " helpless, beside themselves, as it were, while the blood was flowing, and Lord Byron lay pale and senseless, the very image of death, I could have sacrificed their comparatively valueless lives for the one more valuable, of which I thought they had deprived us for ever. I tore off the strings and bands from a part of my dress, cut them into pieces, and made Lord Byron's Italian servant burn them under his Lordship's nose. I rubbed his temples and lips with brandy, and did what I could to save and restore him. At length the blood was staunched, and Lord Byron recovered. He often joked about his weakness, as if he had fainted at the sight of his own blood, like a fine lady ; and reproved me for my violence, as soon as he was informed of the little respect I had shown for the doctors. Thus did he, by his kindness, in a manner, court his own fate. Had he turned them out of doors, and returned to the habits of an English gentleman as to his diet, he would probably have survived many years, to have vindicated with his sword the wrongs of his beloved Greece, and to have heaped contempt on those pretended friends who, since his death, have vilified his glorious nature, because he could or would not believe that a lithographic press, Mr. Bentham's minute legislation, and conning over the alphabet, were the proper and most efficacious means of giving freedom and independence to that suffering and oppressed country."

That Byron himself was deeply perturbed by this attack of epilepsy is evident not only from his subsequent depression and his frequent references to his illness in conversations with Gamba and Parry, but also from a memorandum which he asked Bruno to prepare for him, and in which the symptoms and causes of epilepsy are analysed, and suggestions made as to diet and preventive treatment.

Bruno's memorandum is not a very reassuring document : it held out little hope that the danger would be averted. And so we find Byron on the next day suddenly resuming the diary which he had begun to write at Cephallonia. After recording the details of his fit, he adds some general considerations which clearly illustrate the extent of his uneasiness :—

" This day," he wrote, " though weakly, I feel tolerably convalescent. With regard to the presumed causes of this attack, as far as I know there might be several. The state of the place and the weather permit little exercise at present. I have been violently agitated with more than one passion recently, and a good deal occupied, politically as well as privately, and amidst conflicting parties, politics, and (as far as regards public matters) circumstances. I have also been in an anxious state with regard to things which may be only interesting to my own private feelings, and, perhaps, not uniformly so temperate as I may generally affirm that I was wont to be. How far any or all of these may have acted on the mind or body of one who had already undergone many previous changes of place and passion during a life of thirty-six years, I cannot tell, nor—— But I am interrupted by the arrival of a report from a party returned from reconnoitring a Turkish brig of war, just stranded on the coast, and which is to be attacked the moment we can get some guns to bear upon her. I shall hear what Parry says about it. Here he comes——"

The excitement regarding the brig for the moment diverted Byron's attention from his own sufferings and vexations. He actually wished to take part in the expedition, and was only prevented by the insistence of his two doctors and the fact that his eyes were acutely inflamed as a result of his attack of two days before. He had to lie there and let the others cope with this adventure. Parry had drawn for him, on the back of one of Zambelli's accounts, a plan of how the Turkish brig had stranded—a plan which showed how certain was her capture. But, in spite of this neat little drawing of Parry's, the expedition miscarried. In fact Millingen states that the complete failure of Parry and the rest to prevent the Turks from removing their stores from the brig, and subsequently blowing her up, for the first time shook Byron's unlimited confidence in Parry's efficiency and expert knowledge. Gamba remained on the spot, watching the Turkish brig burning throughout the night. He returned to Missolonghi at 11 o'clock in the morning of Thursday, the 19th of February. On reaching the yard of their house, he noticed that Byron's two small cannon were pointed against the gateway, and on climbing the staircase he discovered the whole staff in dismay, and the foreigners in a panic. It appeared that this time the Souliots actually had risen, and had murdered one of the best of the artillery officers, a Swedish volunteer of the name of Sass, who had come out with Parry. It subsequently transpired that the murder was due largely to a misunderstanding. One of the Souliots, of the name of Toti, had come to the arsenal with the little nephew of Constantine Botzaris, in order to show the child the arms and cannon which were stored there. The sentinel at the door told him that no one was admitted to the arsenal, but the Souliot endeavoured to push him aside. The sergeant of the guard, who was a Hungarian, thereupon ran up and tried to push the Souliot away by force. The latter lost his temper and struck the sergeant, who in his turn clamoured for the guard. Lieutenant Sass, who was the officer of the guard, ran downstairs and, observing the two men locked in a struggle, struck the Souliot on the neck with the flat of his sword. The Souliot thereupon drew his yatagan and his pistol, and severing Sass's left arm with the one, shot him through the head with the other. The Souliot was immediately arrested and imprisoned in the Seraglio. On hearing this, his compatriots crowded round the building and threatened to burn it unless Toti were immediately released.

A council was at once convened at Lord Byron's residence. It was decided that all the Souliots should there and then be asked to leave Missolonghi. If they refused, Lord Byron would himself depart with all the foreigners. On the following day, the 20th of February, the Primates of Missolonghi called upon Byron in a body and requested an immediate loan of 3000 dollars, with which to bribe the Souliots to leave the town. He was obliged in the circumstances to grant this request.

The murder of Lieut. Sass had a further and even more outrageous sequel. Six out of eight English mechanics who had come with Parry refused any longer to remain at Missolonghi, and asked to be repatriated. They claimed that in their contract with the London Committee they had been promised that they were to be employed only in a place of safety. The murder of Lieut. Sass proved, what they had long suspected, that Missolonghi was no such place. Again Byron was obliged to surrender, and the original artillery mission sent out by the London Committee was thus reduced to three only, namely Parry and the only two artificers, Hodges and Gill, who consented to remain.

Byron endeavoured to put the best face possible upon this final humiliation. "Six Englishmen," he wrote to Samuel Barff, "will be soon in quarantine at Zante : they are artificers, and have had enough of Greece in fourteen days. If you could recommend them to a passage home, I would thank you ; they are good men enough, but do not quite understand the little discrepancies in these countries, and are not used to see shooting and slashing in a domestic quiet way, or (as it forms here) a part of housekeeping. If they should want anything during their quarantine you can advance them not more than a dollar a day (amongst them) for that period, to purchase them some little extras as comforts (as they are quite out of their element). I cannot afford them more at present. The Committee pays their passage."

The effect produced on him by the accumulation of these disasters and disappointments was more pronounced than appears from the courageous flippancy of the above letter. "Lord Byron," wrote Stanhope hopefully, "is much shaken by his fit, and will probably be obliged to retire from Greece." At the height of the crisis arising out of Sass's murder, and at the moment when the arsenal was besieged by the Souliot tribesmen, Byron had summoned the chieftains to his house.

" I found him," writes Parry, " in his full dress as Colonel of the brigade, surrounded by the Souliot chiefs, each of whom was in the full costume of his country. They were all fine-looking men, and all being animated by this unfortunate event, formed as fine a picture as the eye could well behold. The report which I had drawn up was read and interpreted. Lord Byron addressed the chiefs, also through the medium of an interpreter, calmness was gradually restored, and the chiefs pledged themselves that justice should be done. They got up, put on their shoes, made a profound obei-sance to Lord Byron, crossing their arms at the same time on their breast, and retired to restore quiet among their soldiers. There was something pathetic in this peaceable conclusion to so threatening an affair; and though Lord Byron was still very unwell, few men, I believe, could have conducted themselves with more dignity and more prudence on so trying an occasion.

" All this, however, harassed him very much, and though he made a fine display when his energies were roused into action, his general health suffered from this excessive mental stimulus and exertion. Greater and increasing debility was the consequence; and, as he had some even still more unpleasant altercations to go through, and still more gratingly unpleasant scenes to witness, he gradually decayed, and soon fell a sacrifice to his own feelings and the improper treatment of those who might have had more respect for the peculiarities of genius."

IV

On Friday the 20th the weather cleared, and he was able to go out riding. He conversed with Gamba in terms of the deepest discouragement. " I begin to fear," he said, " that I have done nothing but lose time, money, patience, and health; but I was prepared for it; I knew that ours was not a path of roses, and that I ought to make up my mind to meet with deception, calumny, and ingratitude." Gamba urged him to retire to Athens and to recuperate his health and spirits. "No," he replied, "no; they would not leave me more tranquil there than here. Besides, I did not come here in search of tranquillity : I am neither undeceived nor discouraged."

From Zante and Cephallonia, where the news of his fit had now been received, his friends Kennedy, Hancock, and Muir wrote begging him to consider his health, and to rest for a while in the Ionian Islands. To Kennedy he replied as follows :—

"MY DEAR DOCTOR,

"I have to thank you for your two very kind letters, both received at the same time, and one long after its date. I am not unaware of the precarious state of my health, nor am, nor have been, deceived on that subject. But it is proper that I should remain in Greece; and it were better to die doing something than nothing. My presence here has been supposed so far useful as to have prevented confusion from becoming worse confounded, at least for the present. Should I become, or be deemed useless or superfluous, I am ready to retire; but in the interim I am not to consider personal consequences; the rest is in the hands of Providence —as indeed are all things. I shall, however, observe your instructions, and indeed did so, as far as regards abstinence, for some time past."

And to Samuel Barff, who also urged him to come to Zante, he replied :—

"I am extremely obliged by your offer of your country house (as for all other kindness) in case my health should require my removal; but I cannot quit Greece while there is a chance of my being of any (even supposed) utility. There is a stake worth millions such as I am, and while I can stand at all, I must stand by the cause.

"When I say this, I am at the same time aware of the difficulties and dissensions and defects of the Greeks themselves, but allowances must be made for them by all reasonable people."

For by then Byron had realised that the only thing he could do for Greece was not to run away.

In the evening of Saturday, February 21st, at 8 o'clock, there was a violent earthquake, to which Byron was not unaccustomed, but which frightened Parry out of his life. As a compensation for this disturbance Colonel Stanhope on the same day left Missolonghi for a visit to the Morea and Athens.

Thus concluded a week of uninterrupted turmoil. "In one week," he said to Parry, "I have been in a fit; the troops mutinied; the Turkish brig burned; Sass killed; an earthquake; thunder, lightning, and torrents of rain—such a week I never witnessed." His health and temper had already broken. "My situation here," he would say, "is unbearable. A town without any resources and a Government without money; imprisoned by the floods, unable to take any exercise, without the means of satisfying them or doing anything either to relieve them or myself."

It was in circumstances such as these that the month of February drew haggardly to its conclusion. On Sunday the 22nd he experienced a slight return of his epileptic attack, with convulsions in the right leg, but it quickly disappeared. By the end of the month the artillery brigade was again reorganised, and several further Philhellenes who had drifted to Missolonghi from the Morea were enrolled in it. Finlay arrived from Athens, bearing messages from Odysseus and Trelawny, inviting Byron and Mavrocordato to a conference at Salona. It was the project of this conference which occupied the remaining weeks of Byron's life, and which will require therefore some further explanation.

V

On leaving Cephallonia in September 1823, Trelawny, as I have said, proceeded to Tripolitza, Argos, Corinth, and finally to Eastern Greece. " I separated from Byron," he wrote to Jane Williams, " at Cephallonia. He was past hope. He trifled four months at that miserable island. Could I longer waste my life in union with such imbecility ? " By January 1824 Trelawny was established in Athens, where he purchased a harem of from twelve to fifteen ladies : " brutti mostri," Gamba described them later to Mrs. Shelley, and one at least appears to have been a negress. While at Athens he attached himself to the ex-Minion of Ali Pasha, the Klepht Chieftain Odysseus Androutzos, for whose character and abilities he conceived a passionate admiration. " A man," he wrote, " of most wonderful mind—a glorious being . . . brave, clever, and noble." And in a few months this connexion was cemented by Trelawny " marrying " Tarsitsa Kamenou, the infant half-sister of Odysseus.

Odysseus himself possessed no very marked Philhellenic sympathies. His policy was dictated solely by a determination to allow no other of the Greek leaders to secure predominance. He succeeded from the first in prejudicing Trelawny against Mavrocordato :—

" A word," the former wrote to Mrs. Shelley, " as to your wooden god—Mavrocordato. He is a miserable Jew, and I hope ere long to see his head removed from his worthless and heartless body. He is a mere shuffling soldier, an aristocratic brute : wants Kings and Congresses—a poor, weak, shuffling, intriguing, cowardly fellow ; so no more about him."

It had not been very difficult perhaps for Odysseus to complete the conquest of Trelawny. The latter, it was obvious, was determined to play a leading part in Greece ; it was obvious also that he was passionately jealous of Lord Byron. It was an easy thing to work upon these passions in order to detach Trelawny from the party of

Mavrocordato. Colonel Stanhope was a more difficult, though far more glorious capture. It is to the credit of Odysseus's diplomacy that he should have realised with remarkable rapidity the weak side of Colonel Stanhope. What Odysseus was after was Byron's money, and the London loan of which Byron and Stanhope would so shortly be able to dispose. For such a prize it was worth while to bow the knee for a moment to the Phanar. Mavrocordato could be disposed of later. Meanwhile the important thing was to secure Lord Byron.

Four days after Stanhope's arrival in Athens the influence had begun to work : " I have," he wrote to Byron on March 6th, 1824, " been constantly with Odysseus. He has a very strong mind, a good heart, and is brave as his sword ; he is a doing man ; he governs with a strong arm, and is the only man in Greece that can preserve order. He puts, however, complete confidence in the people. He is for a strong government, for constitutional rights, and for vigorous efforts against the enemy. He professes himself of no faction—neither of Ipsilanti's, nor of Colocotronis', nor of Mavrocordato's ; neither of the Primates', nor of the Capitani, nor of the foreign king faction. He speaks of them all in the most undisguised manner. He likes good foreigners, is friendly to a small body of foreign troops, and courts instruction. He has established two schools here, and has allowed me to set the press at work. . . . In short, considering his education, his pursuits, and the society by which he has been surrounded, he is a most *extraordinary man.*

" Odysseus is most anxious to unite the interests of Eastern and Western Greece, for which purpose he is desirous of immediately forming a congress at Salona. He solicits your Lordship's and Mavrocordato's presence. . . . I implore your Lordship and the President, as you love Greece and her sacred cause, to attend at Salona. Should you be ill or feeble, which God forbid, we solicit Count Gamba's presence. All delays, even that of a day, will, in the opinion of Odysseus, be injurious, as the Turks will be in motion immediately.   Excuse great haste, and believe me. . . ."

By the same messenger Trelawny wrote as follows :—

" DEAR LORD BYRON,

     "We send another envoy to you on what Ulysses [Odysseus], Col. Stanhope and myself concur in thinking an affair of the greatest and most pressing importance, and on its success the success of the ensuing campaign we think almost entirely depends ! It is to form a treaty of action and active co-operation between Eastern and Western Greece—Missolonghi and Athens—and that without delay !   I am aware there has (*sic*) been proposals and writing about this for some time, but nothing definitely decided on. Ulysses has been with his army before Negropont during the whole winter, which, with the coolness of the western chiefs, has hitherto prevented the completion of this most needful treaty.   There is now no time to be lost—we must be doing !   Ulysses therefore on his part proposes to be at Salona with M. Negris and an able adviser from each separate province that is under his protection.   If Mavrocordato, Lord Byron, and such others as they shall think proper will give him the meeting, Col. Stanhope, who has urged this business on with all might, will postpone his departure from Athens till he hears from you, and I can assure you that Ulysses is perfectly sincere and deeply interested to affect what he has proposed.   Stanhope says he has given you satisfying reasons, and I know if his don't move you, mine will not have much effect : only this I do entreat you, to use your influence in effecting this desirable object of such vital importance to the cause you have so much at heart, and have so gloriously and liberally aided.   Ulysses is the only man I have found in Greece that I think worthy of your confidence and co-operation.   You do not know him,

234

Lord Byron, or we should have had you at Athens—
nor do I despair (if you give us this meeting) of your
making Athens your final situation.

" I say this because you know that from the first
moment I had the honour of knowing you till this
day, in everything in which I have been in action
I have only considered your honour and advantage.
I should have given you a more detailed statement
of things here if I had thought anything I could say
would have influenced you; but you never felt the
curse of writing in vain—and after toiling and
sweating over a composition to have it thrown by
unread, or, what is as bad, unattended to—this kept
me silent—but I am now so imperiously called upon
to pour out to you an opportunity of doing Greece
a greater service than it may ever fall to the lot of
a stranger to have the power of doing.

" I rejoin the army with Ulysses to-day. Corinth
and Negropont are in close blockade. Ulysses
defends the pass of Thermophilly (*sic*) with 3000.
He is the most energetic, active, and enterprising
soldier I have ever met—nor is he deficient in
diplomatic knowledge.

" In pressing haste I

" am as ever

" Dear Lord Byron,

" Yours very faithfully,

" Edward J. Trelawny."

Meanwhile Colonel Stanhope remained at Athens :
he established, with the enthusiastic assent of Odysseus,
a Lancastrian school; he organised a utilitarian society;
" in consequence of the enlightened sentiments " which
Odysseus had expressed in favour of a free press, he engaged
Professor Psyllas as editor at a salary of £50 a year; he
wrote long letters of advice to Odysseus; he " implored "
him to follow the example of America and of Switzerland,
to follow " the example set by England, in the time of

William III " ; he implored him not to tolerate a standing army or to be influenced by the insidious monarchical movement which was doing such damage to the Greek cause in Europe. The General's replies were practical and diplomatic : he asked Colonel Stanhope to procure for him some of the munitions stored at Missolonghi ; he asked for money ; he asked for Byron. And for the rest : "Do not," he wrote to Stanhope, "ask my opinion upon anything. I am not able to give you advice. You are much better acquainted with what is necessary than I am. Do not, therefore, delay to do everything that you shall think desirable for Greece, or likely to advance her liberty." Here unmistakably was a man after Stanhope's heart.

The enthusiasm entertained for Odysseus by Trelawny and Colonel Stanhope was not shared by Byron. He remembered how that unscrupulous brigand had already betrayed the Greek cause at Karystos. Moreover, certain letters in which Odysseus boasted that he had " collared " Stanhope, and hoped similarly to secure Byron, were intercepted at Nauplia, and forwarded to Mavrocordato. Reports reached them that it was the intention of Odysseus to profit by the meeting at Salona to assassinate Mavrocordato, and to secure Byron for himself. Byron decided, none the less, that in all the circumstances it would be wiser to accept the invitation, and he promised therefore to attend at Salona on March 28th. In regard to Colonel Stanhope's request for munitions, he was less accommodating. Relieved as he was at the Colonel's departure from Missolonghi, yet he resented his advocacy of Odysseus, in that it was exploited as implying a division among the English Philhellenes in Greece. "Henceforth," comments Parry, " there were two headquarters for them, two commissioners from the Greek Committee, having different views, and steering different courses, and each attached to a different interest and different party among the Greeks. . . . Henceforth all that Byron had done was to be undone and what he was doing was to

236

be opposed." Byron therefore refused to send the gunpowder and the paper which Stanhope had asked for ;
but he reluctantly allowed the two artificers, Hodges and
Gill, to proceed to Athens.

VI

The month of March dragged on without improvement, and without any conclusive incident. Almost
every day Byron was troubled by intrigues to separate
him from Mavrocordato. He received messages from
Petro Bey, from Colokotronis, and from Sessini, who had
managed to establish an independent enclave at Gastouni.
Mavrocordato was not slow, moreover, to communicate
to Byron any secret information which reached him
regarding the separate policy being pursued by Stanhope
and Trelawny ; nor could Byron blind himself to the
fact that his two assistants were endeavouring to obtain
the stores which the Committee had sent out to Mavrocordato for the use of their Ulysses.

Meanwhile the demands on Byron's purse became even
more insistent. On March 17th the inhabitants of
Missolonghi petitioned him for assistance in repairing
the fortifications of the town. "Without this," they
wrote, " we are full of fear and exposed to danger, as it
has been proved twice already that, owing to our lack of
material, we would have fallen victims to the tyrants, had
not God saved us in time. There are many other dangers
which threaten us : you know them ; you see them ; the
defence against them rests with the wisdom and vigilance
of Your Excellency."

Mavrocordato was even more precise. On March 25th
he wrote to Byron as follows :—

" MY LORD,
        " The till is not only empty, but in debt as well.
All the primates and captains of this place have
resolved to come and see you to beg you to help our

country in this critical moment by making another provisional loan. I send M. Praïdes to you to warn you and to ascertain your views."

Nor were his troubles merely financial. The members of the artillery brigade were becoming unpopular with the townsmen. On March 28th a member of the brigade was found robbing a peasant, and had to be publicly degraded. The other officers of the brigade quarrelled with each other regarding the justice and details of this sentence, and in order to prevent duels Byron was obliged to place them for a night under arrest. " At this moment," records Parry, " there was a combination of circumstances, all tending to irritate the naturally sensitive disposition of Lord Byron and to weaken his hopes of a great and glorious result. He was more a mental being, if I may use this phrase, than any man I ever saw. He lived on thought more than on food. As his hopes of the cause of Greece failed—and they seem to have been the last, and perhaps the greatest his mind was capable of forming—he became peevish ; and, if I may so speak, little-minded. Losing hope, he lost enthusiasm, and became gloomily sensible to his situation. There was no mental stimulus left to make him bear up against his increasing perplexities and nerve his body to resist the noxious effects of a bad climate.

" The difficulties of his own situation, and the coming dangers, had the effect, on the obstinate mind of Lord Byron, of compelling him to remain at Missolonghi. But for these circumstances he would have left it for a time, and have found repose and health."

In the petulant and petty mood thus induced by his ill health and unhappiness he quarrelled with Pietro Gamba. It appears that Gamba had misunderstood some instructions regarding an order for red cloth from Cephallonia, and that Byron, in a fit of temper, had accused him of mismanagement of the accounts. Among the papers found at Missolonghi after Byron's death there is a note, dated March 24th, 1824, in which Gamba endeavours to justify his actions. This letter begins "My Lord," and not as hitherto "Mio Caro Byron." "Herewith," Gamba writes, "I furnish a detailed and accurate explanation of my conduct—you may, if you like, call it my inefficiency or my imprudence—regarding the money spent upon the artillery company." From the explanation which follows it seems that Gamba had advanced out of Byron's private funds the February instalment of the brigade's salary, and that this had been discovered by Parry and reported to Byron. "In whatever manner," Gamba concludes, "you may wish to regard my conduct, I trust that you will not find a worse name for it than ' error of judgment ' or ' disobedience.' For such delinquencies I beg your forgiveness; and whatever punishment you may decide to inflict upon me, I shall accept it willingly, not so much as from a superior officer, as from one who is to me as a father. I must confess, however, that the reproaches you made to me last night have caused me no little pain; but greater than any pain would be the thought that the slightest suspicion could remain in your mind as to my conduct in the management of your household accounts, which you had in the past entrusted to me in all confidence. When it pleased you to confide to me more important and delicate matters I felt that no effort should be spared to secure that these matters should succeed in accordance with your wishes, your interests, and your renown. It is true that I have accomplished little, since circumstances have offered me little to accomplish. But should God give me the occasion, I feel that I possess a sufficiency of intelligence and character to prove to you that the most devoted of your friends will not be the least useful of your servants."

In spite of this touching appeal, Gamba was not immediately forgiven, and their personal intercourse remained for some days suspended. For Byron was no easy master during these days of March. He even quarrelled with Fletcher : only Tita and the page Loukas remained in favour. And the cause of all this was his rapidly declining health. On March 1st he had complained of giddiness and of " very disagreeable nervous sensations," which, he said, " resembled feelings of fear, though he knew there was no cause for alarm." " At no time of his life," records Millingen, " did Lord Byron find himself in circumstances more calculated to render him unhappy. The cup of health had dropped from his lips, and constant anxiety and suffering operated powerfully on his mind, already a prey to melancholy apprehensions and disappointment, increased by disgust. Continually haunted by a dread of epilepsy or palsy—complaints most humiliating to human pride—he fell into the lowest state of hypochondriasis, and vented his sorrows in language which, though sometimes sublime, was at others as peevish and capricious as that of an unruly and quarrelsome child. When he returned to himself, however, he would request us ' not to take the indisposed and sickly fit for the sound man.' "

Meanwhile the *Greek Chronicle*, which Stanhope had fathered, was being edited at Missolonghi by Dr. Meyer, a Swiss doctor, who, although he possessed in Stanhope's eyes all the excellent qualities of a convinced republican, was for Byron an object of intense dislike. For the manners of Dr. Meyer were both arrogant and familiar. The circulation of the *Greek Chronicle*, which had commenced publication on January 1st, was not a large one : Colonel Stanhope in his enthusiasm had forgotten that only a very few individuals in Greece knew how to read. Dr. Millingen estimates that in the whole country there were not more than forty Greek subscribers. Dr. Meyer decided therefore that his republican opinions could be better propagated by the publication of a paper in Italian. Byron, who was evidently uneasy lest the Greek Committee would believe Stanhope's report that he was opposed to liberal principles, had not the force of mind to nip this project in the bud. He adopted another method. He appointed Gamba, whose association with any project he had come to regard as fatal, to be its editor. Dr. Meyer, however, issued on his own a prospectus of this new polyglot paper, which was of so violent a character that the paper was in advance forbidden a circulation in the Ionian islands. Byron retaliated by carefully censoring the first issue of the *Greek Telegraph*, and by suppressing the whole twentieth number of the *Greek Chronicle*, in which Meyer had written a violent attack upon the Austrian Government. He felt, however, that the strong line which he had taken in regard to these two journals would have to be explained to his friends in the islands. " If Lord Guilford is at Zante," he wrote to Barff on the 19th of March, " or, if he is not, if Sig. Tricupi is there, presenting my respects to one or both, you would oblige me by telling them that from the very first I foretold to Col. Stanhope and to P. Mavrocordato that a Greek newspaper (as indeed any other), in *the present state* of Greece, might and probably *would* lead to much mischief and misconstruction, unless under *some* restrictions ; nor have I ever had anything to do with either, as a writer or otherwise, except as a pecuniary contributor to their support in the outset, which I could not refuse to the earnest request of the Projectors. Col. Stanhope and myself had considerable differences of opinion on this subject, and (what will appear laughable enough) to such a degree that he charged me with *despotic* principles, and I him with *ultra radicalism*. Dr. Meyer, the Editor, with his unrestrained freedom of the press, and who has the freedom to exercise an unlimited indiscretion—not allowing any articles but his own and those like them to appear—and in declaiming against restrictions, cuts, carves, and restricts (as they tell me) at his own will and pleasure. He is the Author of an article against Monarchy, of which he may have the advantage and fame ; but they (the Editors) will get themselves into a scrape, if they do not take care.

" Of all the petty tyrants, he is one of the pettiest, as are most demagogues that ever I knew."

VII

Byron had not, however, come out to Missolonghi to censor the articles of Dr. Meyer: he had come to play a leading part in the liberation of Greece. But was he playing a leading part? Was he, in fact, playing any part at all? What if, after all, Trelawny and Stanhope were to steal a march upon him? Obviously, although he disliked the project in principle, it was incumbent upon him to go to Salona. The conference had been arranged for the last week in March, but the incessant rains, the swollen rivers, and the broken bridges, had given Mavrocordato an excuse for delay. And now April was upon them with the hope of spring; Greece would become herself again, arid and luminous; the nightmare of Missolonghi was at an end. Of course he would go, and at once, to Salona. But here again the Souliots intervened to prevent him.

After leaving Missolonghi, the Souliot tribes had drifted towards Arta, but, finding no means of subsistence in that town, they had maintained a somewhat precarious and foraging existence in the immediate neighbourhood of the lagoons. A minor Greek military chieftain, Karäiskaki, had meanwhile established himself at Anatolikon, where he entered into some sort of understanding with the Souliot leader, Djavella. On the 1st of April the nephew of Karäiskaki was wounded in a quarrel with some Missolonghiot boatmen, whom he had asked to convey him to Anatolikon free of charge. Profiting by this excuse, Karäiskaki despatched an armed body of his adherents to Missolonghi to demand redress for the insult. On the approach of these forces a panic seized upon the town: the shops were shut and the bazaars deserted. At the same time it was learnt that Djavella's Souliots were also marching from another direction against the fortifications. Missolonghi was at once placed in a state of defence. On the next morning Djavella occupied the fort of Vasiladi, which completely commanded the entrance to the lagoon. The Turkish fleet at the same moment appeared menacingly in the offing. Missolonghi had been betrayed. In helpless despair they awaited the impending massacre.

The authorities of Missolonghi were galvanised by this menace into feverish activity. They rushed from house to house arresting people indiscriminately and seizing their papers. They arrested Constantine Vulpiotti, who was at that moment living in Byron's house, being the father-in-law of the proprietor. Vulpiotti confessed : he confessed that he and Karäiskaki had been engaged in treasonable correspondence with the Turks; that the sudden appearance of the enemy's fleet was part of a plan for the joint occupation of Missolonghi; that Karäiskaki had hoped in this manner to overthrow the Government and to obtain possession of Mavrocordato, of Byron, and of the Byron dollars. And the plot, to all appearances, had now succeeded.

Byron himself, on the 6th of April, showed admirable calm and courage. He at once placed his services and those of his brigade at the disposal of Mavrocordato. In order to reassure the panic-stricken populace, he rode out for three miles into the country. It was his last ceremonial appearance; it was the last occasion on which he was seen, in full array, by the people of Missolonghi. They crowded there in the open space by the northern gate, watching the cavalcade as it splashed by. First came a detachment of his personal guard, running on foot, their muskets in their hands, their white fustanellas flopping as they jumped the puddles. Behind him clustered his immediate staff, Gamba and Bruno, the page Loukas in his scarlet livery, the burly form of Tita in his chasseur's coat of blue and silver, the exotic figure of the negro groom. An impression of waving plumes, of gold-mounted pistols, of scarlet cloth, of jingling harness ; an impression, predominantly, of a man riding apart from the rest in a little green jacket, flicking his whip absently in his yellow-gloved hand ; an impression of grey curls blowing out from under the gold band of a blue bonnet ; an impression, finally, of a white face, strained and haggard. And in the rear came a second detachment of the bodyguard, hopping along to keep pace with their master, crowding together as they passed under the low red archway of the gate.

On the next day, on the morning of April 7th, the news was more reassuring. The other Souliot leaders had repudiated Djavella : they were, in fact, at that moment marching to the relief of Missolonghi. On hearing of this Djavella suddenly lost courage, and in the night he evacuated the fort of Vasiladi. The Turkish fleet withdrew again to the Gulf of Corinth. The plot had failed ; Karäiskaki was captured within a few hours ; the situation was miraculously retrieved. But the prestige of the Government of Western Greece had been irretrievably shaken ; there was no further talk of the Conference of Salona.

" The volcanic mind of Lord Byron," records Millingen, " was thrown by these events into a violent state of commotion." We may well believe it. For both in prospect and in retrospect the situation in which he now found himself was indeed despairing. He had hesitated all those months at Metaxata to commit himself to any of the Greek parties. In the end, abandoning all hope of securing union, he had identified himself with Mavrocordato, and had staked his own reputation, and the interests of the subscribers to the English loan, upon the success and ultimate predominance of the Government of Western Greece. The subsequent history of the Greek War of Independence proves the wisdom of this decision. But on that 8th of April no such final justification could have been foreseen. The Government of Western Greece had not even the strength to execute Karäiskaki for his treachery ;[1] the Government of Western Greece was non-

[1] Which was perhaps fortunate, since Karäiskaki developed later into one of the heroes of the War of Independence, and was killed while endeavouring to relieve the Acropolis.

existent, and in a few days would arrive the first instalment of the English loan.

Lord Byron's last journey had thus proved a failure : he had failed to reconcile the Greek factions; he had failed to capture Lepanto; he had failed even to attend the Conference of Salona; he had been personally responsible for the Souliots; he had imposed no discipline upon his own brigade; the artillery experts had been a disappointment; the fleet had dispersed; the finances were as bad as ever; Trelawny and Stanhope had deserted him; there was no hope of Napier or Gordon coming to his assistance; the Committee in London were indifferent, if not disapproving. Even in Missolonghi, even within the walls of his own house, he was surrounded by treachery, spying, and intrigue. He had lost his health, his reputation, even his honour. What had he achieved in all those months since August? He had achieved nothing. And what, in the months that might still be accorded, did there remain for him to do?

There was only one thing that there remained for him to do.

CHAPTER XI

April 9—April 19, 1824

I

THE story of Lord Byron's illness and death, the story, that is, of the ten tragic days from Friday, April 9th, to Monday, April 19th, has come down to us in much detail and from several distinct sources. There is, in the first place, the sober and pathetic account given by Pietro Gamba in his narrative; there is the vivid, though less objective chronicle which has been left by Parry; there is the testimony of Dr. Millingen, the value of which is diminished by his embittered bias against Dr. Bruno; there is the detailed statement, which was obtained from Fletcher and published in the *Westminster Review* for July 1824; and there is Dr. Bruno's own defence published in the *Examiner* for August of the same year. These accounts are written by those who, in their several capacities, were present on the occasion. Of second-hand but contemporary records there are the statements of Stanhope and Trelawny, the letters of Lord Sidney Osborne, and the several notices in the English papers, which were based on material supplied by residents in the Ionian islands. From these various sources a very detailed and circumstantial narrative can be compiled.

I have been allowed also to read and to make use of a further document, which, although of primary importance, has not hitherto been published. This document is in the handwriting of Dr. Bruno, and represents the diary of the illness which he prepared for the executors.

Bruno made two copies of this diary, which he surrendered, together with the original, to Hobhouse. It is through Hobhouse's daughter, Lady Dorchester, that the signed document and the two copies came into the possession of Mr. Murray.

To Dr. Bruno's diary is appended the protocol of the post-mortem examination, which was jointly composed and signed, not only by Bruno and Millingen, but also by Drs. Treiber and Vaya, their four signatures being attested by Mavrocordato and his secretary. The original account of the post-mortem concludes with the words : "And to the truth of this the undersigned have affixed their signatures." In the copies, however, which Bruno made of his own diary, to which the account of the post-mortem is attached without a break, he has extended the above wording by a very significant insertion. His amended version runs as follows : "And to the truth of this statement and *of this account of Lord Byron's illness* the undersigned have affixed their signatures." It is manifest that Dr. Bruno wished whoever might see his copies to believe that his own account of the illness was vouched for by the other doctors. In spite of this flaw, however, Dr. Bruno's diary supplements in a very convincing manner the accounts which have hitherto been published ; and, profiting by Mr. Murray's courteous permission, I shall quote, or rather translate literally, the more important passages.

Dr. Bruno's diary, which is written in Italian, begins with the following introduction :—

"The Honourable Lord Byron, being then 37 years of age (*sic*), was by temperament full-blooded and nervous, by constitution robust and plethoric ; he was much addicted to intellectual pursuits, and to indulgence in strong spirits. On arriving at Missolonghi in the beginning of January, he considerably increased the quantity of these libations, being induced thereto by the insinuations and persuasions of a certain Captain, with whom he was in the habit of consorting every evening for his amusement ('per di lui passatempo'). In the middle of February, as a result of incessant mental vexations and his increased addiction to spirits, he was assailed by an attack of epilepsy, which I was able to cure by the following treatment : I applied leeches to his temple and drew four pounds of blood ; I administered purgatives in the form of English salts and magnesia ; I prescribed dieting, frequent and total immersions in warm water, complete abstinence from spirituous liquors or wine, and moderation in all mental exertions.

" By the middle of March, however, being continually tempted by that Captain who had been the indirect cause of his epileptic fit, and in spite of all my protests, his Lordship insisted on changing his diet, on increasing the allowance of meat, and on adding to his victuals such heating condiments as nutmeg, pepper, and ginger. . . . I begged him to abandon these stimulants, to take a little more exercise, to transact less business, and to resume his rigorous diet. But in vain ; he was inclined rather to listen to the suggestions of those who, being ignorant of the art of medicine, sought only to please his Lordship rather than to assist him. He insisted on abandoning the hot baths which I had prescribed for him, preferring to provoke perspiration by the game of single-stick, which he soon carried to excess, and with the effect that his head became over-heated. I warned him to indulge in this sport with moderation, a warning which (such was his lively temperament and his inability to follow a middle course) he completely disregarded. The condition of his Lordship's health was, nevertheless, on the whole satisfactory, although, whether from the effect of his mental exertions or whether from the shock occasioned to his nervous

system by his epileptic fit, he became less good-
tempered, and less satisfied with any favourable
circumstance which happened to him.

"In this condition he continued until the 9th
of April."

On the morning of that day, Friday, the 9th of April,
Byron was cheered by the arrival of the mail from
England. He heard, in the first place, that negotiations
for the Greek loan were proceeding rapidly and with
every hope of success. In the second place, he received
a very favourable account of his daughter's health and
of that of his sister Augusta. He was so enlivened by
the receipt of this intelligence that, in spite of the
threatening weather, he decided to go out riding. Three
miles from the town he and Gamba were overtaken by a
heavy downpour; by the time they reached the spot
where Costa Ghazis was waiting for them with his
canoe they were both in a heavy perspiration and wet
through. Gamba begged Byron to make an exception
to his usual rule, and to ride back the whole way to his
house. It would be very dangerous, he urged, in their
present heated condition to sit in an open boat and to
be rowed back slowly in the pouring rain. Byron would
not listen to this advice. "I should make a pretty
soldier," he replied, "if I were to care for such a trifle."
He insisted therefore upon entering the canoe. Two
hours after his return he was seized with a shivering
fit, and complained of shooting pains in his back and
limbs.

At this point some discrepancy occurs in the various
accounts. Bruno, in his detailed medical record, states
that Byron did not summon him until late in the night
of Saturday the 10th, and implies that his patient had,
during that day, again been out riding. Gamba, on the
other hand, asserts that it was on the night of the 9th
that Bruno was first summoned, that Byron was ill and
in pain during the whole day of the 10th, and that it

was on Sunday the 11th that he took his second ride. As Gamba's account is contradicted not only by Bruno, but by Parry, Millingen, and Finlay, it may be taken that Dr. Bruno's dates are the more accurate, and that it was on Friday the 9th that Byron contracted the chill which was eventually to develop into rheumatic fever,[1] but that in spite of this he rode out again on Saturday the 10th, accompanied by Lambro, the Souliot, and a numerous retinue. On his return from this second ride he was observed to scold his groom for not having changed the saddle, which had been drenched in the downpour of the previous day. On the Saturday evening Finlay arrived, to find him lying on the sofa complaining of rheumatic pains and fever. To Millingen, who also called to speak of the affairs of the dispensary, he mentioned incidentally the old prophecy which years ago had been made to him at Cheltenham. " Beware," the old gipsy had said to him, " of your 37th year, my young Lord : beware ! "

That night the pains increased and he sent for Bruno.

> " He summoned me," Bruno writes, " at a late hour of the night and told me that he had cold shuddering fits followed by burning intervals and wandering pains all over the body. He added that he had not sent for me during the day, since he did not wish to be disturbed in his business by being forced to take medicine. That night he

---

[1] I use the term " rheumatic fever," as I have used the term " epilepsy," since Byron himself, as well as his two doctors, make use of these expressions. I am assured, however, by my friend Dr. Gates, whom I have consulted in the matter, that it is very doubtful whether the attack of February 15th was actually epileptic, while it is practically certain that the final illness was not rheumatic fever. The dominant symptoms of the latter illness, such as acute perspiration and swellings in the joints, are not apparent ; nor, if he had been suffering from this illness, would it have been possible for him, two days before his death, to walk into the adjoining room. Dr. Gates is inclined, rather, to diagnose the malady as either typhoid fever or pernicious malaria.

slept but little and restlessly, and on the morning of Sunday the 11th, he complained in addition of certain local pains caused by his having ridden the day before upon a damp saddle. I ordered him a hot bath, and on the top of it two ounces of castor oil. . . . I begged him to let me bleed him, since I found that his pulses were strong and irregular, but he refused categorically. Instead he agreed to take six doses, one every hour, of 15 grains of antimony powders, and during the evening he perspired a little and slept in snatches throughout the night."

Parry, who visited him during the course of the next day, was somewhat alarmed by his condition. His speech was nervous and disconnected. Parry begged him to proceed at once to Zante, where he would be in a better climate and under efficient medical treatment. Byron, to Parry's surprise, at once consented to this proposal. Meanwhile Parry sturdily approved of his refusal to be bled : " Brandy, My Lord, brandy is the only thing that will save you," and with that he hurried out to make arrangements for their passage to Zante.

On Monday the 12th, Byron took another hot bath and more antimony powders. He again refused to be bled, and insisted upon getting up and attending to his business. He ate nothing but a thin broth with an egg beaten up in it. On Tuesday the 13th he complained of pains in his head and around the eyebrows. At three o'clock in the afternoon of this day the fever suddenly increased, and Bruno asked for permission to call Dr. Millingen into consultation ; the latter, according to Bruno, approved the treatment which had hitherto been accorded. Meanwhile all was ready for the departure for Zante. During the day, however, a hurricane of wind and rain, the sirocco at its worst, descended upon Missolonghi. It was impossible to venture into the gulf : the plan was, for the moment, abandoned.

On the morning of Wednesday the 14th Byron felt

better, and proceeded into the next room for the purpose of transacting business with Gamba. He even spoke of going out again on horseback. " I was afraid," he said to Gamba, who was sitting on the divan beside him, " that I was losing my memory, and, in order to try, I attempted to repeat some Latin verses with the English translation, which I have not endeavoured to recollect since I was at school. I remembered them all except the last word of one of the hexameters."

At midday Dr. Bruno again brought Millingen to see him. They endeavoured between them to induce him to consent to be bled.

" It was not possible," Bruno writes, " to convince him. He even burst into a fit of irritation, saying that he well knew that the lancet had killed more people than the lance. He agreed to take one of his usual pills, and to swallow some black currant tea. The latter rendered him violently sick, and his sleep was disturbed and restless."

II

Until the afternoon of Thursday the 15th it does not appear therefore that either Bruno or Millingen realised that the life of their patient was in any danger. Byron himself seems to have alternated between optimism and an uneasy suspicion that he was more seriously ill than his two young doctors imagined. On the one hand, he told Gamba that he was pleased to have had fever, for he thought it would counteract his tendency to epilepsy. To Fletcher, on the other hand, he appears to have expressed himself with less confidence. He remarked to him repeatedly that he was sure that neither Bruno nor Millingen understood the nature of his disease : " They tell me," he said, " that it is only a common cold, which you know I have had a thousand times." " I am sure, My Lord," said Fletcher, " that you never had one of so serious a nature." "I think I never had," Byron concluded. Fletcher therefore suggested to the two doctors that Dr. Thomas should be sent for from Zante, but they assured him that there was no cause for anxiety.

In the course of that afternoon the fever increased alarmingly, and he was assailed by a raging thirst, which he assuaged by drinking distilled water mixed with cream of tartary and lemon. His pulse was strong, but intermittent. The doctors became seriously uneasy.

"Every argument," records Dr. Bruno, "that I or Dr. Millingen put to him could not move him from his aversion to being bled. I charged his faithful servant, Battista Falcieri, who waited on My Lord the whole day during his illness, to repeat to His Excellency the alarm that I felt, and the fears which I began to entertain that he would not recover, unless he allowed me to bleed him; but My Lord more than once answered 'that I desired to make out that his condition was serious for no other motive than to gain credit by curing him.'

"Meanwhile," continues Dr. Bruno, "his pulse became hourly stronger, more intermittent, and more fully charged. I again urged him, with tears in my eyes, and for the sake of everything that he held dearest in the world, to allow me to bleed him, but My Lord replied, 'I do not like it—I do not like it—you must have understood by now that neither your own prayers nor the chatter of other people will make me consent.'

"We again," remarks Dr. Bruno despairingly, "gave him three pills of calomel, mixed with extract of colocynch. Dr. Millingen met with the same refusal in his attempts to save the illustrious patient."

The whole day the sirocco howled around the house.

It was hopeless to think of Zante. It was hopeless even to send for Dr. Thomas. As Byron lay there isolated and imprisoned in the dark and squalid room, with the rain slashing against the windows, he was assailed suddenly by renewed superstitions. Was he by any chance under the influence of the evil eye? He begged Millingen, with earnest seriousness, to find a witch at Missolonghi who could exorcise the curse which had been put upon him. Millingen consented in order to humour his patient; he even made inquiries in the town. There were several witches available in the district; but Byron did not again recur to this proposal, and no witch was ever summoned to his bedside.

At seven in the evening Parry came to see him :—

" I took a chair at his request, and sat down by his bedside, and remained till ten o'clock. He sat up in his bed, and was then calm and collected. He talked with me on a variety of subjects connected with himself and his family : he spoke of his intentions as to Greece, his plans for the campaign, and what he should ultimately do for that country. He spoke to me about my own adventures. He spoke of death also with great composure, and though he did not believe his end was so very near, there was something about him so serious and so firm, so resigned and composed, so different from anything I had ever before seen in him, that my mind misgave me, and at times foreboded his speedy dissolution.

" ' Parry,' he said when I first went to him, ' I have much wished to see you to-day. I have had most strange feelings, but my head is now better; I have no gloomy thoughts and no idea but that I shall recover. I am perfectly collected. I am sure I am in my senses, but a melancholy will creep over me at times.' The mention of the subject brought the melancholy topics back, and a few exclamations showed what occupied Lord Byron's mind when he was left in silence and solitude. 'My wife! My Ada! My country! The situation of this place, my removal impossible, and perhaps death, all combine to make me sad. Since I have been ill, I have given to all my plans much serious consideration. You shall go on at your leisure preparing for building the schooner, and when other things are done we will put the last hand to this work by a visit to America. To reflect on this has been a pleasure to me, and has turned my mind from ungrateful thoughts. When I left Italy I had time on board the brig to give full scope to memory and reflexion. It was then I came to that resolution I have already informed you of. I am convinced of the happiness of domestic life. No man on earth respects a virtuous woman more than I do, and the prospect of retirement in England with my wife and Ada gives me an idea of happiness I have never experienced before. Retirement will be everything to me, for heretofore my life has been like the ocean in a storm.'

" Then, adverting to his more immediate attendants, he said : ' I have closely observed to-day the conduct of all around me. Tita is an admirable fellow; he has not been out of the house for several days. Bruno is an excellent young man and very skilful, but I am afraid he is too much agitated. I wish you to be as much about me as possible; you may prevent me being jaded to death, and when I recover I assure you I shall adopt a different mode of living. They must have misinformed you when they told you I was asleep; I have not slept, and I can't imagine why they should tell you I was asleep.

" ' You have no conception of the unaccountable thoughts which come into my mind when the fever attacks me. I fancy myself a Jew, a Mahomedan, and a Christian of every profession of faith. Eternity and space are before me; but on this subject, thank God, I am happy and at ease. . . .'

"I had never before," records Parry, "felt as I felt that evening. There was the gifted Lord Byron, who had been the object of universal attention, who had, even as a youth, been intoxicated with the idolatry of men, and the more flattering love of women, gradually expiring, almost forsaken, and certainly without the consolation which generally awaits the meanest of mankind, of breathing out his last sigh in the arms of some dear friend. His habitation was weather-tight, but that was nearly all the comfort his deplorable room afforded him. He was my protector and benefactor, and I could not see him whom I knew to have been so differently brought up thus perishing, far from his home, far from all the comforts due to his rank and situation, far, too, from every fond and affectionate heart, without a feeling of deep sorrow, such as I should not have had at the loss of my own dearest relation. The pestilent sirocco was blowing a hurricane, and the rain was falling with almost tropical violence. In our apartment was the calm of coming death, and outside was the storm desolating the spot around us, but carrying, I would fain hope, new life and vigour to some stagnant part of nature.

"This evening was, I believe, the last time Lord Byron was calm and collected for any considerable period."

III

During that night of Thursday the 15th he was assailed by violent spasms of coughing, which made him vomit. Bruno threatened him with inflammation of the lungs if he did not allow himself to be bled, but he replied again: "You two doctors wish to attribute importance to my illness by representing my state to be more serious than it is; but I will never consent to let you take an ounce of blood from me."

"To this," records Bruno, "I answered that I was astonished to hear such arguments from His Excellency, since he must be sufficiently aware how great was the veneration and affection which I had for him; for this reason alone had I left my widowed and inconsolable mother in order to follow his august person to Greece; that the days I had spent in his service had been signalised by consistent disinterestedness, honesty, and the purest and most exemplary conduct (at which he nodded in affirmation, looking at me with kindly and touching eyes), and that only my deep conviction of the absolute necessity of bleeding him forced me to propose it to His Excellency thus continuously and with such insistence. My Lord was touched by these arguments, and promised me that on the following day he would surrender to my repeated insistence."

That night he slept very little and drank a great quantity of distilled water. The doctors were distressed to observe signs of spasms in his fingers and his toes during his few hours of troubled sleep.

On the morning of Friday the 16th he was worse. The two doctors appeared before him with their lancets, and reminded him of the promise which he had given to Bruno on the previous evening. He again endeavoured to evade this promise, stating that he had passed a better night than he had expected. Dr. Millingen thereupon warned him that only a few hours of hope yet remained, and solemnly assured him that unless he at once consented to be bled, neither he himself nor Dr. Bruno could answer for the consequences. With considerable insight Dr. Millingen added that unless he changed his resolution "the disease might operate such a dis-organisation in his cerebral and nervous system as entirely to deprive him of reason." " I had now," records Millingen, " touched the sensible cord; for, partly annoyed by our unceasing importunities, and partly convinced, casting at us both the fiercest glances, he threw out his arm, and said in the most angry tone : ' Come ; you are, I see, a damned set of butchers ; take away as much blood as you will; but have done with it.' "

In Bruno's account the scene is confirmed as follows :—

> " Rappresentandogli, unitamente al Dottor Millingen, che nella sera mi aveva promesso di lasciarsi cavar sangue, ce lo accordò, dicendo ' Giacchè mi annojate tanto con questo domandare sangue ; cavatelo, e fate presto '—prestando il braccio in una maniera disgustosa."

The lancets were taken from the cases, and the vein was opened. At every moment Byron called out to them to close the vein, but they persisted, and drew a full pound of blood. " The relief obtained," admits Dr. Millingen, " did not correspond to the hopes we had anticipated." His cheeks remained equally flushed, his pulses continued strong and intermittent. They therefore decided to attempt a second bleeding. In Dr. Bruno's account this second bleeding took place within an hour of the first. Dr. Millingen, however, states that the operation was performed next morning, and that in the afternoon of the 17th the vein was opened for the third time.

Dr. Bruno's account is perhaps the most accurate, since it was obviously written down at the time. " Immediately after the second bleeding," he says, " he felt himself relieved and more quiet, and he slept a little, but after three hours his pulse quickened just as if we had not drawn a single ounce of blood." Observing that his expression was becoming fixed, that from time to time he experienced a numbness in the fingers, which appeared to them to indicate that the inflammation was passing to the brain, they proposed a third bleeding. He begged them "not to torment him further with this continual demand for his blood." For the moment they desisted, and contented themselves with twisting cold water bandages around his throbbing temples.

During the night of the 16th the fever increased, and they endeavoured to induce him to allow them to apply leeches. Again he refused, saying that he had no conception how he had ever consented to this treatment on the day of his epilepsy. Shortly afterwards he became delirious, and as a precaution Tita removed the pistols and the stiletto which he always kept beside his bed.

On the morning of Saturday the 17th his temperature had not moderated. Again the doctors begged him to be bled. He swept aside their warnings as to the fatal consequences of a refusal, and merely muttered that they would not again succeed in drawing his blood. During the day, however, feeling that his brain was giving way from lack of sleep, he suddenly consented. Hardly had they opened the vein, however, when he cried out : "Close the vein," and they were able only to draw some ten ounces. They then warned him that in two hours another bleeding would be necessary.

Meanwhile Gamba, who on the 16th had been himself confined to his divan with a sprained ankle, contrived to hobble across to Byron's bedroom. He was appalled by the alteration in his friend's appearance : his countenance "at once awakened the most dreadful suspicions." Byron inquired after Gamba's accident "in the kindest manner, but in a hollow, sepulchral tone." "Take care of your foot," he said. "I know by experience how painful it must be."

"I could not stay near the bed," continues Gamba, "a flood of tears rushed into my eyes, and I was obliged to withdraw."

The news of Byron's condition had by then spread through his own household and out into the town beyond. The hysterical anxiety which Dr. Bruno was unable to conceal communicated itself to the servants. An appalling and terror-stricken confusion seized upon the household; there were no comforts; there was no one in authority; there was no community even of language. Dr. Bruno's English was as unintelligible as Fletcher's Italian; neither Parry nor Tita could speak anything but their native languages; the Greek servants were incomprehensible to everyone. "In all the attendants," writes Parry, "there was the officiousness of zeal; but owing to their ignorance of each other's language their zeal only added to the confusion. This circumstance, and the want of common necessaries, made Lord Byron's apartment such a picture of distress and even anguish during the two or three last days of his life as I never before beheld, and wish never again to witness."

His pulse meanwhile continued, in Bruno's words, to possess "una forza gigantesca." He lay there petulantly refusing a fourth bleeding, and drinking quantities of lemonade. An hour after noon he insisted upon rising in order that his bed might be re-made. Assisted by Fletcher and Tita, he went into his sitting-room. He was obsessed predominantly by the lack of sleep. "I know," he said to Fletcher, "that without sleep a man must die or go mad. I would sooner die a thousand times . . . I am not afraid of dying. I am more fit to die than people think." Bruno had followed them into the room: with tears in his eyes he again entreated Byron to "conquer his pernicious and perhaps fatal aversion from bleeding, which remedy remained the only hope of his salvation." Byron answered: "I don't want you to take any more blood from me; if it is fated that I must perish from this disease, I shall die the same whether you have bled me or whether you leave me all my blood." After saying this he was carried back to his bed, and became silent and depressed. Drs. Millingen and Bruno begged him a second time to allow them to hold a consultation with two other doctors. He would not hear of it. They then conceived the idea of telling him that Prince Mavrocordato had sent his personal physician to examine him, and that ordinary politeness required that he should agree. "Very well," he said, "let the man come in; but he must only look at me and keep silent." Dr. Bruno had already explained to Mavrocordato's physician, a Cephallonian of the name of Lucca Vaya, and to Dr. Treiber, the surgeon of the artillery brigade, the course of the illness and the treatment which had been given. When these two doctors saw Byron, they expressed the view that he was in too weak a condition to be bled any further, and proposed a draft of cream of tartary, boracic, and sugar. They did not consider, and Dr. Millingen agreed with them, that Byron's condition was hopeless. Dr. Bruno, as he himself asserts, was of a different opinion :—

"I told them," he records, "that the medicines they proposed were good enough in their way, but that the principal element in the treatment should be immediate and abundant bleedings, since the great danger was inflammation of the brain." The three other doctors, however, did not share this anxiety, nor did they diagnose any danger of cerebral inflammation. "Very well," answered Bruno, "since I find myself in opposition to all three of you, it is obvious that I must give way, and the responsibility for the life of so great a man will fall upon your own shoulders. It may be that I am mistaken; if this is so, it can only be that the unspeakable affection which I have for the gracious person of My Lord, and the awful fear that he may die, have made me see things in a more serious light than is necessary. From this moment I become a scrupulous executor of all your orders, and with all the more willingness since you with your opinion have given me good hopes, whereas for my own part, since you have now taken from me the remedy of bleeding, I judge My Lord already doomed and dead."

Having delivered this ultimatum Bruno retired into the next room to prepare the draught of boracic and cream of tartar. In a few minutes he was again summoned to the bedside. Lord Byron was fainting. All four approached him, and found that his pulse was weak, and that his feet and hands were cold. The three doctors at once concluded that there had been a " change of diathesis," and that the instant application of stimulants had become necessary. They applied two blisters to his thighs. Byron was by then delirious and in convulsions. In the midst of his delirium he would from time to time recognise his servants and utter a few intelligible sentences. The doctors were able to make him drink some laudanum and ether, but already he experienced great difficulty in swallowing. The whole night he lay there moaning slightly. Further blisters were applied to the thighs and to the nape of the neck, but he did not feel them. The pupil of the eye was shrunken and motionless, the breathing painful, the cheeks the colour of " red lead."

On seeing the effect of the stimulants, which had been applied against his own advice, Bruno again proposed a copious bleeding as a last resort, " but the other three doctors, convinced of their own views of his weak condition, allowed me only to apply on the morning of the 18th of April a few leeches to his temple." By that time, the indications of collapse were already pronounced. The effect of the leeches, according to Bruno, was, however, so beneficial that the condition of the patient " gave the illusion to those who loved that noble person that he could still recover from the fatal danger in which he found himself."

It was by then Easter Sunday, the 18th of April. In order that Lord Byron should not be disturbed by the celebrations usual on that day, the town guard patrolled the streets, warning the inhabitants to keep quiet. The artillery brigade was marched out of the town to provide a counter attraction.

Millingen and Bruno watched beside him. Byron himself had by then abandoned all hope. " Your efforts," he said to Millingen, " to preserve my life will be in vain. Die I must : I feel it. Its loss I do not lament ; for to terminate my wearisome existence I came to Greece. My wealth, my abilities, I devoted to her cause. Well, there is my life to her. One request let me make to you. Let not my body be hacked, or be sent to England. Here let my bones moulder. Lay me in the first corner without pomp or nonsense."

" It is with infinite regret," records Julius Millingen, " that I must state that, although I seldom left Lord Byron's pillow during the latter part of his illness, I did not hear him make any, even the smallest, mention of religion. At one moment I heard him say : ' Shall I sue for mercy ? ' After a long pause he added : ' Come, come, no weakness ! Let's be a man to the last.' "

At noon Gamba came to the bedside. He was still conscious. A letter had that morning arrived from the Metropolitan Ignatius at Leghorn reporting that the Sultan had in full divan proclaimed Byron an enemy of the Sublime Porte. Gamba thought it wiser to withhold this information. There was another letter from the deputy Luriottis, partly in Greek and partly in French, reporting upon the loan negotiations in London. Byron insisted on reading it, and on himself translating the Greek portion. There was a passage in it which displeased him : " I wish," he sighed, " that Napier and Hobhouse were here : we would soon settle this business."

A few hours later further letters arrived. They came from England. There was one letter from Douglas Kinnaird and three from Hobhouse. The latter told him of the conclusion of the Greek loan in London, and of the favourable dispositions of Mr. Canning. He transmitted to him a vote of thanks and gratitude from the Greek Committee for his great services and exertions on behalf of Greece. " Nothing," Hobhouse wrote, " can be more serviceable to the cause than all you have done; everybody is more than pleased and content. As for myself, I only trust that the great sacrifices which you have made may contribute (which I have no doubt they will) to the final success of the great cause. This will indeed be doing something worth living for, and will make your name and character stand far above those of any contemporary. At the same time, do not, I pray, expose yourself to dangers, either by flood or field—'Non missus ad hoc.'"

"I am in no fear now," Hobhouse wrote, "of your taking a sudden leave of the cause and the country. . . . Above all take care of your health, and do not go to the feverish marshes of the Morea, where you were once so ill."

"Your monied matters," Hobhouse wrote, "Kinnaird will tell you, are going on swimmingly; you will have—indeed you have—a very handsome fortune; and if you have health, I do not see what earthly advantage you can wish for that you have not got. Your present endeavour is certainly the most glorious ever undertaken by man. Campbell said to me yesterday that he envied what you are now doing (and you may believe him, for he is a very envious man) even more than all your laurels, blooming as they are. Go on and prosper."

"All friends," Hobhouse wrote, "make many inquiries after you, and hope you will take care of yourself in Greece, and return here after the good fight has been foughten."

A few days, a few hours before, such letters would have meant everything in the world to Byron. But when they reached Missolonghi he had already become unconscious. "He had lost his senses," records Gamba; "it was too late."

IV

By 4 p.m. on that Easter Sunday he appeared to be sinking. They gathered round his bed and waited.

THE END

Millingen and Fletcher broke down completely and left the room. Tita, who was also in tears, was unable to follow them, as Byron held him by the hand. Byron looked at Tita steadily and muttered, half smiling : " O questa è una bella scena." Rousing himself again he said, " Call Parry." But Parry arrived to find him again delirious ; he was shouting aloud in English and Italian : " Forward ! Forward—courage—follow my example—don't be afraid."

At 5 p.m. the delirium left him and he sent for Fletcher. " It is now nearly over," he panted, " I must tell you all without losing a moment."

Fletcher's narrative continues :—

" I then said, ' Shall I go, my Lord, and fetch pen, ink and paper ? '—' Oh, my God ! no, you will lose too much time, and I have it not to spare, for my time is now short,' said his Lordship ; and immediately after, ' Now, pay attention ! ' His Lordship commenced by saying, ' You will be provided for.' I begged him, however, to proceed with things of more consequence. He then continued, ' Oh, my poor dear child ! My dear Ada ! My God ! could I but have seen her ! Give her my blessing, and my dear sister Augusta and her children —and you will go to Lady Byron, and say—tell her everything—you are friends with her.' His Lordship appeared to be greatly affected at this moment. Here my master's voice failed him, so that I could only catch a word at intervals ; but he kept muttering something very seriously for some time, and would often raise his voice and say, ' Fletcher, now if you do not execute every order which I have given you, I will torment you hereafter if possible.' Here I told his Lordship, in a state of the greatest perplexity, that I had not understood a word of what he said ; to which he replied, ' Oh, my God ! then all is lost, for it is now too late ! Can it be possible you have not understood me ? '—' No, my Lord,' said I ; ' but I pray you to try and inform me once more.' ' How can I ? ' rejoined my master ; ' it is now too late, and all is over ! ' I said, ' Not our will, but God's be done ! ' and he answered, ' Yes, not mine be done—but I will try——' His Lordship did indeed make several efforts to speak, but could only repeat two or three words at a time—such as ' My wife ! my child ! my sister !— you know all—you must say all—you know my wishes ! ' The rest was quite unintelligible."

The doctors meanwhile had decided, in despair, to give him a strong draught of quinine. They asked Parry to induce him to swallow it.

" At the moment," records Parry, " of administering the bark he seemed sensible ; I spoke to him, and said, ' My Lord, take the bark, it will do you good, it will recover your Lordship.' He took my hand, and said, ' Give it me.' He was able to swallow only a very small quantity, about four mouthfuls, I think. Dr. Bruno seemed satisfied, however, and said, ' That will do.' When he took my hand, I found his hands were deadly cold. With the assistance of Tita, I endeavoured gently to create a little warmth in them ; and I also loosened the bandage which was tied round his head. Till this was done he seemed in great pain, clenched his hands at times, gnashed his teeth, and uttered the Italian exclamation of ' Ah, Christi ! ' He bore the loosening of the band passively ; and after it was loosened he shed tears. I encouraged him to weep, and said, ' My Lord, I thank God, I hope you will now be better ; shed as many tears as you can, you will sleep and find ease.' He replied faintly, ' Yes, the pain is gone, I shall sleep now,' and he again took my hand, uttered a faint good-night, and sank into a slumber; my heart ached, but I thought then his sufferings were over, and that he would wake no more."

Some incoherent mutterings were all they could catch of the last words of Byron. "Augusta—Ada—Kinnaird—Hobhouse." He mentioned sums of money, and the names of places. In a sudden lucid outburst he exclaimed: "Why was I not aware of this sooner? Why did I not go home before I left for here?" And then again, "Poor Greece—poor town—my poor servants. Io lascio qualche cosa di caro nel mondo."

At six in the evening he said to them: "I want to go to sleep now," and he closed his eyes. They watched beside him all that night of Sunday the 18th, raising his head from time to time to ease his breathing. He continued in a condition of profound stupor, the blood discharged by the leeches pouring down his face. On Monday the 19th of April his breathing became stertorous and his pulse intermittent. He remained unconscious, moaning a little from time to time, but not apparently in great suffering. Outside, the afternoon waned wet and sullen, and with sunset came the sound of thunder in the gulf. They waited there in the little room; from time to time Fletcher would raise his master's head from the pillow. At 6.15 p.m. Byron was seen suddenly to open his eyes and close them again. "Oh, my God!" exclaimed Fletcher, "I fear his Lordship is gone."

The doctors bent over the bed and felt his pulse. "You are right," they said, "he is gone."

V

They stood there beside the darkened bed, gazing across to each other through the gathering dusk: Millingen and Tita, Gamba and Parry, Fletcher and Bruno—congruous only in their joint exhaustion and their joint despair. Slowly the night descended, wet and thunderous, over the lagoons.

They roused themselves to action : they called for lights ; they removed the basins and the stained and twisted towels ; they summoned a village woman to lay out the body ; they sent for Mavrocordato. Throughout the night Praïdes and Gamba remained in the adjoining room docketing and sealing the papers that they found there. And with the dawn came the boom of cannon firing the last salute.

The body was embalmed. The four doctors gathered in the death-chamber to make their autopsy. They lifted the corpse on to the table and stripped it naked. "We could not refrain," writes Dr. Millingen, " from pausing in silent contemplation on the lifeless clay of one who but a few days before was the hope of a whole nation and the admiration of the civilised world. We could not but admire the perfect symmetry of the body . . . which might have vied with that of Apollo himself." After which the doctors bared their arms and set to work. Dr. Meyer, Editor of the *Greek Chronicle*, was there to help them. He had been present at the autopsy on Madame de Staël ; it would have been a pity if he had missed so analogous an occasion. For over an hour the five of them hacked and sliced and weighed and dumped things into separate pails. The brain and skull interested them particularly : the *dura mater*, it appears, was firmly attached to the internal wall of the cranium ; they had to tug and lever between them to get the two apart. They found the vessels of the membrane completely injected with blood ; there were adhesions in the convolutions of the brain itself ; the sutures of the skull, as in extreme old age, had fused together. The cerebrum and the cerebellum, without the membranes, weighed six pounds ;[1] the lungs were crepitant and healthy ; the liver diseased ; the heart enlarged. In any case, they concluded, Lord Byron could not have lived another

[1] "Libbre mediche "—an unknown measure.

seven years. It had been a highly interesting autopsy, and when it was all over they put him more or less together again, and fitted the parts of the skull back into each other, and sent for the undertaker.

There was no lead to be procured at Missolonghi; all they could find was an oblong packing-case lined with tin, and some earthenware jars for the intestines. The body was disposed accordingly, and when the work had been completed a receipt was drawn up by the undertakers and witnessed by the authorities. The translation of this curious document, which is in Italian, runs as follows :—

"We, the undersigned, bear witness that in the large case, which has been sealed with the seals of the Provisional Government, is to be found the authentic body of the Honourable Lord Byron, peer of England; that we ourselves placed the said body in the case, closed it hermetically, and thereupon affixed thereto the seals above mentioned.

"We bear witness also that in the smaller case will be found the honoured intestines of the said noble and respected Lord Byron ('Le rispettabili viscere del sullodato nobile e benmerito Lord Byron'), that is to say, the brain, the heart, the liver, the spleen, the stomach, kidneys, etc., contained in four separate jars. The lungs, which are missing, were deposited, in deference to the repeated representations of the citizens of Missolonghi, in the church of San Spiridione, in the hope that the most noble and respected family of the Illustrious Lord would grant them to Missolonghi, of which town My Lord had accepted the honorary citizenship.

"Given at Missolonghi 25th/13th April, 1824.

$$\left\{\begin{array}{c}\text{Signed}\\\text{in}\\\text{Greek}\end{array}\right\}$$ " APOSTOLOS CAPSALIS.
SPIRIDION RASIS.
NICOLA LANIOTIS.

" The Governor-General of Western Greece bears witness that the above signatures are written by the hands and in the writing of Messrs. Apostolos Capsalis, Spiridion Rasis, Commissary of Police, and Nicola Laniotis, secretary to the Government, and that to them can be accorded full and indubitable Faith.

" A. MAVROCORDATO."

" Missolonghi Ap. 20 (*sic*), 1824.

Which certificate, if it does nothing else, disposes for ever of the legend that it was Byron's heart which was buried in the Heroon.

VI

In ever-widening circles the news of Byron's death spread out from Missolonghi. The guns which at daybreak on the 20th of April had echoed over the lagoons were replied to with salvos of rejoicing by the Turkish garrisons at Lepanto and Patras. Trelawny, journeying from Athens on the business of Ulysses, was told of it at the ford of the Evvenus. He hurried on to Missolonghi, and was in time, before they closed the coffin, to examine and to handle the deformed foot which had for so long excited his curiosity. From Zante the news was forwarded by express to Europe. It reached Lady Blessington at Naples and Leigh Hunt at Florence; it crashed upon the Guiccioli at Bologna. At 8 a.m. on the morning of May 14th Hobhouse was aroused from his bed at the Albany by a loud knocking at his door. A special messenger had arrived with a letter. It was a blue official envelope franked by Sidney Osborne; it bore the red official seal of the Ionian Government and Lord Sidney's private seal in black. It had been addressed to Hobhouse, Care of Douglas Kinnaird at Messrs. Ransome's, and had arrived during the night. There was also a short note from Kinnaird himself. Hobhouse began with the latter : it ran as follows :—

> " MY DEAR H.,
>
> " If you cannot come to me on the receipt of this, I will come to you. Nobody knows it as yet. But it must be known in a few hours, as I cannot take upon me to keep back the letters (of which a heap came in the bag) from their addressees. Let me know therefore by bearer if I may come to you. I have put off my friends from dining here.
>
> " Yours truly and ever.
" D. K."

With trembling hands Hobhouse proceeded to open the larger envelope. It contained several letters in different handwritings and four flimsy sheets of printed Greek. The first of these papers was an illegible but heart-broken scrawl from Gamba. It was dated April 21st from Missolonghi. In an " agony of grief " Hobhouse proceeded to read the more detailed letters from Fletcher and Lord Sidney Osborne.

Within a few hours it was known in London that Lord Byron had died at Missolonghi.

VII

Meanwhile at Zante they were squabbling over the remains. The packing-case in which the body rested had been painted black for the state funeral held at Missolonghi on April 22nd. On the 23rd it was carried back to his house, and on the 29th it was closed and secured with iron hoops. Several holes were bored though the wood and the tin, and the case was then deposited in a large barrel containing 180 gallons of spirit. On the 3rd of May the barrel and its contents were shipped across to Zante, and deposited, while they squabbled, in the lazaretto. Trelawny and Stanhope were of opinion that the body should be buried at Athens, either in the so-called Theseion or in the Acropolis itself. Lord Sidney Osborne wisely opposed the choice of so precarious a resting-place; the Turks, he argued, might at any moment recapture Athens; their first act, in such an eventuality, would be to desecrate the tomb. He advised that the remains should be provisionally interred at Zante pending an expression of Lady Byron's wishes. Millingen, for his part, and with some inconsistency, recalled to them the wishes Byron had expressed to him when dying: "One request," he had said, "let me make to you. Let not my body be hacked or sent to England. Here let my bones moulder. Lay me in the first corner without pomp or nonsense." He had expressed the same wish to Lady Blessington at Genoa, and to Trelawny at Argostoli; but to Gamba, Parry, and Fletcher he had said the contrary. The controversy which these discrepancies excited at Zante became somewhat heated. In the end it was agreed that the barrel must be shipped at once to England.

On April the 21st the brig "Florida" had arrived at Zante with Captain Blaquière and the first instalment of the English loan. It was decided that the "Florida" should return immediately with the body of Lord Byron. It was to be accompanied by Bruno, Fletcher, Tita Falciere, Lega Zambelli, and the negro groom. Pietro Gamba was refused a passage, and proceeded faithfully to England in another vessel. His place was taken by Colonel Leicester Stanhope, who, as a result of the protests of Lord Strangford to the Foreign Office, had been summarily recalled by the Adjutant General. The "Florida" left Zante on the 25th of May, and on June 29th anchored in the Downs. From there she proceeded to the London Docks.

I find the following entry in the manuscript of Hobhouse's diary for July 5th:—

"I went with Mr Hanson and proved Lord

Byron's will at Doctors Commons. Then I went to London Bridge and, getting into a boat, we rowed to London Dock Buoy, where the ' Florida ' . . . . was anchored. Messrs. Woodeson, the undertakers, had been previously sent on board, and I found them employed in emptying the large cask enclosing the chest that contained the body. It was a long black box hooped with iron, something like a coffin— the best that could be made at Missolonghi. The leaden coffin brought by the undertakers was placed alongside of the chest, and a canvass covering having been drawn round them, everyone except the household withdrew. I retired to the cabin, and to distract my attention looked over the papers which Lord Byron had sealed up at Cephallonia and left there. Captain Hodgson of the ' Florida,' his father, Fletcher, and myself minutely examined them. There was no testamentary document in them of any kind, and we signed a paper to that effect.

" Mr. Woodeson came to me and told me the body had been removed into the coffin, and asked me if I wished to see it. I believe I should have dropped down dead if I had looked at it. He told me, as also did Bruno the physician, that it had almost all the freshness and firmness of life. The chest, containing the vases in which the heart and brain and intestines were deposited, was not opened. I covered the coffin with a plane lid and the ship's flag, and watched by it whilst the Captain went on shore for the customs permit for its removal. Lord Byron's large Newfoundland dog was lying at my feet. A young man, whom I did not know, came on board and begged leave to see the body. He did this in terms so moving and was so much affected that I could not help promising him a sight of it before interment. He took up a bit of the cotton in which it had been wrapped and placed it carefully in his pocket-book.

" At last the Custom House order arrived and the coffin was lowered into the undertakers' barge. There were a good many boats round the ship at the time, and the shore was crowded with spectators. I left the servants to take care of the effects, and carrying the papers with me went on board the barge. We passed quietly up the river, and landed at Palace Yard Stairs, at a quarter to five in the afternoon. A black cloth was strapped round the coffin, and it was removed on the shoulders of six men to the house prepared for its reception, 20 George Street. The removal across Palace Yard was quite unobserved."

For seven days the coffin lay in state in the front parlour of Sir Edward Knatchbull's house, Great George Street. The room was draped with black and lighted by wax tapers. Mr. Hanson informed Hobhouse that it would be his duty as executor to identify the body. Mastering his repulsion, Hobhouse entered the room, and gazed upon the coffin. The decaying face that glimmered in the light of the candles was not the face of Byron : Hobhouse was able to identify the body by raising the red velvet pall and glancing at the foot.

On Friday the 16th of July at 4.20 p.m. Lord Byron was buried, in a manner befitting an English country gentleman, in the vault at Hucknall Torkard.

APPENDICES

I. Further Notes on the Minor Characters which have Figured in this Narrative

II. A List of the Main Publications upon which this Narrative is Based

APPENDIX I

FURTHER NOTES ON THE MINOR CHARACTERS WHICH HAVE FIGURED IN THIS NARRATIVE

THE subsequent adventures of Trelawny are, I presume, already familiar. Having satisfied his curiosity by peering at Byron's deformity and by reading such of the dead man's letters as were still lying about his rooms, Trelawny turned his attention to securing for his brother-in-law Odysseus what remained of Byron's organisation at Missolonghi. "Everyone here," he wrote to Stanhope on April 28th, "now wish to join Odysseus, or, at least, leave this hole : I know you will say I have seduced them." On the next day he wrote again, pointing out that with Byron's death Stanhope had become the sole representative of the London Committee, and urging him at once to transfer the whole of the Committee's stores to Athens. Fortunately Blaquière had by that time arrived in the "Florida" at Zante with the first instalment of the loan, and was at once informed of these intrigues by Mavrocordato. Stanhope, who was under orders to return to England, and whose enthusiasm for the cause of Greek republicanism was already on the wane, left the decision in the hands of Blaquière ; and Blaquière, being a wise man, decided, in so far as was still possible, to continue the policy initiated by Byron. Trelawny returned in disgust to Athens. Odysseus, after failing to secure for himself a share of the English loan, decided to throw in his lot with the Turks. In December 1824, accompanied by Trelawny, he visited the camp of Omer Pasha, and in return for his appointment as Captain of Eastern Greece concluded a treaty

277

of alliance. His treachery was before long unmasked and punished. In April 1825 the Greek government forces defeated the combined troops of the Turks and Odysseus at Daulis. Odysseus himself was captured, and a few months later was executed for his treachery by being thrown from the Acropolis. Trelawny had already retired to a cave on Mount Parnassus in which Odysseus had taken the precaution of hiding his family and his treasure. While in this stronghold Trelawny was shot in the back by Messrs. Fenton and Whitcombe, who had been suborned for the purpose of this assassination by the Greek Government. For weeks he lay there recovering from his wound, and was eventually rescued by Commodore Rowan Hamilton, whose intervention, as appears from a MS. in the British Museum, had been obtained through the good offices of J. C. Hobhouse. Trelawny proceeded with his wife to Cephallonia, and subsequently to Zante. A daughter was born in June of 1826, and died a few months later. Meanwhile Trelawny had quarrelled with Tarsitsa, whom he relegated to a convent. As a final revenge he sent her in a little box the dead body of their infant daughter.[1] He then returned to England. We hear of him in 1828 living quietly in Cornwall and later visiting Landor at Florence. In 1831 he published "The Adventures of a Younger Son," and in 1833 he proceeded to America. On his return to England he figured for a brief period as a lion in London society, exploiting his past intimacy with the man whom he had so cynically deserted. In 1846 he retired to Putney, and subsequently to Monmouthshire. In 1858 he published his "Recollections of the Last Days of Shelley and Byron," which he reissued twenty years later under a new title and in an amended form. For several years he lived at 7 Pelham Crescent, Brompton, retiring finally to the

---

[1] I am aware that this story has been authoritatively contradicted. It was, however, recently confirmed to me by Mr. Wood of Patras, who had received it direct from his great-uncle, Mr. Charles Hancock.

village of Sompting, near Worthing, where he died in August 1881. In the last years of his life he was painted by Millais in the subject picture entitled " The North-West Passage."

Of those others who accompanied Byron to Greece the records are less abundant. Stanhope on his return to England contented himself by succeeding to the title of Earl of Harrington and living a mildly liberal existence. He died in 1862. Of Millingen I have already spoken. Bruno, after attending the funeral at Hucknall Torkard, returned to London, where he refused to accept from the executors any fee for his services, and thereafter disappears into the unknown.

Pietro Gamba, after assisting Hobhouse with the winding up of Byron's estate, returned to Italy, and from there, again, to Greece, where he was appointed a Colonel in the Greek army. He was seen at Argos by the Rev. Mr. Swann in July 1825. There exist in the British Museum two letters addressed by him to Hobhouse from Nauplia in September 1825 and January 1826, regarding the inexplicable procrastination of Lord Cochrane. In 1827 he contracted typhoid fever and died. He was buried in the fort of Diamantopoulos, on the isthmus of Metana. This fort is no longer extant, nor is there any trace of the grave of Pietro Gamba.

Parry, for his part, returned in May 1824 to England, where he succeeded in extorting £400 from the Greek Committee, published his book, and within a few months drank himself to death upon the proceeds. Dr. Treiber lived on for many years at Missolonghi. Dr. Meyer was killed in the famous sortie of April 1826. Costa Ghazis, the boatman, died in 1890. Tita Falciere was subsequently employed in Greece both by Henry Bulwer and Benjamin Disraeli. To the latter he became deeply attached, and after residing many years at Hughenden, where his portrait is still preserved, and after marrying Mrs. Disraeli's maid, was appointed Home Service messenger in the India Office. The subsequent destinies

APPENDIX I

of Fletcher and Lega Zambelli are best illustrated by the following letter, addressed by the former to Hobhouse.

> " 10 *Cobourgh Place,*
> " *Bayswater,*
> " *June 6th,* 1835.

" Hond. Sir,

 " I hope Sir John you will pardon me the liberty i have taken in thus addressing you But your very great kindness in saying that Anything you could serve me in you promised to do, I was then in hopes that i with the small Annuity that you Sir and Mr Hanson was so very kind to propose for me would have been quite sufficient with aeconomy to have served my every wish and want. But not wishing to remain in Idleness i was tempted to try in establishing a Maccaroni Manufactory with Lega Zambelli wherein we expended the greater part of our small capital by having all our machinery and 2 men from Italy then we had many difficulteys to strive against by many famileys who thought none could be good but what was made in Italy but after many exertions on our parts and great sacrifices which we was at first obliged to make we at length succeeded in getting it established so far that had not Mr Thompson taken the duty off the foreign maccaroni we should have netted at least from three to four hundred per annum before this period but after that dreadfull blow we was compleatly ruined. My ever to be lamented Lord and Master very justly observed 2 days before the fatal day which deprived England of its greatest ornament and me of the *best* of Masters, My Lord said ' Fletcher, one thing very much disturbs my mind which is that i have not provided for you which after the many ups and downs we have had togeather you have never forsaken me and have served me with honesty and fidelity and at times ive been cross with you. But

you well know i did not mean it but we are loseing
time, bring me pen ink and paper. Not but I
think my sister and Mr Hobhouse will take care
and provide for you as they know it is my wish
and will. I even mentioned to Hanson when he
was over at Venice when you was obliged to be a
witness that should anything happen to me that
you should be provided for, and he told Colonel
Stanhope the same the day after His Lordship was
attacked by an Epelopesey fit that he was sorry
he had not provided for me but in case His Lordship should be taken before he had made the pro-
vision for me he hoped the Col. would remember
to state to the Honble. Mrs. Leigh and to you
Sir John that it was is wish i should be provided
for as in is old will I was mentioned for 50 pounds
per annum which was made many years before is
Death and i have had many narrow escapes both
by sea and land since then. Now Sir John knowing
the mutual friendship exisiting beween my ever to
be lamented Lord and you could he Look Down
he would Bless you if you will but place me in
either a Door Keeper's place at either Houses of
Parliament or even Porter or any trifling thing in
the India House . . . I hope Sir John you will not
refuse or it will be fatal to me. My poor afflicted
Lord when he found he could not write said ' Well
there is no way of making sure for you than by
taking the box of dollars.' I replied, ' No, My
Lord, not one single Dollar i would starve first.'

" I remain, Sir John, your obedient servant
" W. FLETCHER."

It does not appear that this appeal produced any very
substantial improvement in Fletcher's condition, for three
years later he was confined for debt in White Cross Street
prison, from which he only obtained his discharge
through the intervention of Mrs. Leigh (herself, by then,

impoverished) and the ability of his solicitor Mr. Edward Spence, whom he rewarded with a lock of Byron's hair. According to tradition Fletcher is buried in the church-yard of Hucknall Torkard; but I have been unable to find the grave or to ascertain the date on which he died.

APPENDIX II

A LIST OF THE MAIN PUBLICATIONS UPON WHICH THIS
NARRATIVE IS BASED

(*The more important are indicated by an asterisk*)

Editions of Byron's Works.

**" The Works of Lord Byron." 7 vols. Published by
John Murray, 1898–1904, and edited by E. H.
Coleridge.

**" Letters and Journals." 6 vols. Published by John
Murray, 1898–1904, and edited by R. E. Prothero
[Lord Ernle].

**" Lord Byron's Correspondence." 2 vols. Published
and edited by John Murray, 1922.

*" Works," edited by W. E. Henley. (Vol. I only.)
1897.

General Biographies.

*Galt, John. " The Life of Lord Byron." 1830, 1908.

Gordon, Sir Cosmo. " The Life and Genius of Lord
Byron." 1824.

*Jeaffreson, John Cordy. " The Real Lord Byron."
2 vols. 1883.

*Karl, Elze. " Lord Byron." Berlin, 1870. Trans-
lated 1872.

Lake, J. W. " The Life of Lord Byron." 1826.

Macaulay, Lord. " Lord Byron." 1853.

**Mayne, Ethel C. " Byron." 2 vols. 1912.

**Moore, Thomas. " Life, Letters, and Journals of
Lord Byron." 1830.

Specific Works.

*Blessington, Lady. " Conversations with Lord Byron."
 1824.

*——. " Idler in Italy." 2 vols. 1839.

*Broughton, Lord (John Cam Hobhouse). " Recollec-
 tions of a Long Life."

——. " Travels through Albania and other Provinces
 of Turkey." 1813.

Brydges, Sir S. " Letters on the Character and
 Poetical Genius of Lord Byron." 1824.

——. " An Impartial Portrait of Lord Byron as a
 Poet and a Man." 1825.

Dallas, A. R. C. " Recollections of the Life of Lord
 Byron, 1808–1814." 1824.

*Edgcumbe, Richard. " Byron : The Last Phase."
 1909.

**Gamba, Pietro. " A Narrative of Lord Byron's Last
 Journey to Greece." 1825.

Graham, W. " Last Links with Byron, Shelley, and
 Keats." 1898.

Guiccioli, Teresa. " Lord Byron jugé par les témoins
 de sa vie." 1868. Translated, 1869.

Hayman, H. " Lord Byron and the Greek Patriots."
 Harper's Magazine, Feb. 1894.

*Hunt, Leigh. " Lord Byron and Some of his Con-
 temporaries ; with Recollections of the Author's
 Life and of his Visit to Italy." 3 vols. 1828.

*Kennedy, James. " Conversations on Religion with
 Lord Byron and Others." 1830.

" Life, Writings, Opinions and Times of the Rt. Hon.
 George Gordon Noel Byron." By an English
 gentleman in the Greek military service. 3 vols.
 1825.

Mackay, C. " Medora Leigh." 1869.

Medwin, T. " Journal of the Conversations of Lord
 Byron." 1824.

Milbanke, Ralph (Lord Lovelace). " Astarte." 1905.
 (Privately printed.)

*Millingen, Julius. " Memoirs of the Affairs of Greece ; . . . with Various Anecdotes relating to Lord Byron and an Account of his Last Illness and Death." 1831.

**Parry, William. " The Last Days of Lord Byron : with His Lordship's Opinions on Various Subjects." 1825.

Salvo, C. de. " Lord Byron en Italie et en Grèce." 1825.

*Stanhope, Leicester. " Greece in 1823 and 1824."

Stendhal. " Lord Byron en Italie." 1816.

**Trelawny, E. J. " Records of Shelley, Byron and the Author." 2 vols. 1858, 1878.

Works on the Greek War of Independence.

*Blaquière, Edward. " The Greek Revolution, its Origin and Progress." 1824.

*——. " Narration of a Second Visit to Greece, including Facts connected with the Last Days of Lord Byron." 1825.

Dalling and Bulwer. " An Autumn in Greece." 1826.

Ferriman, Z. D. " Some English Philhellenes (Byron, Napier, Hastings, Church, Guilford, Gordon, J. P. Kennedy)."

Finlay, George. " History of the Greek Revolution." 1863.

Gordon, T. " History of the Greek Revolution."

Hughes, Rev. T. S. " Travels in Greece and Albania." 1830.

*Isambert, G. " L'Indépendance grecque et l'Europe." 1900.

Jebb, Sir R. " Modern Greece."

Leake, W. M. " Travels in Northern Greece." 1835.

——. " Travels in the Morea." 1830.

——. " A Historical Outline of the Greek Revolution." 2 vols. 1826.

APPENDIX II

*Mendelssohn-Bartholdy. " Geschichte Griechenlands."
2 vols. 1870–1871.

Napier, C. " The Colonies, of the Ionian Islands in
Particular." 1833.

*Phillips, W. Alison. " The Greek War of Indepen-
dence." 1897.

Pouqueville, F. C. " Histoire de la régénération de la
Grèce." 4 vols. 1824.

Prokesch Osten, Count A. " Geschichte de Abfalls
der Griechen vom Turkischen Reiche."

Soutzos, A. " Histoire de la Revolution Grecque."

INDEX

INDEX

288